RACE AND HUMAN DIVERSITY:
A BIOCULTURAL APPROACH

RACE AND HUMAN DIVERSITY:
A BIOCULTURAL APPROACH

Robert L. Anemone, Ph.D.
Department of Anthropology
Western Michigan University
Kalamazoo, Michigan

Routledge
Taylor & Francis Group
LONDON AND NEW YORK

First published 2011 by Pearson Education, Inc.

Published 2016 by Routledge
2 Park Square, Milton Park, Abingdon, Oxon OX14 4RN
711 Third Avenue, New York, NY 10017, USA

Routledge is an imprint of the Taylor & Francis Group, an informa business

ISBN: 9780131838765 (pbk)

Library of Congress Cataloging-in-Publication Data

Anemone, Robert L.
Race and Human Diversity: A Biocultural Approach/ Robert L. Anemone.—1st ed.
    p. cm.
    Includes bibliograpical references.
    ISBN-13: 978-0-13-183876-5 (alk. paper)
    ISBN-10: 0-13-183876-8 (alk. paper)
    1. Race—Social aspects.   2. Anthropology.   I. Title.
    HT1521.A55 2011
    305.8—dc22

                                    2010005271

Printed and bound in the United States of America by
Edwards Brothers Malloy on sustainably sourced paper

Now, any fool can see that a Chinese is not a Negro. And if telling a Dutchman from an American Indian were all there is to distinguishing races, this book would not have happened.

Earl W. Count, *This Is Race* (1950:xiii)

This book is dedicated to my wife, Dr. Joyce Kubiski, without whom it would have never been completed. Joyce is the heart and soul of our family and the glue that holds us together. She has been a source of constant encouragement, love, and support for me as I worked on this book and every day and in every way for our four children. Together we have created a multiracial family in Kalamazoo, Michigan, with genetic roots in Poland, Ethiopia, Italy, and Ireland. Without her hard work and vision, we would never have succeeded.

This book is also dedicated to our four children: Giancarlo, Wondimu, Helen, and Wondissen.

CONTENTS

PREFACE

Race has long been a topic of great interest to anthropologists of all types, including biological, cultural, archaeological, and linguistic anthropologists. In fact, the roots of anthropology can clearly be seen in the 19th-century fascination with racial differences and their meanings. I come to the study of race late, having spent most of my research career as a biological anthropologist working in other areas of inquiry, particularly the study of human and primate evolution. But as a result of developing and teaching a course over the past decade at Western Michigan University titled "Race, Biology, and Culture," I have become fascinated with both the history of anthropological attempts to deal with human diversity and the ways in which modern anthropology can lead to a new understanding of human variation. This book is a result of that fascination.

As a teacher on race and human diversity at the university level, I have been struck by the absence of a text that deals with anthropological notions of race and human difference from the dual perspectives of biology and culture. While many fine texts written by cultural anthropologists and sociologists provide a cultural critique of racial notions, none includes much biology. Similarly, one can find books that document at great length the biological intricacies of human diversity, but they typically devote scant attention, if any, to the cultural side of things. Of course, the gulf between anthropologists who study human biology (biological or physical anthropologists) and those who study culture (social or cultural anthropologists) is one of the central features of academic anthropology today. The few departments that retain a four-field approach seem to do it mostly through lip service, and increasing specialization in both research and teaching has become the norm for most professional anthropologists. My goal in writing this book is to attempt to bridge this gap with a textbook that critically analyzes race from both a biological and a cultural perspective.

The biocultural perspective is necessary if we as anthropologists and teachers are to be successful in explaining what I like to refer to as the "central paradox of race." The paradox refers to two claims that are often made by anthropologists: (1) that race does not exist and (2) that race is extremely important. The biocultural perspective resolves the paradox by clarifying that race fails (i.e., it doesn't exist) as a biological concept but that race as a social phenomenon can sometimes hold life-or-death significance (i.e., it is important). While some chapters of this book mostly explore biological details (e.g., chapters 2, 3, 5, and 6) and others cover primarily cultural or historical material (e.g., chapters 1, 4, and 9), my goal is to provide a synthetic, biocultural approach as often as possible. Chapters 7 (on nutrition and health) and 8 (on race and intelligence), for example, provide a cultural and historical background and context for primarily biological data on aspects of human difference. Each chapter has a list of discussion questions at the end, and most chapters include one or more boxes in which interesting related topics are set off from the main narrative. The overall message of this book is that race makes little sense as biology but needs to be understood as an aspect of culture—indeed, a very significant part of American culture.

The book follows the structure of my Race, Biology, and Culture class, but instructors may assign the chapters in almost any order that suits their teaching. The book begins with a short chapter that lays out some of the basic problems of a biological theory of race, in particular the arbitrariness of most racial classifications based on biological differences between populations. Chapters 2 and 3 provide the biological and evolutionary background to a consideration of the biology of human differences. Chapter 4 provides a historical look at the ways that anthropologists have conceptualized and studied racial differences since the first scientific racial classification was proposed by Linnaeus in 1758. Chapters 5 and 6 return to a study of the biological basis for human variation by considering how humans have adapted to life in stressful environments (e.g., hot, cold, and high-altitude environments). My approach to the study of biological differences in humans is dynamic and processual, and it is always informed by evolutionary theory. So these two chapters also discuss evolutionary scenarios that explain why and how human populations have evolved different body shapes, sizes, cardiovascular physiology, and skin colors in different environments. Chapter 7 provides a biocultural look at human diet, nutrition, and patterns of sickness and health. Chapter 8 looks at the long and sordid history of scientific attempts to create a racial hierarchy of supposed inborn differences in human intelligence. Finally, Chapter 9 describes the historical record of race as a cultural phenomenon in the United States, including government legislation, Supreme Court decisions, citizenship, and a brief history of the civil rights movement of the mid-20th century.

My hope is that students who read this book will learn how anthropologists thought about race in the past and think about it today and will consequently be able to analyze issues of race and ethnicity more thoughtfully in their own lives and become better prepared for their roles as citizens of a multiracial 21st-century America.

I would like to thank my editors at Pearson–Prentice Hall, especially Nancy Roberts, who first encouraged me to consider writing this book, and Sarah Holle, who got me through the final stages. Most of all, I thank my family for their support and encouragement during the long process of researching and writing this book.

Robert L. Anemone
Kalamazoo, Michigan

ACKNOWLEDGMENTS

I wish to thank the following reviewers of this book for their valuable insights.

Pamela C. Ashmore *University of Missouri, Saint Louis*

Tom D. Brutsaert *State University of New York, Albany*

Janis Hutchinson *University of Houston*

Sunil K. Khanna *Oregon State University, Corvallis*

Wesley Niewoehner *California State University, San Bernardino*

Tyler G. O'Brian *University of Northern Iowa, Cedar Falls*

Paul W. Sciulli *Ohio State University, Columbus*

Beth A. S. Shook *California State University, Chico*

Linda Taylor *University of Miami, Coral Gables, Florida*

Mary Willis *University of Nebraska, Lincoln*

Race and Human Diversity:
A Biocultural Approach

CHAPTER 1

Race and Biological Diversity in Humans

"A 'race' is a physical division of mankind, the members of which are distinguished by the possession of similar combinations of anatomical features due to their common heredity."

HOOTON 1937:152

"There are no races, there are only clines."

LIVINGSTONE 1962:279

"The inhabitants of different parts of the world are often visibly different, and the differences are in part genetic. This, in a nutshell, is the essence of race as a biological phenomenon."

DOBZHANSKY 1968:78

"Pure races, in the sense of genetically homogenous populations, do not exist in the human species today, nor is there any evidence that they have ever existed in the past."

AMERICAN ASSOCIATION OF PHYSICAL ANTHROPOLOGISTS 1996:569

ON THE NONEXISTENCE OF HUMAN RACES

Since its beginnings in the 19th century, anthropology has been concerned, some might say obsessed, with the study of human racial variation. One could also say that race has been an American concern for an even longer period of time, perhaps dating back to August 1619, when the first shipload of 20 African slaves arrived at Jamestown, Virginia, a year before the arrival of the Pilgrims on the *Mayflower* at Plymouth Rock (Bennett 1964). Yet as the quotations that open the chapter make clear, there is no consensus among anthropologists on some basic questions about race in humans, including whether race even exists. What are human races, and how should they be defined? How many races are there today? Should anthropologists even name races and attempt to classify individuals into racial categories? What is the connection between

1

FIGURE 1.1 An artist's depiction of the 1619 arrival of the first African Americans in Virginia.
Courtesy of the New York Public Library Picture Collection.

the existence of racial classifications and the ugly fact of racism? These are still important questions for anthropologists today.

Over the past century, anthropologists have published hundreds of books and articles in which they have offered differing definitions of the concept of biological race and proposed a wide variety of racial classifications of humans. These classifications have been based on a wide variety of anatomical traits, ranging from skin color to blood group genetics, and as a result, they have varied tremendously in their details. A brief examination of three important anthropological works published shortly after World War II highlights the wide range of opinion concerning the meaning of the race concept that was a hallmark of anthropological inquiry for much of the 20th century. In two popular texts published in 1950, we find strong support for the validity of biological race but equally strong differences of opinion on the number of races that exist among humans and the specific traits that should be used to define races. Coon et al. (1950:115) focused on the fact that members of a race resemble each other and differ from members of other races in physical features and defined a race as "a somatically unique population or collection of identical populations." They listed 30 different living races and combined these into six larger units they called "racial stocks": Negroid, Mongoloid, White, Australoid, American Indian, and Polynesian. The races in this classification were defined on the basis of different sets of physical characteristics. For example, one of the two races of Australian aborigines, the Murrayian, was said to have a "stocky build, brown skin, abundant beard and body hair" (Coon et al. 1950:115), while the Hindu race was defined as "light-brown to dark-skinned Mediterranean, usually skinny in build" (Coon et al. 1950:129). By contrast, Boyd (1950:207) defined race as "a population which differs significantly from other human populations in regard to the frequency of one or more of the

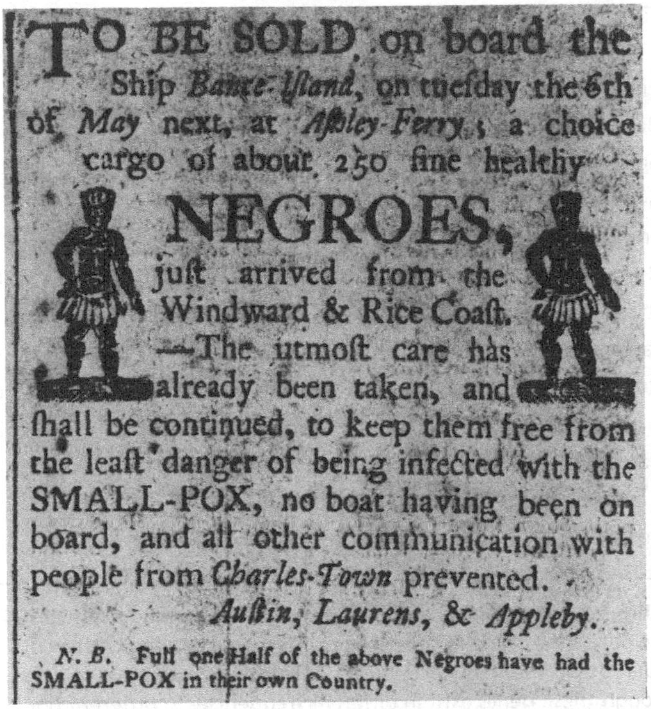

FIGURE 1.2 An advertisement for a cargo of human chattel from Boston.

genes it possesses" and then named five living races (and one "hypothetical" race!) based on the genetics of several common blood groups (e.g., ABO, MN, and Rh). For example, his African or Negroid race is characterized by a "tremendously high frequency of the gene Rh+, a moderate frequency of Rh− . . . [and a] rather high incidence of gene B. Probably normal M and N" (Boyd 1950:268). In both texts, the authors recognize to some extent the arbitrariness of their race concepts, the existence of intermediate populations existing between their named races, and the fact that their races fade gradually one into another. Coon et al. (1950:140) explicitly admit this when they state that "the foregoing list of 30 'races' might have been ten or 50: the line of discrimination in many cases is arbitrary." Boyd (1950:269–270) states that his classification "corresponds well, omitting the inevitable intermediates, with geography" but that "it must not be thought that the divisions between our genetic races will be absolutely sharp, any more than is the difference between races characterized by any other method." By contrast, in a book published eight years earlier, Montagu (1942) argued that the notion of race among humans was completely unsupported by the biological facts and that racial classifications are arbitrary social or political instruments that pose a great danger to human existence. Claiming that race is a dangerous myth and a biological fallacy, Montagu asserted that all racial schemes are inherently racist and that the term *race* should be dropped from scientific and public discourse and replaced by *ethnic group*.

Today, the situation is not much different from 1950, with many anthropologists discounting the very existence of biological race among humans while others continue to use the concept in their research and teaching. Among anthropologists who still support racial classifications, there is no agreement concerning the best traits to use in determining racial classifications or the number of races that should be recognized. Society as a whole seems confused by the lack of agreement among biologists and anthropologists concerning race. In particular, people are puzzled when they hear anthropologists state that race does not exist. Aren't the obvious differences between Nigerians and Swedes self-evident proof of the existence of race? What do anthropologists mean when they say that race is a social construction? Why is it that after all this study, we seem no closer to agreement on the nature and very existence of human races?

	Freq A	Freq B	Freq O
English	.250	.050	.692
Belgians	.257	.058	.684
Spanish	.294	.068	.645
Swedes	.301	.073	.616
French	.276	.088	.632
Bulgarians	.283	.113	.607
Italians	.213	.118	.678
Japanese	.279	.172	.549
Russians	.250	.189	.565
Chinese	.220	.201	.587
Iraqis	.226	.208	.581
Chinese	.193	.250	.554
Egyptians	.272	.250	.459

FIGURE 1.3 ABO blood group gene frequencies from Boyd (1950:224–225). These data show some of the genetic differences between different populations in the frequencies of the three genes of the ABO blood group. Although these genes exist in different frequencies in different populations, these data cannot be used to objectively distinguish different "races."

Many anthropologists currently argue that biological race is a figment of the human imagination, a "folk concept" remaining from a prescientific era when Europeans first ventured beyond their shores and discovered a new world of human diversity. These critics regard race as a social construction, a set of ideas about the meaning of human variation invented by people at a particular time and place for a particular purpose. While admitting the existence of enormous amounts of biological variation among humans in a wide variety of physical traits (including but not limited to skin color), these anthropologists (among whom the author of this book counts himself) suggest that we should recognize and study human biological variation directly, not through the cloudy lens provided by racial classification. While downplaying the biological theory of race, they suggest the need to recognize that in the social realm, race is an important, sometimes life-or-death matter. From this perspective, race continues to matter in 21st-century America, but as a social or cultural reality, not a fact of nature or biology.

Other anthropologists continue to support the notion that biological differences between humans from different parts of the globe should be formalized in the naming of different races. They argue that racial variation is self-evident and sometimes accuse the opponents of biological race as being "politically correct" advocates of a social or political agenda while asserting that their own position on the reality of race is purely scientific and completely devoid of any political influences. Furthermore, they suggest that in certain fields, notably in forensics and medical studies, race is an important variable that can yield significant insights into the identification of human remains in criminal investigations or in understanding patterns of health and illness.

What are we to make of the inability of anthropologists to agree on something as fundamental as the number or even the existence of human races? In this book, we will explore the historical and present-day controversies concerning human biological diversity and race, using both the biological and the cultural perspectives provided by modern anthropology. This biocultural approach allows us to take a holistic view of human race, one that recognizes the importance of both biological and social or cultural dimensions of the race question. Whether or not race exists as a strongly supported dimension of human biology, we will see that as a social marker and dividing line between individuals and groups, race continues to be of the utmost importance in modern American society. W. E. B. Du Bois (1903:3) recognized this fact more than a century ago when he identified the main problem facing the United States in the 20th century as "the problem of the color line." Forty years later, Gunnar Myrdal (1944) proclaimed race "an American dilemma." In the 21st century, race continues to be a significant social issue for all Americans. Racism still exists in American society, and issues such as affirmative action continue to divide us. Neighborhoods and schools in our cities and towns continue to be racially segregated, and crime, poverty, imprisonment, and even sickness and health reflect the persistent racial inequalities of life in America. One analysis of race in modern American society by a prominent political scientist (Hacker 1992) was titled *Two Nations: Black and White, Separate, Hostile, Unequal*. Although the fight against racism has made great progress in America over the course of the past century, the racial problems that remain are serious. It is therefore important for all Americans to grapple with the anthropological and scientific meanings of race and to form their own opinions based on the best knowledge provided by both natural science and social science on this important topic.

DEFINING RACE

One difficulty encountered by people attempting to discuss race today is the confusion of different definitions used by scientists, anthropologists, journalists, and the public. For example, people often refer to the "Jewish race," the "Hispanic race," or the "Irish race" as if somehow these different uses of the term *race* all refer to the same thing. Among anthropologists and biologists, however, race has historically been *an idea about the geographic patterning of human biological variation*. Essentially, it reflects the observation made by seafaring Europeans several hundred years ago that the inhabitants of the different continents were different with respect to certain physical traits, notably skin color. The term *race* is never used by modern anthropologists to refer to religious groups (e.g., the "Jewish race" or "Hindu race"), linguistic groups (e.g., the "Hispanic race"), or nationalities (e.g., the "Irish race" or "English race"). Religion, language, and nationality are important parts of human culture, but they have little to do with human biology and therefore should not be used in connection with the concept of race. Note that I am not minimizing the importance of, for example, being Anglo or Hispanic in Texas. Nor do I mean to ignore the importance of being Jewish or Muslim in Jerusalem or of being Serbian or Bosnian in Sarajevo. These cultural markers play important roles in shaping identities and structuring lives, but culture does not reflect biological differences, and therefore cultural differences are not relevant to discussions of biological race.

In addition to the cultural variations that distinguish individuals and groups, there are also anatomical or morphological differences between people and populations that reflect underlying biological differences. Some morphological differences are visible to the naked eye, including skin, eye, and hair color and body size and shape. Some other biological differences are just as real but are not as easily seen; these include blood type, fingerprint patterns, and disease susceptibilities. Considering all of these traits that differ among members of our species, there is no doubt that *Homo sapiens* is a species with considerable biological variation. Looking a little deeper, we can see that there is a geographic pattern to some aspects of this biological variation. People with dark skin color can be found in high frequencies in certain parts of the world, including sub-Saharan Africa, Australia, and certain islands in the Pacific, while people with very fair skin are more frequent in other parts of the globe (e.g., Scandinavia and northern Europe and Asia). This kind of geographically patterned biological variation is the traditional raw material of racial classifications. We can define *race*, then, as *the geographic pattern of variation in some biological traits that distinguish different human populations*. A belief in the existence of biological race within the human species is usually associated with the attempt to classify all human populations into a finite number of races based on some set of features such as skin color or blood type. But as we shall see, anthropologists have a long history of disagreeing on how this business of classifying humans into races is to proceed, with no apparent resolution in sight.

THE NATURE OF BIOLOGICAL VARIATION IN *HOMO SAPIENS*

If we look closely at the individuals within any population of *Homo sapiens*, whether the population consists of the inhabitants of a small town or village or a large city, we will be struck by the amount of morphological diversity within the population. No two people look exactly alike, and diversity is often the rule when it comes to the different shades of skin, hair, and eye color represented by individuals within the population. Body size and shape vary, as do a wide variety of genetic traits such as blood type. This within-population biological variation is known as *polymorphic variation*, and it reflects the genetic diversity packaged within populations of our species. Alternatively, the kind of biological variation often used to justify the recognition of different races is *between-population* or *polytypic variation*. Polytypic variation includes the fact that Africans tend to have darker skin color than Scandinavians, while polymorphism refers to the fact that within an African population such as the Yoruba of Nigeria, many individuals differ with respect to skin tone or blood type. Note that both polymorphic variation and polytypic variation are present in traits that are observable in the individual *phenotype* (e.g., skin, eye, or hair color), as well as in phenotypic traits that are not visible to the naked eye, such as blood type. The important point here is that *Homo sapiens*, like all biological species, features some degree of both polymorphic differences within a single population and polytypic differences between populations. We can say, therefore, that *Homo sapiens* is a polymorphic and polytypic species. One of the problems with the position that humans should be classified into races is that this point of view emphasizes the polytypic variation within our species but ignores or minimizes the polymorphic variation that is just as real and just as important. If we name a "Caucasian race," the implication is that all people so classified are somehow the same, ignoring the wide range of morphological and genetic differences between European, Middle Eastern, and North African peoples typically included within this race. A balanced approach to the study of human biological diversity must highlight differences both within and between populations in order to achieve a clearer understanding of the global nature of human diversity. In fact, the most recent attempts by geneticists to measure the relative importance of polymorphic and polytypic variation in *Homo sapiens* demonstrates that the great majority of human genetic variation (85 to 90 percent) is found within the three major continental "races" (Africans, Asians, and Europeans), while only 10 to 15 percent is found between them (Jorde and Wooding 2004). An easily observable example of this phenomenon might be differences in stature between European and African populations. While the average height of Africans may be somewhat greater than that of Europeans, the difference between the shortest and the tallest populations in Europe or Africa is much greater than the difference between the average African and the average European. In Europe, the difference in height between the shortest Sicilian and the tallest Scandinavian is quite large, comparable to that in Africa between the shortest Pygmy and the tallest Bantu. Ignoring polymorphic variation in *Homo sapiens* limits our ability to understand the full spectrum of human biological difference and its geographic patterning.

THE ARBITRARINESS OF THE RACE CONCEPT

If we can accept the presence of polytypic variation in *Homo sapiens*, why not accept the existence of races based on this variation? In other words, if I can tell a Swede from a Nigerian, doesn't this prove that biological race exists? But if biological race is so obvious, how can we explain the long history of disagreement among anthropologists concerning the details of racial classifications? When an anthropologist decides to create a racial classification scheme, one of the first decisions he or she must make is which polytypic trait or traits should be used in the classification. As I have mentioned, a wide variety of traits can be found in human populations living in different parts of the globe. While skin color is the most commonly used racial trait, it is far from the only trait on which one could base a classification of human races. Why not classify humans into races based on nose size and shape, ABO blood type, hair type, or body size or shape? Simply put, there are no rules in place concerning the choice of racial traits; different anthropologists have chosen different traits over the years and as a result have created different racial classifications. The choice of traits on which to base a racial classification is therefore completely arbitrary and subjective: one simply uses the traits that one thinks will yield the best "set" of races and ignores all other traits.

This approach could work and yield a consistent set of races if the different polytypic traits used by different anthropologists actually varied in a consistent manner across different populations. That is, if skin color variations went hand in hand with variations in blood types (i.e., if the genes for skin color and blood type *covary*), a classification based on either trait would be the same. For example, if all African peoples had blood type A while all Europeans had blood type B and all Asians had blood type O, traditional racial classifications based on skin color or blood type would give us the same three basic races. But alas, the true situation of human biological diversity is much more complex. Most polytypic traits do not covary, so classifications based on different traits usually yield different results. For example, while skin color clearly distinguishes European populations living around the Mediterranean from African populations, the presence of the sickle-cell gene (a genetic condition that leads to the sometimes fatal disease known as sickle-cell anemia, which we will discuss in greater detail later) links many sub-Saharan African populations with Caucasians living around the Mediterranean. Which trait is the better racial trait, then, skin color or the presence of the sickle-cell gene? The choice is up to the individual anthropologist, and the arbitrary choice of racial traits is an important reason for the lack of consensus among anthropologists concerning the number of biological races.

Another problem contributing to the arbitrary nature of most racial classifications stems from the manner in which most traits vary within populations. This problem arises from the pattern known as a *normal distribution* or *bell curve* that characterizes most traits used to define races. For example, skin color varies continuously and follows a normal distribution both within and between populations. Skin color can be quantified with an instrument known as a skin reflectometer, which measures the amount of light reflected by a patch of skin (usually measured on the inner arm, an area typically unexposed to direct sunlight and hence untanned). The darker the skin, the less light is reflected, and vice versa. If we were to measure the skin reflectance of a large population from any part of the world, we would find continuous variation in skin reflectance and skin color. Similarly, if we were to measure the skin reflectance of populations across the globe, we would also find continuous variation from the lightest-skinned to the darkest-skinned peoples. Clearly, both polymorphic variation and polytypic variation in skin color are present in *Homo sapiens*. Problems arise when one tries to create discrete, nonoverlapping human races based on a biological trait such as skin color that is continuously variable. Where does one draw the line between a "dark" and a "light" race? The same problem arises if one attempts to divide the world's peoples into tall and short "races." There is obviously significant variation in stature both within and between human populations, but the variation is continuous and follows a normal distribution. There is no single way to break up a continuous curve into a finite number of different groups. Rather, there are an infinite number of ways to do it, but each one is arbitrary and hence no more scientific than any of the alternatives. Standards of tallness are different in the NBA and at the racetrack: a tall jockey would be an extremely vertically challenged basketball player, and even the shortest basketball players are too tall to expect much success as riders at the racetrack. One draws the same conclusion when races are defined by skin color. How dark must one's skin be to qualify as a member of a dark-skinned race? Southern Europeans are darker than northern Europeans, but should they be classified into a separate race because of this fact? And if so, what do we do about the intermediate skin colors of central Europeans? Again, racial classifications that distinguish populations based on traits that display continuous variation are arbitrary and subjective and therefore nonscientific.

To sum up, the reasons that anthropologists have been unable to agree on the exact number of human races is rooted in the very nature of human biological diversity. A variety of biological differences exist both within and between human populations all over the planet, including but certainly not limited to skin color. Anthropologists arbitrarily select one or two of these traits to build racial classifications, but the choice of traits will necessarily affect the resulting classification because different traits vary independently of each other. Thus a classification based on skin color will differ

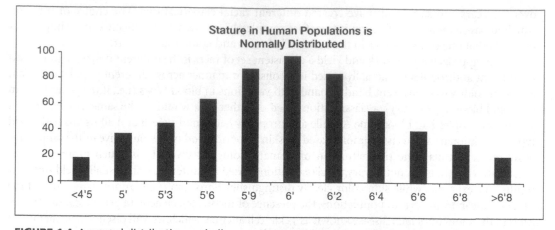

FIGURE 1.4 A normal distribution, or bell curve, characterizes many continuously variable traits among humans, including stature, weight, and skin color. Trying to divide a normal distribution into any number of discrete categories or classes is not scientifically valid because the data are continuously distributed, with no obvious gaps between data points. Any resulting classification is necessarily arbitrary: How would you classify the population represented in this figure with respect to stature? Would we all agree where to make the breaks between "tall," "medium," and "short" individuals?

from one based on blood type. Second, most of these traits vary continuously along a normal distribution or bell curve, and there is no single solution to the problem of how to divide such a distribution into a few, discrete groups. Using skin color to create different races is, in principle, no different from using stature for the same purpose. The same difficulties in scientifically and objectively defining a tall and a short race are found in attempts to define a black and a white race. The result can be seen in the history of anthropological attempts to answer the question "How many human races are there?" Different scholars, using different traits or different dividing lines between the same traits, have come up with completely different classifications. This problem is so severe that perhaps it is time to recognize that we have been asking the wrong question all these years and to try to change our whole approach to the study of the geographic pattern of biological variation in *Homo sapiens*. Rather than continue in these futile attempts to determine how many races exist, perhaps it is time for anthropologists to try a different approach to the study of human race.

AN ALTERNATIVE APPROACH TO THE STUDY OF HUMAN DIVERSITY

The real lesson of 250 years of racial classifications is that attempting to classify people into different races based on the geographic patterns of biological variation between populations is doomed to failure. How many races exist is simply the wrong question for anthropologists to ask, since there is clearly no single objective and scientific answer to this question. Biocultural anthropology suggests a new way to study human biological diversity, one based on two different but complementary theoretical approaches provided by biological and cultural anthropology.

Genetics and Darwin's model of evolution by natural selection provide the specifically biological theory that will allow a new and better understanding of human biological diversity. In place of the classificatory approach that anthropologists have used in the past, an evolutionary approach seeks an understanding of the adaptive significance of racial differences. Rather than determining the correct racial box in which to place all "dark-skinned" populations, this new approach aims to understand the evolutionary and adaptive significance of population-level variations in human skin color. The question becomes "Why do human populations in the tropics tend to have darker skin than populations living in the world's temperate zones?" Rather than static classifications of the *patterns* of racial difference, the evolutionary approach seeks to understand the dynamic, evolutionary *processes* behind the geographic patterns of biological diversity seen in *Homo sapiens*. The goal of this approach is to understand the evolutionary and historical processes that led to the patterns of biological diversity that we see in human populations today. The discussion of the principles of evolutionary theory in chapters 2 through 4 provide the needed biological background for the analysis of human racial differences from an evolutionary perspective.

The cultural part of the biocultural approach recognizes that the notion of race has a multitude of cultural meanings separate from any questions concerning its status as a biological concept. This approach is sensitive to the historical development of the notion of race as a cultural construction and to the fact that race is constructed differently in different societies and even in the same society at different points in time. Examples of different cultural constructions of race will be discussed later in this text, but we can take a quick look at the different ways that the system of racial classification works in Brazil and in the United States as an example. In Brazil, many more gradations of skin color are recognized than in the United States, where one is typically considered to be black, white, or Asian. The anthropologist Marvin Harris (1964) elicited 40 different racial names from a sample of 100 Brazilians! In addition, one's socioeconomic status in Brazil greatly modifies one's position in the racial hierarchy. It is said that "money lightens the skin" in Brazil and in so doing raises one to a higher "racial" level or category. By contrast, in the United States, skin color trumps economic considerations to the extent that even rich and famous African Americans may be as likely as poor blacks to experience racism. Throughout much of American history, a single black ancestor made one black to the legal authorities, regardless of the number of white ancestors! These kinds of racial distinctions are clearly in the realm of culture rather than biology, and a full understanding of what race means today requires a consideration of its biological, cultural, and historical dimensions.

The biocultural approach advocated here is a synthesis of the often dichotomized biological and cultural aspects of the race concept. It confronts race as both a biological and a cultural notion and critically evaluates its usefulness on both fronts. It replaces the old-fashioned typological or

FIGURE 1.5 A reflection of the significance of being black or white in New Orleans in the aftermath of Hurricane Katrina. Note the different verbs used by the news agencies to describe the behavior of desperate people wading through the flooded streets of New Orleans in search of food when they are white ("finding") or black ("looting").
Courtesy of Chris Graythen/Getty Images b) Courtesy of Dave Martin/AP Photo.

classificatory approach of earlier centuries with a new approach that seeks to understand the dynamic processes that have led to the biological diversity that is recognized in different ways by various human societies today. Informed by an equal dose of evolutionary principles and cultural understanding and with a keen sense of the historical development of the race concept, the biocultural approach evaluates both the biological (i.e., evolutionary and genetic differences between and within populations) and the cultural aspects of race formation and race classification (i.e., the different meanings associated with racial membership in society). Only by combining biological and cultural approaches can anthropology clarify the intellectual and social muddle surrounding race today. I cannot think of a more important task for anthropology to confront as we move through the 21st century.

A NOTE ON TERMINOLOGY: USING THE "R" WORD

Should a book that purports to critique the notion of biological race use the terms *race* or *racial variation* when referring to biological variation between human populations? One could reasonably argue that using these terms may unconsciously and unintentionally confuse some students and readers and sabotage the author's intended message that race as biology is very problematic. In this book, I have decided to use the term *biological race* unabashedly (i.e., without quotation marks, italics, or apologies) to refer to a concept that has historically been used to classify human populations on the basis of assumed biological differences. The reader should be aware that by using terms like *biological race* or *racial traits*, I am not suggesting that these concepts are valid biological notions or that they have stood up to the scrutiny of modern biologists or biological anthropologists. Instead, I am only arguing that they are legitimate linguistic usages that have had historical currency in the West for nearly 400 years. As a result, these terms are essential linguistic tools to build an intelligible argument about the historical development of race and changing scientific and anthropological opinions about the meaning of race. Race has always been an idea about biological variation in *Homo sapiens*; I will interrogate it as biology and find it lacking. I will argue that while the concept of race originated as a kind of folk biology, it fails as modern biology. Today, race is best considered as a social or cultural construction. One could say that race exists in our heads, not in the real world.

Discussion Questions

1. In what ways does arbitrariness creep into any attempted racial classification, and how does this help clarify the difficulty that anthropologists have had in answering the question as to how many races exist?

2. What does it mean to say that *Homo sapiens* is both a polymorphic and a polytypic species?

3. Can you think of any regional variations in racial terminology within the United States? For example, are there some parts of the country that recognize and name races differently than in other parts of the country?

4. Compare the shift in the analysis of race practiced by modern biological anthropologists to the way that anthropologists approached the study of race in the past.

5. What are some examples from the text of the misuse of the term race that we might hear today on the street but not from the mouths of anthropologists? Why are these terms considered to reflect a misunderstanding of the historical meaning of race?

CHAPTER 2

Charles Darwin and Evolutionary Theory

"Nothing in Biology makes sense except in the light of evolution."

DOBZHANSKY 1973:125

DARWIN AND THE GALAPAGOS

Like Newton, Freud, and Einstein, Charles Darwin is one of the very few scientists who can be credited with ushering in a genuine scientific revolution. He was born in 1809 in the English town of Shrewsbury, the son of a prosperous doctor whose high expectations that Charles would follow in his footsteps and become a medical doctor were soon to be dashed. As a child, Charles gave no indication of future scientific greatness. He was a mediocre student who struggled with the classical curriculum of the day, with its emphasis on mathematics and the Greek and Latin classics. Conceding to his father's wishes, he entered Edinburgh University in Scotland in 1825 to study medicine but soon found out that he was no match for the primitive and harsh realities of medical practice of the time. While at Edinburgh, he had the misfortune of observing two surgical operations that, in this era before the use of chloroform or other kinds of anesthesia, were gruesome and difficult procedures. Unable to bear watching the suffering of the patients, one of whom was a child, he had to leave the operating room before the procedures were completed. Many years later, he would write in his autobiography that "these two cases fairly haunted me for many a long year" (Barlow 1958:48). He left Edinburgh after two years and completed his higher education at Christ's College at Cambridge University, where, following his father's wishes, he studied theology and prepared for a career as a minister in the Church of England. Unknown to his father, however, Charles had already lost his faith, and it is unclear how far he was willing to indulge his father's wishes about becoming a minister after graduation. Luckily for him, another career path appeared just as he graduated from Cambridge in 1831.

At Cambridge, Darwin had studied with several of the leading scientists of the day, including the geologist Adam Sedgwick and the botanist John Henslow, and his love for nature (the study of which was called "natural history" at the time) had made a very strong positive impression on these influential scientists. Under their tutelage, Darwin learned the latest theories in geology, zoology, and botany, and he soon realized that he would much rather collect beetles, dissect fish, and take long walks through the countryside observing the geological terrain than preach the word of God. When Henslow was asked to make a recommendation for a scientist to serve as "ship's naturalist"

FIGURE 2.1 Portrait of Charles Darwin (1809–1882) at age 31, by George Richmond, 1840.
Courtesy of DEA Picture Library/Getty Images.

aboard HMS *Beagle*, a British naval vessel about to sail around the world, he recommended Darwin. The main purpose of the *Beagle*'s voyage was to map the coastlines of South America, but her captain, a man named Robert Fitzroy, wanted to have a scientist aboard whose duties would be to study the geology and zoology of the many places visited during what would turn out to be a five-year voyage. Darwin was understandably thrilled at his good luck and opportunity, and with some help and support from his uncle Josiah Wedgewood (the early industrialist of Wedgewood porcelain fame), he was able to convince his father to give his blessing and allow him to take the job. Little did his father suspect that as a result of his son's scientific contributions, the voyage of HMS *Beagle* would become the most famous British scientific expedition of the 19th century and that the experiences Charles would have on this trip would lead him to make one of the most momentous discoveries in the history of biology.

During the voyage of the *Beagle*, Darwin would spend time engaged in the study of all facets of natural history in many interesting and exotic places, including Australia and Hawaii, but nearly three of the five years would be spent mapping the coastlines of South America. Darwin experienced an earthquake while hiking in the Andes Mountains, found fossils of long-extinct mammals in Argentina, and studied the origin of coral reefs in the South Pacific. But the most important place he visited, in the sense of making the observations that would propel him to develop his theory of evolution, was an archipelago of small volcanic islands situated about 600 miles west of Ecuador in the Pacific Ocean known as the Galápagos Islands. It was here that as a result of his studies of the unique

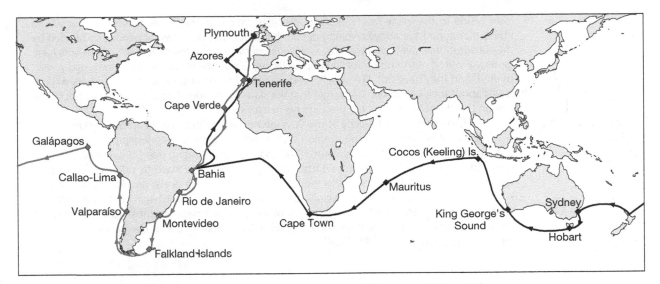

FIGURE 2.2 HMS *Beagle* circumnavigated the globe over the course of five years (1831–1836). Note the location of the Galápagos Islands, situated along the equator in the Pacific Ocean, 600 miles west of Ecuador, to which country they belong today.

BOX ONE
Charles Darwin on Slavery

Although the British government had outlawed the transatlantic slave trade in 1807 and eventually abolished slavery in the British Empire in 1833, during the five-year voyage of the *Beagle* (1831–1836), Darwin saw at first hand some of the ugly realities surrounding slavery and its effects on both slaves and slaveholders in South America. Throughout his life, he was a committed and outspoken abolitionist who strongly supported the monogenist position for the unity of the human species (details of the debate between the monogenists and polygenists appear in chapter 5). In his published journal, *The Voyage of the Beagle*, published in 1839, Darwin describes his impassioned and empathic reaction to slavery as a result of his own experiences during the voyage:

On the 19th of August we finally left the shores of Brazil. I thank God, I shall never again visit a slave country. To this day, if I hear a distant scream, it recalls with painful vividness my feelings, when passing a house near Pernambuco, I heard the most pitiable moans, and could not but suspect that some poor slave was being tortured, yet I knew that I was as powerless as a child even to remonstrate. I suspected that these moans were from a tortured slave, for I was told that this was the case in another instance. Near Rio de Janeiro I lived opposite to an old lady, who kept screws to crush the fingers of her female slaves. I have staid [*sic*] in a house where a young household mulatto, daily and hourly, was reviled, beaten, and persecuted enough to break the spirit of the lowest animal. I have seen a boy, six or seven years old, struck thrice with a horsewhip (before I could intervene) on his naked head, for having handed me a glass of water not quite clean: I saw his father tremble at a mere glance from his master's eye. These latter cruelties were witnessed by me in a Spanish colony, in which it has always been said that slaves are better treated than by the Portuguese, English, or other European nations. I have seen at Rio de Janeiro, a powerful negro afraid to ward off a blow directed, as he thought, at his face. I was present when a kind hearted man was on the point of separating forever the men, women, and little children of a large number of families who had long lived together. I will not

(continued)

even allude to the many heart-sickening atrocities which I authentically heard of:—nor would I have mentioned the above revolting details, had I not met with several people, so blinded by the constitutional gaiety of the negro, as to speak of slavery as a tolerable evil. Such people have generally visited at the houses of the upper classes, where the domestic slaves are usually well-treated; and they have not, like myself, lived amongst the lower classes. Such enquirers will ask slaves about their condition; they forget that the slave must indeed be dull, who does not calculate on the chance of his answer reaching his master's ears.

. . . Those who look tenderly at the slave-owner, and with a cold heart at the slave, never seem to put themselves into the position of the latter:—what a cheerless prospect, with not even a hope of change! Picture to yourself the chance, ever hanging over you, of your wife and your little children—those objects which nature urges even the slave to call his own—being torn from you and sold like beasts to the first bidder! And these deeds are done and palliated by men, who profess to love their neighbors as themselves, who believe in God, and pray that his Will be done on earth! It makes one's blood boil, yet heart tremble to think that we Englishmen and our American descendants, with their boastful cry of liberty, have been and are so guilty. [Darwin 1962:496–498]

and strange fauna and flora of these islands, Darwin would begin to question the prevailing scientific opinions of the time concerning the origins of biological organisms and the reasons for the diversity seen in the world of living things.

Like most of his contemporaries during the 1820s and 1830s, Darwin was a believer in a notion that came to be known as "special creation." This is essentially the biblical story (told in Genesis, the first book of the Bible) that God created all living things in their present form and placed them in appropriate environments on the earth. Species did not evolve according to this view, nor did they ever go extinct, and the world and its living things were considered to be quite young. Some people had tried to date the world based on a literal reading of the life spans of the ancient patriarchs presented in the book of Genesis. Counting back 20 generations from Abraham to

FIGURE 2.3 Some of the unique life forms of the Galápagos Islands, including the large land tortoise that gives the islands their Spanish name and two marine lizards. These are the only ocean-dwelling lizards in the world. Courtesy of Thinkstock by Getty Images.

Adam and Eve, it had been suggested by a certain Archbishop Usher that the creation had occurred in 4004 B.C.E. (beginning at 8:00 p.m. on Saturday, October 22!). Animals (and plants) were well adapted to their environments as a direct result of God's divine plan and his omnipotence. This explanation for the adaptive features of living things was known as the "argument from design" and is best known from the writing of William Paley, an author whose work was familiar to Darwin from his student days. In *Natural Theology* (1803), Paley presented his famous analogy of the watch and the watchmaker in making a case for the argument from design and for the existence of God. Paley suggested that a close examination of the inner workings of a watch would indicate that this complex machine must have been skillfully designed by a watchmaker for the obvious purpose of telling time. Thus the presence of design and purpose as evidenced by the watch are proof of the existence of a watchmaker. By analogy, the existence of living things with clearly designed features that serve some purpose or function in life (e.g., the sharp teeth and claws of carnivorous animals for eating meat, the lungs of mammals for breathing air, and just about any other anatomical or physiological feature one might think of) implies the existence of some rational, intelligent designer of these living things. Surely, Paley and his contemporaries argued, living things could not have arisen randomly or by chance, in the same way that a functioning watch could not simply arise by the chance or random mixing of wheels, gears, and levers. So in this way, design and adaptation within biology was reduced to and explained by the creation story of a single religious tradition from the ancient Near East. Furthermore, Paley and his followers used the evidence of design and purpose in nature as a philosophical proof of the existence of God. This was the pre-evolutionary "biology" that Darwin learned at university and brought with him on the voyage of the *Beagle*, but it would soon be shattered on the volcanic rocks of the Galápagos Islands. The observant reader can hardly fail to note the similarities between the early-19th-century argument from design and the modern "alternative" to evolutionary theory known as intelligent design. Modern proponents of intelligent design also suggest that the living world is simply too complex to have arisen without the guiding hand of some omniscient designer. They too are wrong.

The Galápagos are a group of about a dozen volcanic islands that rose from the Pacific sea floor as a result of repeated underwater eruptions over the last several million years. In spite of the fact that they have never been connected to the mainland of South America, the fauna and flora of the Galápagos Islands show close similarities with those of Central and South America. Many of the animals and plants that Darwin saw there, however, are endemic to the Galápagos. That is, they

BOX TWO

Intelligent Design: A Modern Argument from Design?

The argument from design was a popular 19th-century idea that suggested that the presence of complexity and adaptation among all living things proved that life must have been designed by some divine intelligence. In 1803, Archbishop William Paley used the famous analogy of the watch and the watchmaker to argue that adaptations in living things also required a designer, because they could not have appeared by random processes, only by purposeful design. This idea actually has very deep roots in Western thought and can be traced back to Greek philosophers (e.g., Plato and Aristotle) in the fourth century B.C.E. and Roman thinkers (e.g., Cicero) in the first century B.C.E. In the 13th century C.E., the Catholic theologian Thomas Aquinas argued that the presence of complexity and design in nature and in all living things was a clear proof of the existence of God. Like all well-educated Englishmen of the early 19th century, Darwin was very familiar with Paley's watchmaker analogy and its inescapable implication that all living things were perfectly designed by an omniscient divine being. When he developed his theory of evolution by natural selection, however, Darwin presented a very different picture of the world of nature. Rather than argue that living things showed signs of perfect design, he cited many

(continued)

examples of clearly less than perfect design in the way that animals and plants were put together or lived their life. For example, on the Galápagos Islands, Darwin saw flightless cormorants, large seabirds who, like all members of the cormorant family of birds, dive and swim underwater in the ocean to feed on small fish. In spite of the fact that, uniquely among the approximately 40 known species of cormorants, these birds are flightless, they still bear the anatomical remnants of an evolutionary past when their ancestors could fly: a set of small, useless wings. In fact, nature is full of flightless birds, and in every case, they retain vestiges of a flying past. Darwin wondered why a divine designer of all life would provide reduced and functionless wings for birds that never flew, like the kiwi, ostrich, emu, cassowary, and penguin? Other examples of vestigial organs are common in nature, including the appendix in humans and the remnants of eyes in functionally blind subterranean mammals such as the subterranean mole rat or the naked mole rat of the genus *Spalax*. Darwin suggested that the presence of vestigial organs in nature suggested that living things are not perfectly designed, and he recognized that this evidence seriously weakened the argument from design. The presence of vestigial organs was better explained as a result of the historical development and evolutionary relationships of living organisms. The fact that flightless birds retain the useless vestiges of wings is proof positive that at some time in the past, these birds had flying ancestors. When they lost the ability to fly, they also lost much of the associated anatomical specializations required for flight, including large flight muscles, a powerful keel on the breastbone for their attachment, and most of the wing feathers. But enough of these features remain in the vestigial wings of flightless birds to clearly demonstrate that flightless birds are the evolutionary descendants of once-flying birds. In this way, Darwin's logic disproved the notion that living things were perfectly designed by an almighty designer and supplanted the argument from design.

A challenge to Darwinian evolution that echoes the argument from design has recently appeared from within biological science itself. Known as intelligent design, the theory is most fully developed in the book *Darwin's Black Box: The Biochemical Challenge to Evolution*, written by Lehigh University biochemist Michael Behe (1996). Whereas the traits considered as reflecting design in the 19th century were complex anatomical features such as the mammalian eye, modern advocates of intelligent design like Behe have moved the argument to the molecular level. In *Darwin's Black Box*, Behe used the term *irreducible complexity* to refer to complex physiological or molecular features of living organisms that in his view are too complex to be explained by natural selection alone and must therefore have been created by an "intelligent designer." Irreducibly complex traits are thought to include multiple interacting parts in which the removal of any part would destroy the function of the complex whole. Behe's main examples include the flagellum or tail-like structure of bacteria such as *E. coli*, the blood-clotting system of vertebrates, and the immune system. Behe provides a modern update of Paley's watchmaker analogy in his example of the mousetrap as a structure marked by irreducible complexity. He argues that the mousetrap consists of five interacting parts—base, catch, spring, hold-down bar, and hammer—all of which must be present for it to function properly. The removal of any of these interdependent pieces will destroy the function of the trap, and since the trap functions only with all five pieces in just the right relationships, Behe argues that there can be no intermediate, evolutionary steps that will lead to a functioning whole of this sort. Consequently, in Behe's view, irreducible complexity must require some form of intelligent design.

One of the main problems with Behe's view of irreducible complexity in the thinking of the overwhelming majority of biologists today is that it ignores the fact that many complex biological structures may have had different functions in ancestral forms. Complex biological adaptations such as the mammalian eye or the vertebrate immune system can in fact evolve by natural selection as simpler versions change in function or in efficiency of operation. The evolution of the eye can be traced in living things from organisms with simple light-sensitive pigments on the skin to the development of a depression in the light-sensitive tissue that allows greater visual acuity to the development of a small aperture through which light enters as it does in a pinhole camera to the fully fledged and extremely complex mammalian eye, with its separate lens, retina, optic nerve, and muscles. At each stage of this hypothetical evolutionary sequence, natural selection would have acted on variations present in the population with respect to the anatomy and function of the evolving eye. Even tiny advantages or disadvantages in the ability to see would have provided more than enough raw material for natural selection to act on. Over many millions of years, the result could well be the appearance of the complex eye we see today in mammals, without any need to call on the help of an imagined "intelligent designer."

One of the most cogent critics of intelligent design and irreducible complexity is Brown University biologist Kenneth R. Miller, whose 2008 book *Only a Theory* points out many flaws in the creationist arguments. Miller cogently argues that neither mousetraps nor bacterial flagellae nor any of the other

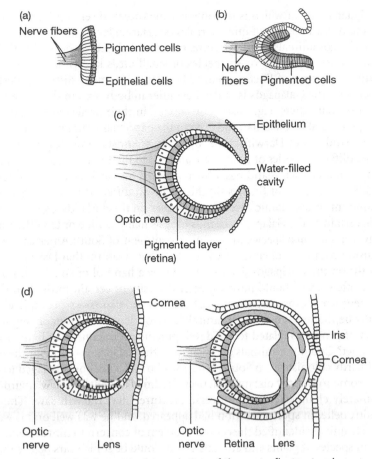

FIGURE B2.1 Stages in the evolution of the eye reflect natural selection, not intelligent design.

examples cited by Behe truly demonstrate irreducible complexity. Simpler versions exist for each of these adaptations, sometimes serving different functions, but always plausibly fine-tuned and modified by natural selection. My sense of the scientific community's reaction to the notions of irreducible complexity and intelligent design is that these ideas have been completely rejected as untestable, unnecessary, and irrelevant to the teaching of biology. In its *Kitzmiller* v. *Dover Area School District* decision in 2005, the U.S. Supreme Court agreed that intelligent design is a form of creationism and thus a religious doctrine rather than a scientific theory. Requiring that it be taught in public schools would therefore violate the establishment clause in the First Amendment of the U.S. Constitution, which states that "Congress shall make no law respecting an establishment of religion." While the debate continues in many American communities and school boards, the scientific and legal arguments are clear: intelligent design is simply a modern form of the argument from design, part of the scientifically discredited theory of creationism, and as such should play no role in science education in America.

are unique species found nowhere else on earth. They are also an obviously nonrandom selection of animals and plants: the animal community is dominated by reptiles and birds, while the only mammals present were goats, dogs, pigs, and rats that were brought (either intentionally or inadvertently) to the islands by human colonizers. The most notable of the original inhabitants of the Galápagos are the giant land tortoises that are found throughout the archipelago and for which the island chain is named (*galápago* is the Spanish word for "tortoise"). The Galápagos also boast the presence of two species of large iguana, one of which is the only marine (ocean-dwelling) iguana in the world. The other is a large and fierce-looking but quite harmless vegetarian land dweller.

But the Galápagos animals that have come to be most closely associated with Darwin and his theory of evolution are the dozen or so species of small birds known as Galápagos or Darwin's finches. The different species of finches seem to be adapted to many different lifestyles, diets, and local environments on the Galápagos Islands: they differ in body size, in the size and shape of their beaks, in their customary diets (e.g., insects or plants), in their preferred habitat (upland forests, mangrove swamps, coastal woodlands), and even in the particular island on which they are found. It seems (and much study since Darwin's time, by many scientists, provides strong support for this position) that the different species of finches are adapted to fill different *ecological niches* on the various islands. For example, each island has a finch adapted for catching and eating small insects on the wing, but different species of finches fill this niche on different islands. There seems to be an extraordinary amount of taxonomic diversity of finches on these islands, especially when one considers that while certain of the Galápagos Islands have as many as nine or ten different finch species, there exists only a single finch species in the entire continent of South America! To a lesser extent, the same conclusion could be drawn for many of the other creatures that Darwin saw and collected during his months on the Galápagos. He wondered why a handful of small volcanic islands in the middle of the Pacific Ocean should have a greater diversity of certain birds than the entire South American continent while other large groups of animals and plants were completely absent. Could this pattern really be the result of a supernatural cause or divine creation, or might it reflect some other, natural set of processes related to the development and migration of living things across the surface of the planet? Could the animals and plants on the Galápagos represent the evolved descendants of a set of hardy colonists from South America who had somehow managed to cross 600 miles of Pacific Ocean sometime in the distant past, been modified under these new environmental conditions, and ultimately changed into the diverse creatures that Darwin saw? The first cracks in Darwin's orthodox belief in special creation had appeared, and he was well on his way to becoming an evolutionist. He quickly identified the central problem of concern to him as being the nature and origin of different species of plants and animals, but it would be some years before the full outline of his theory of *evolution by natural selection* would crystallize.

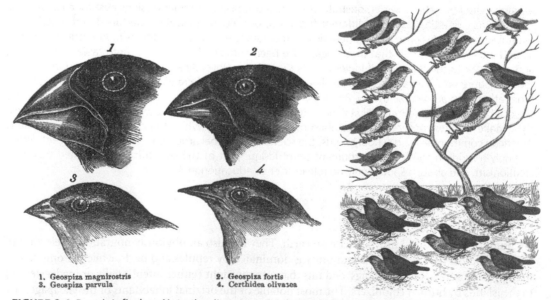

1. Geospiza magnirostris
3. Geospiza parvula
2. Geospiza fortis
4. Certhidea olivasea

FIGURE 2.4 Darwin's finches. Note the diversity in beak size and shape and habitat among these closely related birds. Courtesy of Universal Images Group/Getty Images.

BOX THREE

Darwin's Finches: A Case Study in Evolution

Because most biologists and anthropologists think that the finches that Darwin saw on the Galápagos Islands played a large role in the development of his evolutionary theory, it is quite surprising to find out that in fact Darwin himself did not think (or write) very much at all about the finches that have come to bear his name. *The Voyage of the Beagle* is full of discussions of the iguanas (he grabbed one's tail and pulled it from its burrow!) and tortoises (he rode on the back of one!), but about the finches, he only mentions their lack of fear of humans: he didn't even know that they were all finches, thinking that some were blackbirds, wrens, and warblers. It wasn't until the ornithologist John Gould studied the 31 stuffed specimens that Darwin brought back to London that the birds were all properly classified as members of the finch group.

One of the few mistakes that Darwin made in his pioneering work as a globe-trotting naturalist was in not labeling the island of origin for each of the specimens he collected in the Galápagos. It wasn't until one of the local inhabitants mentioned to him that the tortoises varied from island to island that he began to label his specimens as to their island of origin. He states in *The Voyage of the Beagle:* "I never dreamed that islands, about fifty or sixty miles apart, and most of them in sight of each other, formed of precisely the same rocks, placed under a quite similar climate, rising to a nearly equal height, would have been differently tenanted" (Darwin 1962:394). But that is exactly the story for the birds and other animals of the Galápagos: the finches on different islands differ in many details of body size, beak size and shape, and plumage colors. They also differ with respect to the habitats in which they dwell, their diets, and other behaviors. But all of this would have been news to Darwin, since much of our knowledge about the evolutionary biology of Darwin's finches has come long after Darwin's death in 1882, as the result of the work of a number of ornithologists, notably Peter and Rosemary Grant, a husband-and-wife team of Princeton University biologists whose study of Darwin's finches on the island of Daphne Major has become one of the landmark studies in all of evolutionary biology (Weiner, 1994).

Beginning in 1973 and continuing every year for more than 30 years, the Grants have returned to the Galápagos Islands to study two finch species on Daphne Major, the medium ground finch (*Geospiza fortis*) and the cactus finch (*G. scandus*). Their study is basic, low-tech field biology: they capture, identify, weigh, and measure the birds and track their attempts at raising a family before releasing them; they do the same thing every field season. In recent years, they have added the collection of a few drops of blood for genetic tests of relatedness back in the lab. As a result of this long-term study of individual animals and their descendants over many generations, the Grants have painted a detailed and fine-grained picture of how evolution actually occurs in nature. Perhaps the most surprising result from this amazing study is how quickly evolution by natural selection can modify phenotypic traits in a natural population in response to climate change. The Grants have documented that beak size in the ground finch became larger in drought years, when the plants that produce the majority of small seeds were wiped out, and as a result, the larger-beaked ground finches were at an advantage because they could eat the still available large seeds. Similarly, during very wet years when the cactus plants did poorly but there was an abundance of small seeds from other plants, the beak shape of the cactus finches became blunter as they began to eat more small seeds.

The work of Peter and Rosemary Grant has demonstrated that animals do indeed track environmental changes and respond to climate shifts in understandable ways. It also suggests that the process of evolution by natural selection can be studied on a much shorter time scale than many would have thought, including Darwin himself, who thought that evolutionary change proceeded at far too slow a pace to allow one to observe it in nature. This research has enormous implications for our modern world and ecosystems in light of the now overwhelming evidence for global climate change under the influence of human industrial activities. While we may not be able to predict exactly how the world's ecosystems will be affected by global warming, we can be certain that increasing temperatures will exert selective pressures on animals and plants and that there will be winners and losers among living creatures.

FIGURE 2.5 Down House, where Darwin lived his entire life after the voyage of the *Beagle.* Just outside London, it is today a museum dedicated to Darwin's life and work, run by the Natural History Museum in London. © Adrian Chinery / Alamy.

Upon returning to England at the conclusion of the voyage of the *Beagle* in 1836, Darwin found that his situation in life and prospects for the future were radically different than they were five years earlier, at the beginning of the voyage. He met and became friends with many of the leading scientists in England, including Thomas Henry Huxley and Charles Lyell, who would support him in his new and revolutionary work. He published his journal of the voyage in 1839, and it was well received by both the scientific community and the buying public, and Darwin was quickly recognized as one of the most promising young naturalists in the United Kingdom. Other books on the origins of coral reefs, earthworms, and barnacles solidified his reputation as a first-rate biologist. He soon married his first cousin, Emma Wedgewood, the daughter of his uncle Josiah Wedgewood, the man who in 1831 had convinced Charles's father to allow him to sail on the *Beagle.* Charles and Emma quickly settled down in a large country house outside of London where they would live the rest of their lives and raise a large family and where Charles would do most of the writing for which he is so famous today. Most important, Darwin returned to England after the voyage of the *Beagle* deeply skeptical of the pre-evolutionary ideas (special creation and the argument from design) that he had been taught in school and church, preferring to seek a natural explanation for the origins, distribution, and adaptive features seen in the biological world.

SCIENTIFIC PRECURSORS TO DARWIN

It is important to realize that Charles Darwin was neither the "inventor" of the concept of biological evolution nor the first modern scientist to speculate about an evolutionary theory. In fact, his own grandfather, Erasmus Darwin, had published a long, philosophical poem called *Zoonomia* in 1794 in which he suggested an evolutionary development of life. Certainly the most famous evolutionary precursor to Darwin was the French scientist Jean-Baptiste de Lamarck, whose *Philosophie Zoologique* (1809) was the first influential evolutionary treatise published in modern Europe. In Lamarck's view, organisms had an inborn "desire" or "drive for perfection" that naturally (i.e., without any intervention by a supernatural agent) led to organisms' becoming well adapted to their environment. According to Lamarck, organisms were able to become adapted to environmental conditions through their own exertions, coupled with this inner drive. In addition, he thought that once organisms acquired adaptive features through the use (or nonuse) of their organs or body parts, they could pass these adaptive features on to their offspring through a process known as the "inheritance of acquired characteristics." Lamarck's classic example of the process of evolutionary change was his explanation for the origin of the long neck of the giraffe. He suggested that individual giraffes lengthened their necks as a result of using them to stretch higher and higher to reach leaves that were high on trees. Having acquired longer necks as a result, they were then able to pass their longer necks to their offspring. Many generations of this kind of striving to become adapted would naturally lead to the evolution of the long neck of the modern giraffe. Unfortunately for Lamarck, many European biologists soundly criticized his theory as untestable and unscientific. In the 1880s, the German biologist August Weismann would definitively disprove the notion of the inheritance of acquired characteristics with an ingenious set of experiments. Weismann cut off the tails of mice and bred these mice for many generations in an attempt to create a tailless mouse through Lamarck's proposed mechanism. But in spite of many generations of tail amputations, each newborn mouse was born with a perfectly normal tail. Weismann suggested that whatever biological material was passed from parents to offspring (he coined the term *germplasm* for this material), it was not affected by changes acquired during life by the physical body of the individual (what Weismann called the *soma*), and therefore somatic or bodily characteristics that were acquired during one's life were not inherited by offspring. Perhaps the most important and influential aspect of Lamarck's work was the notion that all living things were well adapted to their environments as the result of some kind of interaction between organism and environment. Darwin would never accept the notion that organisms had some mysterious inner drive toward becoming adapted, but he recognized that Lamarck was correct to highlight the relationship between organism and environment, and this idea would be a major part of his own still-to-be-developed evolutionary theory.

FIGURE 2.6 Jean-Baptiste de Lamarck (1744–1829). Lamarck was an early evolutionist whose theory of how evolution occurs (through the "inheritance of acquired characteristics") has been superseded by Darwin's theory of natural selection. © Mary Evans Picture Library / Alamy.

FIGURE 2.7 Charles Lyell (1797–1875), whose uniformitarian theory of geology greatly influenced the young Darwin. In spite of his influence on and support of Darwin's work, Lyell never fully embraced Darwin's evolutionary theory.
Courtesy of De Agostini Picture Library/Getty Images.

Two other important influences on the development of Darwin's evolutionary ideas were Charles Lyell and Thomas Malthus. Lyell's contribution to Darwin's thought was the geological doctrine known as uniformitarianism, which Darwin first learned about during the voyage of the *Beagle* as a result of reading Lyell's three-volume *Principles of Geology* (1830–1833).

Uniformitarian geology involved several ideas that were ultimately useful to Darwin, including the great antiquity of the earth, the complete reliance on natural rather than supernatural causes to explain geological change, and the idea that geological events in the past could be understood through the study of present-day processes. Darwin used each of these scientific principles in the development of his own ideas about biological change in a direct way that makes clear his scientific debt to Lyell. For example, the notion that all life had evolved from simpler common ancestors to the diversity and complexity that we see in the world today required an antiquity of the planet and of its life that was far greater than allowed by the restricted chronologies of a few thousand to a few hundred thousand years that were generally accepted during the 18th century. For Darwin's evolutionary theory to be plausible required an earth history of millions of years, and Lyell provided him with just this kind of chronology. Uniformitarian geology was in part a reaction to earlier, theologically inspired geological theories that relied on biblical events to explain aspects of earth history. These theories relied on supernatural powers and events mentioned in the Bible (e.g., Noah's flood) to explain aspects of the earth's history. Lyell was a thoroughly modern scientist in his reliance on natural causes to explain the record left in the rocks. The key to the success of uniformitarian geology can be seen in the motto of the early uniformitarians: "The present is the key to the past." They relied on present-day, observable processes of geological change to explain the geological record. For example, a study of the deposition of silt in today's Mississippi River delta allows geologists to interpret similar features in the rock record of the earth (and even of other planets such as Mars) as the result of the deposition of silt by rivers in the past; there is no need to offer explanations based on the actions of gods or other supernatural causes. For Darwin, the uniformitarian motto became a guiding principle in his attempts to develop a theory of biological evolution. Like Lyell, Darwin relied on present-day, natural, and observable processes to explain the history of life, and he never had recourse to supernaturalism or theology to explain difficult facts or observations in the biological realm.

Thomas Malthus was an English cleric who wrote a small book about human population size that was to have an immediate and extraordinary effect on Darwin's thinking about the nature of evolution. In his autobiography, Darwin describes how one day in October 1838 while he was reading Malthus's *On Population Size* "for amusement" (Barlow 1958:120), he hit upon the germ of the idea of evolution by natural selection. Malthus was writing about human populations, how they increase over time, and some of the unpleasant results of unrestrained population growth. He noted that human reproductive capacity could, under the right circumstances, lead to very rapid population growth. Imagine how quickly a human population could increase in size if each married couple had ten children. Although very large by modern American standards, this family size is well within the normal range of human fertility and one that is still often reached or surpassed in societies that place a high cultural or economic value on large families and that do not practice birth control. Malthus argued that this kind of exponential population increase would quickly outstrip the available food and other resources needed to sustain the rapidly growing population. These circumstances would inevitably result in increased competition for the scarce resources necessary for life, and what Malthus called a "struggle for existence" would ensue. Ultimately, competition for scarce resources and more crowded living conditions would act to limit human population size increases

FIGURE 2.8 Thomas Malthus (1766–1834), whose work on human population size and the "struggle for existence" led to Darwin's development of the theory of natural selection.
Courtesy of Heritage Images/Getty Images.

through a series of catastrophes such as the spread of epidemic diseases, widespread famine, or warfare. Population size would crash, and the cycle would start all over again. Although Malthus was speaking of human populations and human history, Darwin's genius was to immediately see the significance and applicability of these demographic ideas to the questions he was asking about the populations and histories of species in nature. Darwin realized that what Malthus suggested for humans was equally or even more valid for other living things, but he took the argument further than Malthus had. The tendency of population size to increase at a faster rate than the increase in resources required for life would lead to a "struggle for existence" in every species living in nature. Furthermore, if the result of this competition were to be the differential survival of individuals who were smarter, quicker, or more efficient in whatever manner (i.e., better adapted to their environment), perhaps this could explain the origin of adaptive design in the biological world. Animals and plants were adapted to their environments as a result of the strict competition to survive in nature; only the fittest could survive, reproduce, and leave offspring. Over many generations of this "natural selection," populations and species could change in response to the requirements of their environments. He would later note the significance of reading Malthus in his autobiography: "Here, then, I had at last got a theory by which to work" (Barlow 1958:120). With this insight derived from his reading of Malthus, his observations during the voyage of the *Beagle*, and Lyell's principles of uniformitarianism, Darwin was on his way to the development of the most important biological theory of the 19th century.

THE ELEMENTS OF THE THEORY OF NATURAL SELECTION

Darwin's theory of evolution by natural selection can be explained as a set of natural facts or observations and some logical deductions that result from these facts. This kind of analysis makes it clear that Darwin's great contribution was to synthesize a set of biological observations and logical ideas that were for the most part common knowledge and were generally available to many other scholars of his time. His genius was not in thinking of something completely new under the sun but in synthesizing existing knowledge to answer, in a strikingly original manner, the most important biological question of the day concerning the origin of species and of their adaptations. One of his contemporaries, upon first reading *The Origin of Species* and noting that its argument was so simple, logical, and obvious, is said to have exclaimed, "How stupid not to have thought of it oneself."

   1. **The existence of inherited variation in natural populations and species.**   Darwin's interest in and knowledge of plant and animal breeding suggested to him that all species were characterized by high levels of genetic variation. Animal and plant breeders used (and still use) a technique known as "artificial selection" to choose certain desired traits among domestic animals or plants. In Darwin's day, breeders of dogs, pigs, cattle, orchids, and many other plant and animal species were able to create new varieties or breeds in spite of their almost complete lack of understanding of the principles of genetics. They simply knew that if they allowed only the animals or plants with the desired traits (e.g., large size and aggressiveness in dogs) to reproduce, over several generations they could create breeds with maximal expression of the desired trait. This was clear evidence that the genetic variation was present from the start and simply required artificial selection to increase (or decrease) its expression. Think of the amount of genetic variation that must have been present in the ancestral wolf populations to allow for the creation of the multitude of dog breeds known today. So the presence of large amounts of inherited variability in all species of living things provides the raw material for evolutionary change.

   2. **Populations tend to increase much faster than available resources.**   Darwin discovered this fact through his reading of Malthus's famous essay on human population size and quickly realized its relevance to the biological world of animals and plants. Mathematically, the argument is that population size tends to increase at an exponential (i.e., multiplicative or geometric) rate while resources increase at a significantly slower linear (i.e., additive or arithmetic) rate. Over time,

resources cannot support the increasing demands of the rapidly growing population. This leads to competition for resources or, as Malthus called it, a struggle for existence.

3. A struggle for existence occurs between individuals in all populations.   If all individuals in a population are genetically different and if population size tends to outstrip available resources necessary for life, it follows that a competitive struggle for existence must occur in which the individuals with the best available traits are more likely to survive than those with less than optimal characteristics. Darwin simply applied the logic of Malthus to the world of nature to arrive at this deduction. We should note, however, that not only survival but also reproduction counts in the Darwinian struggle for existence. Living to adulthood is a necessary but not a sufficient condition for fitness in the biological world: one must also reproduce and leave descendants. We can only truly know who the winners and the losers are in the struggle for existence by determining differential rates of survival and reproduction over several generations. The key to success in the Darwinian world is not simply the "survival of the fittest" but differential success in reproduction. We call this process natural selection.

4. Natural selection leads to genetic changes in populations, adaptation to different environments, and ultimately to the origin of new species.   Over many generations, natural selection leads to adaptation, to evolutionary change within a species, and sometimes to the origin of new species. This process results from the differential survival and reproduction of individuals with different combinations of inherited characteristics. These different characteristics either increase or decrease an individual's ability to compete with other members of their species, and so the frequency of these traits are likewise increased or decreased in the population over time with the passing of generations. One can imagine that in early human prehistory, the frequency of hunters with severe myopia (nearsightedness) might have been reduced in favor of hunters who were better able to see and strike their prey with their weapons and thus guarantee food on the table with greater consistency. So natural selection should lead, in the short term, to a greater degree of adaptation between a species and its environment. In the long term, as environments change and populations migrate to different habitats, natural selection should lead to the origin of new species.

THE MAKING OF *THE ORIGIN*

Although Darwin had developed these ideas into a coherent theory of natural selection and clearly understood the importance of this work by 1838, it is surprising to discover that he did not publish on natural selection until 1859. He did develop his ideas "in a very brief abstract of my theory in pencil in 35 pages" (Barlow 1958:120) in 1842 and an expanded 230-page manuscript in 1844, but he published neither of these, choosing instead to simply distribute both manuscripts to several of his closest colleagues and friends for comments. Recognizing the unorthodox nature of his work and the likelihood that its conclusions would be welcomed by neither the scientific nor the religious world, he hoped to build a convincing case by amassing documentation and support for his ideas. He was also busy in these years writing several other books on a wide variety of biological and geological topics, including the better part of eight years (1846–1854) spent working on his book on the barnacles! So in spite of the fact that he had resolved the two most important theoretical questions in 19th-century biology (does evolution occur? and if so, by what mechanism does it act?), he didn't publish his conclusions for more than 20 years.

In 1856, Lyell advised Darwin that he must publish his work on natural selection soon or take the risk of some other biologist winning the credit for his discovery. Darwin ignored this good advice and continued to delay publication until his hand was forced by the receipt of a manuscript sent to him by Alfred Russell Wallace in the summer of 1858. Wallace was a naturalist who, like Darwin, had spent years collecting plants and animals in many exotic locales around the world, including throughout the Malayan archipelago in the South Pacific. Also like Darwin, Wallace had read Malthus's essay and had been similarly struck by the applicability of his argument concerning the "struggle for existence" to the biological questions surrounding the origin of species and their evolution. But unlike Darwin, Wallace quickly wrote a manuscript developing these ideas and sent it to Darwin, by now a well-respected naturalist, for his comments and advice on publication. Darwin was shocked and heartbroken to discover that Lyell's prediction had indeed come true and that while he had been spending decades building evidence for his theory, Wallace had independently developed the theory of natural selection and was ready to publish. Darwin's first inclination was to destroy his own manuscripts and to defer publication of the theory to Wallace, since he feared that some might accuse him of stealing Wallace's idea. Luckily, his friends and colleagues, who knew full well that Darwin had developed the theory independently and long before Wallace, were able to arrange for joint presentation of Wallace's paper and a brief paper of Darwin's at a meeting of the Linnaean Society in London in the fall of 1858 and for publication of both papers in the Linnaean Society's *Proceedings* later that same year. Darwin finally got serious about publishing, and *On the Origin of Species, or the Preservation of Favored Races in the Struggle for Existence* became available on November 24, 1859. The entire first run of 1,250 books sold out on the first day, and a second run of 3,000 additional copies sold out soon thereafter. Although both Darwin and Wallace share credit for independently developing the theory of evolution by natural selection, Darwin's name is more closely associated with the idea because of the lifetime of work he devoted to it and the fullness of the documentation that he developed in support of it.

Although publication of *The Origin* led to a storm of controversy within the religious elements of Western societies (some of which continues to this day in the debates over the teaching of creationism or intelligent design as alternatives to evolution in American schools), the scientific community was largely won over by the force and elegance of Darwin's argument. Forced by circumstances into publishing his revolutionary ideas in 1859, Darwin promptly retired from the loud public debates over the validity and meaning of his theory, leaving the fight to such longtime scientific

FIGURE 2.9 Alfred Russell Wallace (1823–1913), the codiscoverer of the theory of evolution by natural selection. Courtesy of Hulton Archive/ Getty Images.

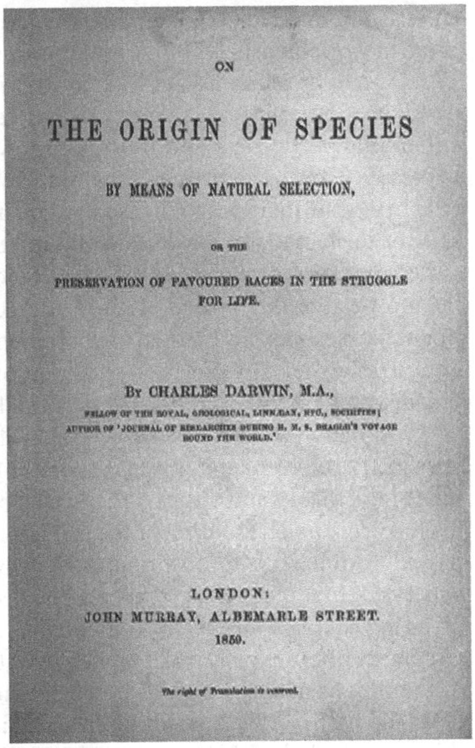

ON

THE ORIGIN OF SPECIES

BY MEANS OF NATURAL SELECTION,

OR THE

PRESERVATION OF FAVOURED RACES IN THE STRUGGLE
FOR LIFE.

By CHARLES DARWIN, M.A.,

FELLOW OF THE ROYAL, GEOLOGICAL, LINNÆAN, ETC., SOCIETIES;
AUTHOR OF 'JOURNAL OF RESEARCHES DURING H. M. S. BEAGLE'S VOYAGE
ROUND THE WORLD.'

LONDON:
JOHN MURRAY, ALBEMARLE STREET.
1859.

The right of Translation is reserved.

FIGURE 2.10 Darwin's *Origin of Species* was published in 1859 and went through six editions during Darwin's lifetime. This is the title page of the first edition. Courtesy of GraphicaArtis/Getty Images.

FIGURE 2.11 Thomas Henry Huxley (1825–1895), know as "Darwin's Bulldog" was the grandfather of Aldous Huxley, the famous author of *Brave New World.* © *Photo Researchers / Alamy.*

allies as Thomas Henry Huxley, who referred to himself as "Darwin's bulldog." He did, however, continue to work on aspects of his evolutionary theory, publishing his thoughts on human evolution in *The Descent of Man and Selection in Relation to Sex* in 1871. In this important book, Darwin also developed an evolutionary mechanism to explain the appearance of characters that are thought to enhance attractiveness and thus to improve an organism's ability to compete for mates but don't necessarily improve, or may even hinder, the ability of the individual to survive or compete for resources. The male peacock's feathers are perhaps the best-known example of a trait that evolved in spite of the fact that it may hinder the ability of an individual bird to survive in nature. Darwin suggested that elaborate traits of this sort could evolve if the females preferred to mate with males with the most elaborate trains of brightly colored feathers. Perhaps the reader can speculate on traits that might have evolved in male and female members of our own species as a result of sexual rather than natural selection. Today, sexual selection continues to be an important part of the much larger body of Darwinian theory that has arisen in the 150 years since publication of *The Origin*.

Although Darwin's argument for evolution by natural selection stood up to a barrage of criticism generated by religious thinkers, one of the early scientific criticisms identified the one real weakness of the theory and struck a nearly fatal blow. The weak link in Darwin's argument had to do with his incorrect understanding of the principles of inheritance by which novel adaptive traits would be passed from parents to offspring. Essentially, Darwin suggested a form of "blending inheritance," in which parental traits were somehow blended together in the act of sexual reproduction, resulting in offspring having a mixture or combination of the traits shared by their parents. If the father were tall and the mother short, Darwin thought that the offspring would inherit a blended or averaged version of the genetic material relating to height and would be intermediate in height compared to the parents. Some of Darwin's scientific critics quickly recognized that natural selection could not work if this were really how the process of inheritance worked. The problem is that any novel trait that improved the level of adaptation of an individual (and presumably increased the survival and reproduction of its bearer) would quickly be blended out of existence over several generations. The process would be analogous to blending red and white paint together over and over: one would lose the distinctive red and the unblemished white in favor of a nondescript pink. Darwin recognized the validity of this criticism but was never able to resolve it despite much effort over the years and many revised editions of *The Origin*. Ironically, the true nature of inheritance had already been determined and published in 1865 by an obscure Austrian monk and amateur botanist, Gregor Mendel, but this work was completely unknown to Darwin and his allies and was to remain hidden for 35 years.

Discussion Questions

1. Darwin did not invent the idea of evolution. Rather, he synthesized lots of biological information from a variety of sources to come up with his theory of natural selection. Briefly describe the elements of Darwin's theory that he borrowed from each of the following people or disciplines.
   a. Thomas Malthus
   b. Charles Lyell
   c. The professional breeders of animal and plants

2. We have seen how Lamarck's theory "explained" the long neck of the giraffe. How do you think a modern Darwinian would explain it?

3. What was quickly recognized as the major problem with Darwin's theory?

4. What is the argument from design, and what two things does it seek to explain or prove?

5. Is the expression "survival of the fittest," which was coined by Herbert Spencer and never used by Darwin, an accurate shorthand way of referring to the theory of evolution by natural selection? Why or why not?

CHAPTER 3

Genetics from Mendel to the Human Genome Project

"Research is to see what everybody has seen and to think what nobody has thought"

Szent-Györgyi 1957.57

"Thus I felt slightly queasy when at lunch Francis winged into the Eagle to tell everyone within hearing distance that we had found the secret of life"

Watson 1968:115

GREGOR MENDEL AND THE BIRTH OF GENETICS

Gregor Mendel lived most of his adult life as a monk at the Saint Thomas Monastery in the city of Brno, the capital of Moravia, which at the time was a part of the Austro-Hungarian Empire. Today it is the second-largest city in the Czech Republic, with nearly 400,000 inhabitants. Mendel had been trained in science and mathematics at the University of Vienna and was a science teacher at the local *Gymnasium* (high school) until he became abbot of the Augustinian monastery in 1868. During his years there, he performed a series of breeding experiments on the common pea plant (*Pisum sativum*) in the greenhouses and gardens of the monastery. His results, which were published in 1865 by the Natural History Society of Brno in a paper with the modest title "Experiments in Plant Hybridization," are today recognized as the starting point for all of modern genetics, in particular Mendelian genetics, the branch that bears his name. Essentially, Mendel discovered the principles of the inheritance of traits or characteristics within all sexually reproducing organisms, from fish to the members of the band Pfish. Let's take a closer look at Mendel's experiments, his results, and the explanatory model that he developed in order to explain his results and to build the foundation of Mendelian genetics. In so doing, we will see how Mendel's work, and the understanding of the nature of inheritance that it allowed, solved the problems posed by Darwin's mistaken ideas on blending inheritance.

FIGURE 3.1 Gregor Mendel (1822–1884), the father of modern genetics.
© World History Archive / Alamy

Mendel's first set of breeding experiments involved the simple crossing (*hybridization*) of pea plants that differed in one easily visible characteristic. In one set of these *monohybrid cross* experiments, he crossed plants that were tall with short plants. He already knew that his tall and short plants were "true-breeding," meaning that if he self fertilized a tall plant, all offspring always resembled the parents and were also tall. Remember that self-fertilization is possible in many plants that, like the common pea plant, are true hermaphrodites and have reproductive organs of both sexes: male *stamens* and female *pistils*. Mendel's short plants were also true-breeding, as were each of the six other easily distinguished traits he worked with (wrinkled or round seeds, green or yellow seeds, white or gray seed coat, terminal or axial flowers, etc.). Darwin postulated that inheritance was a process involving the blending of parental "blood line" that resulted in the offspring's being a mixture or average of the parental traits. This suggested that the offspring of a tall and a short pea plant would be of medium height. Mendel's experiments yielded the surprising result that all offspring of this kind of cross resembled the tall parent in height. The same result was obtained for each of the other six sets of traits: the offspring always resembled one of the parents and were never a blended average of the parental traits. Mendel called the trait that appeared in these hybrid offspring the *dominant* trait, and he called the one that seemingly disappeared the *recessive* trait. But what had happened to the recessive trait? Had it truly disappeared, never to occur in any of the descendants of the original parental pair? Or did it remain within the first generation hybrids while showing no outward evidence of its presence? Mendel explored this question by self-fertilizing the tall offspring of the original cross (we refer to the original, true-breeding parents as the P or parental generation, the first set of hybrid offspring as the F_1 or first filial generation, the second set of offspring resulting from the crossing of the F_1 plants as the F_2, and so on). Again his results were surprising in that both

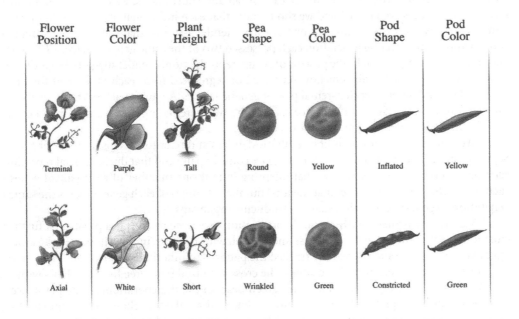

Flower Position	Flower Color	Plant Height	Pea Shape	Pea Color	Pod Shape	Pod Color
Terminal	Purple	Tall	Round	Yellow	Inflated	Yellow
Axial	White	Short	Wrinkled	Green	Constricted	Green

FIGURE 3.2 Mendel's experiments involved crosses between pure-breeding pea plants for seven different characteristics. While all first-generation (F₁) plants always showed the dominant trait, his second-generation (F₂) results revealed a 3:1 ratio of plants with dominant and recessive traits. Courtesy of Field Museum Library/Getty Images.

the dominant and the recessive traits appeared in the F_2 generation of plants. So the recessive trait had not disappeared; it was merely masked by the presence of the dominant trait in the F_1 hybrids.

At this point in his experiments, Mendel made the critical decision to count the number of tall and short plants in the F_2 generation to see if any pattern might emerge from a mathematical or statistical analysis of his results. Working with each of the other six traits, he replicated his results for tall and short. For each pair of true-breeding traits, one of the pair was found in all of the F_1 individuals (the dominant trait) but the other trait (the recessive trait) reappeared in one of every four F_2 plants, yielding a 3:1 ratio of tall (or dominant) to short (or recessive) plants. In the final step in this set of hybridization experiments, Mendel self-fertilized each of the F_2 plants. This final cross allowed him to determine if the tall and short plants of the F_2 were genetically identical to the pure-breeding tall and short plants of the parental generation. It turned out that the short plants of the F_2 were pure-breeding in the same way that the parental generation short plants were (i.e., they always yielded short plants upon self-fertilization), but the situation was a bit more complex with the tall F_2 plants. One of every three F_2 tall plants was pure-breeding tall, while two of every three tall plants, upon self-fertilization, yielded tall and short offspring in the familiar 3:1 ratio. In other words, two-thirds of the F_2 tall plants were genetically identical to the original F_1 tall hybrids. What initially seemed to be a 3:1 ratio of tall to short plants was in reality a 1:2:1 ratio of true-breeding tall (dominant) to hybrid tall to true-breeding short (recessive) plants. Mendel recognized that rather than being a blending process, inheritance was actually a *particulate* process, and that the actual material that was inherited from parents to offspring maintained its existence as particles from generation to generation. Inheritance was clearly a more complex and more interesting subject of study than Darwin ever imagined, and Mendel now had enough information to allow him to develop a theory to explain these results.

Mendel's theory suggested that each of the traits that he studied was determined by the presence of a pair of inherited factors. In the case of tall and short plants, we can speak of a dominant factor *T* and a recessive factor *t*, and we should note that each individual plant has either two dominant factors, two recessive factors, or one of each. Mendel assumed that the pure-breeding tall and short plants of the parental generation each possessed two of the same genetic factors (*TT* for the tall and *tt* for the short plants). In the process of sexual reproduction, Mendel suggested that the pairs of genetic factors for each trait somehow separated or segregated from each other, and the offspring inherited one member of each parental pair of genetic factors. A pair of each of these genetic factors must be present in each offspring, since each of the two parents supplied a single member of each pair. Today these genetic factors are known as *genes*.

We can now formalize this first result of Mendel's and refer to it as his first law, or the Law of Segregation. It states that genetic factors or genes come in pairs and that during sexual reproduction, each pair segregates or separates so that offspring inherit one member of each pair of genes from each parent. Segregation ensures that the total number of copies of each gene remains the same from generation to generation in all sexually reproducing organisms.

Mendel performed another set of hybridization experiments with pea plants that further elucidated the nature of the genetic process and the behavior of genes in inheritance. In these *dihybrid cross* experiments, he simultaneously tracked the patterns of inheritance of two different characteristics over several generations. For example, he cross-fertilized true-breeding tall plants with yellow peas with pure-breeding short plants with green peas. In the F_1 generation, all the plants were tall with yellow peas, suggesting (as Mendel already knew) that tall and yellow were dominant to short and green, respectively. Presumably, all of the F_1 plants carried one each of the dominant and recessive traits for height and color (*TtYy*), while the parental plants carried two identical copies of the dominant (tall and yellow, *TTYY*) or recessive (short and green, *ttyy*) genes. When Mendel

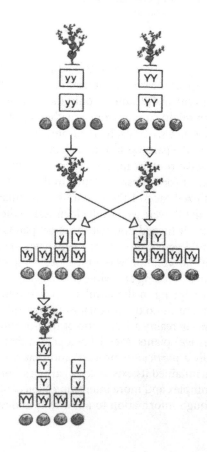

FIGURE 3.3 Mendel's monohybrid cross of pure-breeding yellow and green peas yielded all yellow peas in the first generation, and a 3:1 ratio of yellow to green in the second generation. Yellow is thus dominant to green, which is recessive to yellow. From results like these, Mendel formulated his Law of Segregation.

cross-fertilized the F₁ hybrids, he found four different kinds of plant in the F₂ generation, in the striking ratio of nine tall and yellow, three tall and green, three short and yellow, and one short and green. Notice that nine plants were dominant for both traits (tall and yellow), three plants were dominant for the first trait and recessive for the second (tall and green), three plants were recessive for the first and dominant for the second (short and yellow), and one plant was recessive for both traits (short and green). Notice also that for every 12 tall plants, there are 4 short ones, and for every 12 yellow plants, there are 4 green ones. Mendel noticed these 3:1 ratios and determined that the 9:3:3:1 ratio was simply the result of two different and independent 3:1 ratios for each of the two sets of traits in his dihybrid crosses. In other words, the tall and short genes were segregating normally, as were the yellow and green genes, suggesting that segregation held for different pairs of genes too. He built his second law, the Law of Independent Assortment, on his interpretation of these results, stating that different pairs of genes segregate or assort independently of each other during sexual reproduction. It was clear to him that his particulate model of inheritance worked when looking at a single inherited trait or at two or more traits (the mathematical ratios quickly get messy, but the principle works for as many pairs of genes as one cares to study).

By demonstrating that inheritance is a particulate process rather than a blending process, Mendel solved Darwin's problem of the loss of new and useful variation. In the Mendelian world of particulate inheritance, genetic adaptations that improved an individual's ability to compete in the Darwinian struggle for existence could spread rapidly through the population over a few generations, leading to the kinds of adaptive improvements and evolutionary changes that Darwin argued for. Mendel also demonstrated that genes come in pairs, that these pairs can be inherited independently of each other, and that the presence of certain genes could mask the presence of others. Mendel's work forms the basis for the

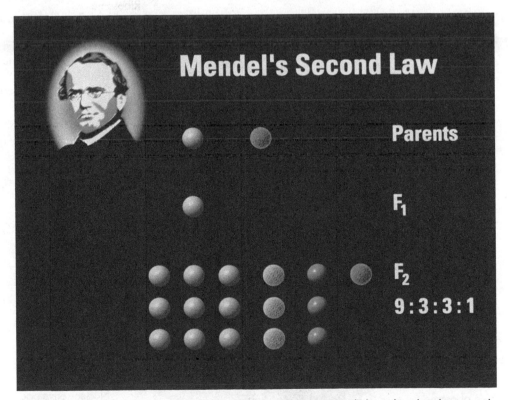

FIGURE 3.4 Mendel found a 9:3:3:1 ratio in the second generation (F₂) results when he crossed true-breeding plants for two different traits. In this example, the peas are either yellow (dominant) or green (recessive) and either smooth (dominant) or wrinkled (recessive). This dihybrid cross led to Mendel's second law, the Law of Independent Assortment.
Credit: Laguna Design/Science Photo Library.

modern science of genetics, and he is today rightly considered the father of genetics. His experiments clearly distinguish between what we call today the *genotype*, the actual genes that an individual carries for some trait (e.g., *TT* or *Tt* or *tt*), and the *phenotype*, the observable trait of interest that is influenced by some genotype (e.g., tall or short pea plants). Unfortunately for Darwin (and for Mendel), Darwin was completely unaware of Mendel's results and of their importance to his own ideas on evolution, in spite of the fact that they were published in 1865, only six years after the appearance of the first edition of *The Origin of Species*. But in 1900, three different European botanists independently rediscovered Mendel's publication and quickly recognized its significance. While we know a lot more today about the processes of inheritance than we did in 1865 or 1900, Mendel's laws are still as true and as important as ever. They continue to provide the foundation for understanding the nature of the inheritance of many congenital diseases, as well as of many other inherited traits in all life forms from bacteria to humans.

GENES, CHROMOSOMES, AND CELL DIVISION

When Mendel's work was rediscovered in 1900, biological science was poised on the brink of important new discoveries about the biology of the cell, the mysteries of cell division, and the nature and location of Mendel's "genetic factors" within the cell. With new and better microscopes, cell biologists were gradually able to identify the major components of the cell and to suggest that all living things were constructed of cells. Today we know that there is a great diversity of living cells, ranging from nerve cells to blood, muscle, and fat cells. For the purposes of our discussion (i.e., understanding evolution and genetics), we will focus on one set of cellular actors, the

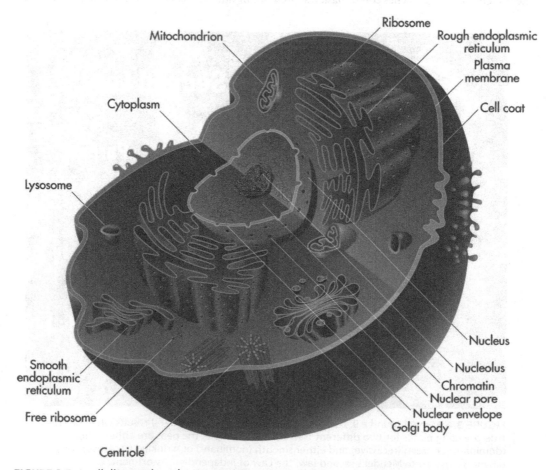

FIGURE 3.5 A cell slit open in order to reveal its parts. Note the nucleus, where the chromosomes are found, and the many organelles found in the cytoplasm (outside the nucleus).

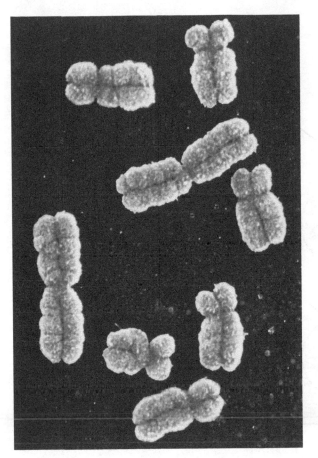

FIGURE 3.6 Chromosomes are paired structures of different size and shape that are found in the cell's nucleus. They carry the hereditary material known as DNA, which makes up the genes.
Credit: Biophoto Associates/Science Photo Library.

chromosomes, and ignore much of the rest of the complex biology of cells. In particular, we seek to understand the behavior of chromosomes during cell division and sexual reproduction and to relate this to what we already know about the transmission of Mendel's "genetic factors."

Leaving plants behind for the moment, there are two kinds of cell division that occur in cells in the bodies of animals: *mitosis* and *meiosis*. Mitosis yields *somatic cells*, which account for most cells in the body, while meiosis yields *gametes* or reproductive cells, which are found exclusively in the testes of males (sperm cells or *spermatozoa*) and the ovaries of females (egg cells or *ova*). Note that except for the reproductive or germ line cells, all of the varied types of cells that exist in the body (e.g., muscle, nerve, blood, liver, bone) are somatic cells. Mitosis explains part of the quandary of how a complex adult organism made up of billions of cells can begin life as a single cell (i.e., an ovum fertilized by a sperm cell). In mitosis, a somatic cell can replicate itself and then divide into two "daughter" cells, each with all the same cellular components as the original "parent" cell. The early cell biologists were able to determine that mitosis began with duplication of the cell's chromosomes: these were then divided equally into each of two daughter cells. For example, in humans, normal somatic cells have forty-six chromosomes organized into twenty-three similar or *homologous pairs*. We call the number of chromosomes in a somatic cell the *diploid number* (2N = 46 in *Homo sapiens*), while the number of homologous pairs is known as the *haploid number* (N = 23 in *H. sapiens*). In mitosis, a single diploid cell divides into two diploid daughter cells.

Meiosis is a somewhat more complex process whose purpose is to regulate the number of chromosomes that are passed on to each offspring in sexual reproduction. Since sexual reproduction involves the fusion of two reproductive cells or gametes (sperm and ovum) to form a new organism, how can the proper diploid number of chromosomes be maintained from generation to generation? It should be clear that if the sperm and ova were themselves diploid cells, the fertilized

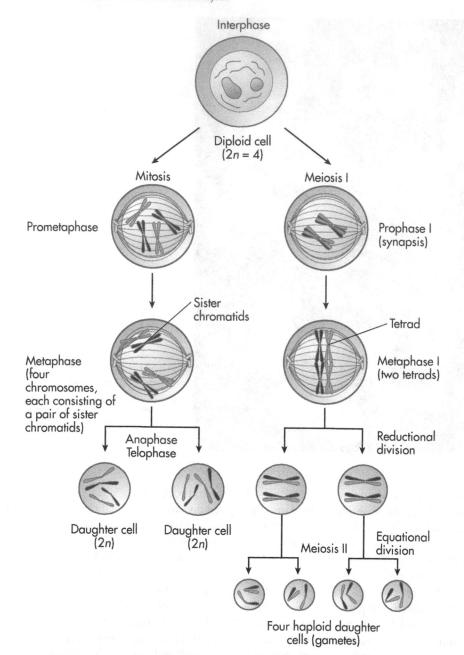

FIGURE 3.7 The two kinds of cell division are known as mitosis and meiosis. Mitosis occurs in somatic cells and yields two diploid daughter cells from the division of a diploid parent cell. Meiosis yields four haploid daughter cells after two divisions from a diploid cell, resulting in the formation of gametes or reproductive cells.

ovum (also known as the *zygote*) would have twice the diploid number of chromosomes ($2 \times 46 =$ 92 in *H. sapiens*), a prescription for developmental disaster. Meiosis ensures that this does not occur by reducing the number of chromosomes in gametes from diploid to haploid (i.e., from 46 to 23 in *H. sapiens*). The happy result is that the fertilized ovum or zygote has the diploid number of chromosomes. Meiosis achieves this result through two separate divisions, starting with a diploid cell, which then duplicates its chromosomes (i.e., from 46 to 92 in *H. sapiens*), to yield four cells with the haploid number of chromosomes (i.e., 23 chromosomes in *H. sapiens*). In meiosis, each daughter cell receives one member of each pair of homologous chromosomes.

Once the behavior of chromosomes during meiosis had been seen under the microscope, certain similarities were immediately noticed between these processes and the patterns of inheritance proposed by Mendel. Both Mendel's genetic factors and chromosomes come in pairs and are passed on from parents to offspring, only one of each pair is passed on to an individual sperm or ovum, and the pair is re-formed in the fertilized ovum or zygote. A closer look reveals that both of Mendel's laws have parallels in the actions of chromosomes during meiosis.

Mendel's Law of Segregation, in which pairs of genetic factors end up in different gametes, is mirrored by the separation of the members of each chromosomal pair into different gametes when the number of chromosomes is reduced from diploid to haploid. The Law of Independent Assortment, in which different pairs of genetic factors segregate independently of each other, is reflected in the independent separation of different homologous pairs of chromosomes during meiosis. To explain these striking similarities, Walter Sutton and Theodor Boveri independently hypothesized in the first decade of the 20th century that Mendel's genetic factors (*genes*) must be part of or reside on the chromosomes. Thus was born the *chromosomal theory of inheritance*, to which all of modern genetics still subscribes.

With the chromosomal theory of inheritance in place, biologists were finally able to make sense of the patterns of inheritance of many different traits in humans and other organisms. One essential tool for determining the results of different genetic crosses was developed by the geneticist Reginald Punnett and is known as the *Punnett square*. Using a simple 2-by-2 matrix to model the result of a monohybrid cross, the Punnett square allows us to illustrate how the processes of meiosis, Mendel's laws, and sexual reproduction predict the kinds and frequencies of offspring that will be born to parents with certain genetic traits. For example, the accompanying figure demonstrates how a Punnett square can be used to determine the probability of a child's being born with the recessive disease known as cystic fibrosis to two parents who are both heterozygous carriers of this recessive gene. Today the Punnett square is a very useful tool for both the genetic counselor and the anthropologist, allowing us to use our knowledge of inheritance to predict the genotypic and phenotypic results of any simple genetic cross.

An interesting and important exception to the standard Mendelian ratios was discovered in the "Fly Room," the Columbia University laboratory of Thomas Hunt Morgan where breeding experiments

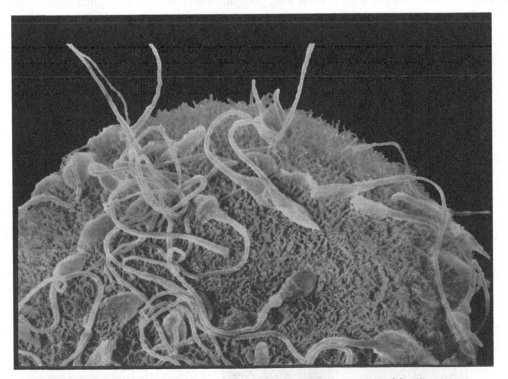

FIGURE 3.8 An ovum with many sperm cells on its surface at the moment of fertilization.
Credit: Dr. Yorgos Nikas/Science Photo Library.

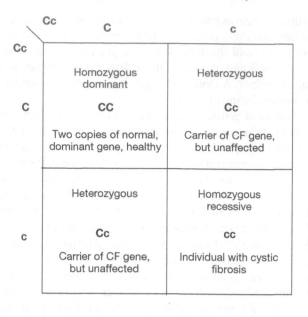

	C	c
C	Homozygous dominant **CC** Two copies of normal, dominant gene, healthy	Heterozygous **Cc** Carrier of CF gene, but unaffected
c	Heterozygous **Cc** Carrier of CF gene, but unaffected	Homozygous recessive **cc** Individual with cystic fibrosis

FIGURE 3.9 Punnett square showing the results of a mating between two individuals who are both heterozygous carriers (Cc) of the recessive cystic fibrosis gene. Note that one-fourth of their offspring will have the disease, one-fourth will be normal, and half will be carriers, like the parents.

on the fruit fly *Drosophila melanogaster* were conducted in the early 1900s. This exception to the newly formed genetic rules helped illuminate several important genetic processes including *mutation*, the chromosomal mechanisms of *sex determination*, and the phenomenon of *genetic linkage*. Normal fruit flies have bright red eyes, but on a spring day in 1910, Morgan noticed the presence of a single male fly with white eyes. Assuming correctly that he had chanced upon the result of a new genetic mutation, Morgan began a set of breeding experiments with this unique fly. After breeding it with some of his normal, red-eyed sisters, Morgan determined that the resulting progeny of the F_1 generation all possessed red eyes. This was not a surprising result: if the new mutation were recessive, this is just what Mendel would have predicted. The surprise came when Morgan allowed his red-eyed F_1 flies to breed with each

FIGURE 3.10 Thomas Hunt Morgan (1866–1945).
Courtesy of Gamma-Keystone/Getty Images.

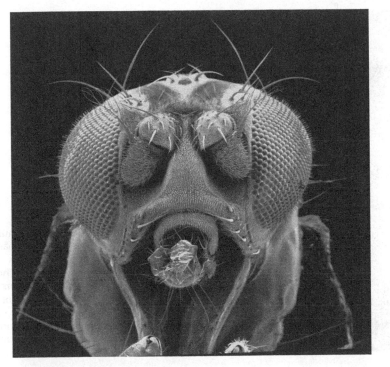

FIGURE 3.11 A wild-type, red-eyed fruit fly.
Credit: Eye of Science/Science Photo Library.

other. The F_2 generation included red-eyed females, red-eyed males, and white-eyed males but no white-eyed females. Somehow this new genetic trait had been passed down from the grandfather to his grandsons but not his granddaughters. At this point, Morgan and several of his brilliant and soon-to-be-famous students recognized that the gene for white eyes must somehow be related to the chromosomal mechanisms of sex determination, and in the following years, they managed to unravel this puzzle, for which Morgan was awarded the Nobel Prize for Physiology or Medicine in 1933.

Morgan had discovered the phenomenon of sex linkage, in which certain genes are present on what we call the *sex chromosomes*, X and Y. In mammals and fruit flies, one pair of chromosomes determines the sex of the individual: males have XY, while females have XX. Males are said to be *heterogametic* because the sex chromosomes are not homologous (i.e., they don't look at all similar and don't carry the same genes), while females are *homogametic* by virtue of their possession of two similar X chromosomes. The other 22 pairs of chromosomes in humans are called *autosomes*, to distinguish them from the sex chromosomes. In the same way that individuals inherit one copy of each pair of autosomal chromosomes from each parent, one of our sex chromosomes enters the zygote via the sperm and the other via the ovum. Females obviously inherit an X chromosome from each of their parents, while males inherit their X chromosome from their mother and their Y chromosome from their father. The gene for eye color is found on the fruit fly's X chromosome, so it is said to be *sex-linked* or *X-linked*. As a result, males will normally carry only one copy of the gene on their single X chromosome, while females will have a pair of eye color genes on their two X chromosomes. Knowing that the gene for red eye is dominant to the white eye gene, we can use the Punnett square to illustrate the mechanisms of sex-linked inheritance in the fruit fly. Alternatively, we can explore this process by examining the human inheritance patterns of *hemophilia*, a serious medical condition in which the blood fails to clot properly, caused by a recessive, sex-linked gene on the X chromosome. Hemophiliacs are typically the children of a heterozygotic mother, who carries one copy of the normal clotting gene and one copy of the recessive hemophilia gene on her two X chromosomes, and a normal father, who carries the normal clotting gene on his one X chromosome. As the Punnett square reveals, one-half of all male children born to these parents would be expected to inherit the

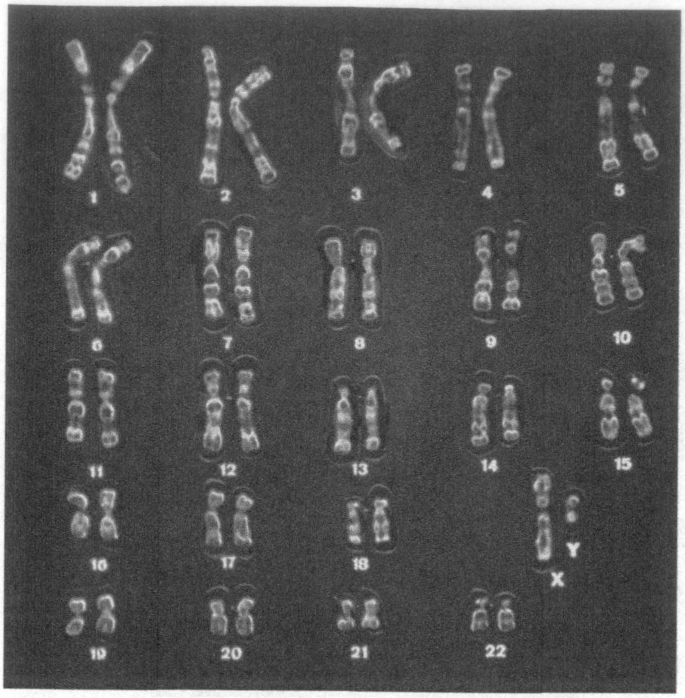

FIGURE 3.12 A human karyotype, a special cell preparation in which the chromosomes are visible under the microscope. The 23 pairs of human chromosomes are arrayed and numbered from largest to smallest. This karyotype is from a male: notice the unmatched sex chromosomes, X and Y.
Credit: CNRI/Science Photo Library.

hemophilia gene, and since males only have one X chromosome and the Y does not carry the same genes as the X, all of these males would be hemophiliacs. Notice that none of the female children of this cross would be hemophiliacs: one-half of these females would, however, be heterozygous *carriers* of the recessive gene (like their mothers) and would be expected to pass the disease on to half of their sons. *Red-green color blindness* is inherited in humans in exactly the same fashion as hemophilia (it is sex-linked and recessive) and is also much more common among males than females.

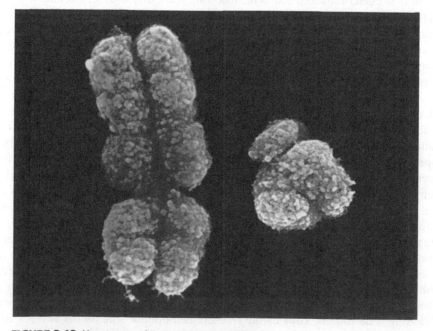

FIGURE 3.13 Human sex chromosomes Y and X.
Credit: Biophoto Associates/Science Photo Library.

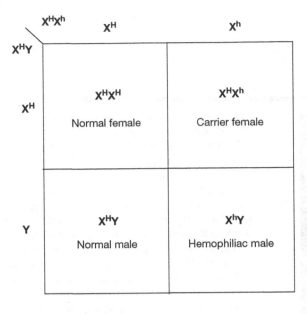

FIGURE 3.14 Punnett square for the recessive, sex-linked genetic trait of hemophilia. Half of the male offspring of this cross between a carrier mother and normal father will be hemophiliacs, and half will be normal. Half of the female offspring will be carriers, and half will be normal.

THE WATSON-CRICK MODEL OF DNA

By the end of the 1940s, it was clear that genes, found along the length of the chromosomes in the cell's nucleus, were responsible for the patterns of inheritance that had been worked out during the 19th century by Gregor Mendel. The replication and subsequent division of chromosomes during cell division and the processes of sexual reproduction were understood as the mechanisms for passing genes on from generation to generation. The next great puzzle to be solved concerned the structure and function of the genetic material itself. What chemical constituents made up the chromosomes and genes, and what did this genetic material actually do in the living cells to ensure the proper development of an individual? New model organisms and new analytical techniques had to be developed to do some of this work, and as for the earlier work on *Drosophila* in Morgan's lab, Nobel Prizes were eventually awarded to several of the scientists responsible for this work.

The first major advance was the *one gene, one enzyme* hypothesis of George Beadle and Edward Tatum, which suggested that genes carried the information for the biochemical production of enzymes and other protein molecules. While supporting evidence for this theory came from certain inherited metabolic diseases that sometimes afflict humans, the actual work was done in a far simpler organism than humans or even fruit flies. Beadle and Tatum decided to use a culture of a simple bread mold known to biologists as *Neurospora crassa* to investigate the biochemical functioning of genes. After determining the minimum growth requirements for this mold (air, water, salt, and sugar), they created, through exposure to X-rays, mutant forms that were unable to survive on this standard medium. Since these mutants could survive if additional nutrients were added to the growth medium, the researchers were able to determine that the mutated genes were responsible for the synthesis of certain enzymes that were a critical part of biochemical pathways involved in the processes of nutrition and metabolism. Beadle and Tatum determined that the enzyme produced by the mutated gene did not function properly, resulting in the breakdown of an essential biochemical pathway and the death of the mold. Significantly, they found that these biochemical flaws could be inherited, suggesting that the information for the production of enzymes was somehow carried by the genes. Today we know that the genes do indeed carry the codes for the production of protein molecules, including but not limited to enzymes. Structural proteins—the collagen in our bones, tendons, and ligaments; the oxygen-carrying molecules hemoglobin and myoglobin; neurotransmitters in our brains, including serotonin and dopamine; and the actin and myosin proteins that allow our muscles to contract—are some of the other essential proteins that

BOX ONE

Hemophilia: The Royal Disease

FIGURE B3.1 Queen Victoria, the original carrier of hemophilia in the European royal families.
Courtesy of Popperfoto/Getty Images.

As noted in the text, hemophilia is a sex-linked, recessive genetic disease that typically afflicts males, while females serve as carriers of the disease, passing it on to roughly half of their male children but rarely suffering from it themselves. This is of course because among males, it takes just one copy of the hemophilia gene to cause the disease, since males only have a single X chromosome. Because the disease is recessive, females would need to have two copies of the hemophilia gene in order to be afflicted with the disease, and this is a very rare event indeed. More commonly, females inherit a single copy of the hemophilia gene from their carrier mothers, and they in turn become carriers. Throughout much of the 19th and 20th centuries, hemophilia was popularly known as the "royal disease" because of the frequency with which it affected male members of the royal families of Europe. Genetic studies of the occurrence of hemophilia among these royal families has led to the inescapable conclusion that the original carrier of the hemophilia gene was none other than Queen Victoria (1819–1901), wife of King Albert, whose reign of 63 years as queen of the United Kingdom was the longest of any British monarch and whose time is now known as the Victorian era. The pedigree or family tree shows that Queen Victoria passed the hemophilia gene on to two of her daughters (Alice and Beatrice), each of whom had hemophiliac sons, and to her son Leopold, who died at the age of 30. In further generations, the disease would spread to other royal families of Europe as a result of the tendency of members of royal families to marry other royals. The disease ultimately spread to the royal families of Spain, Germany and Russia.

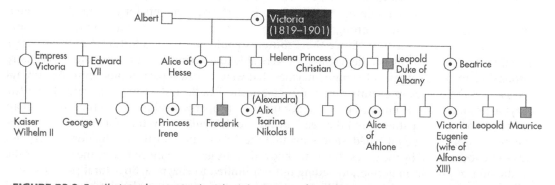

FIGURE B3.2 Family tree demonstrating the inheritance of hemophilia among the royal descendants of Great Britain's Queen Victoria and King Albert.

are coded by genes. Indeed, the information resident in the genes can be said to control the development of an individual organism from the single-celled zygote to a complex adult comprised of billions of cells of thousands of different functional types. While the work of Beadle and Tatum in *Neurospora* solved the puzzle of gene function, it brought us no closer to understanding the chemical structure of genes or the details of how they accomplished this task. This work would await the collaboration of an American, James Watson, and a British scientist, Francis Crick, at England's Cambridge University in the early 1950s. The Watson-Crick model would explain not only the structure of genes on the chromosomes but also how the genes actually function in the synthesis of protein molecules.

Watson and Crick knew that chromosomes were comprised mainly of a nucleic acid with the decidedly unwieldy name of *deoxyribonucleic acid* (DNA). They were also convinced of the importance of determining the structure of DNA as a prelude to understanding the mechanisms of inheritance. The urgency with which they attacked this problem was heightened by the intense competition between themselves and the famous American chemist Linus Pauling, who was also seeking to determine the structure of DNA in his lab at the California Institute of Technology in Pasadena. Building on the work of many other biologists and biochemists, Watson and Crick successfully created a model for the structure of the DNA molecule in 1952 and were awarded the Nobel Prize (along with one of their collaborators, Maurice Wilkins) in 1962. The Watson-Crick or *double-helix* model of DNA suggested that genes could be understood as the functional units of a very long, linear DNA molecule in the shape of a double helix. Each chromosome is essentially one very long DNA molecule that might carry hundreds or thousands of different genes. The beauty of the Watson-Crick model for DNA structure can be found in the elegant manner in which the proposed structure of the molecule helps explain how chromosomes duplicate themselves and how genes work in protein synthesis.

FIGURE 3.15 James Watson (left) and Francis Crick in Cambridge, 1953.
Credit: A. Barrington Brown/Science Photo Library.

FIGURE 3.16 Linus Pauling won two Nobel Prizes (Chemistry in 1954 and Peace in 1962) but lost out to Watson and Crick in the race to decipher the structure of DNA. © Roger Ressmeyer/CORBIS

The DNA molecule is composed of a repeating series of linked subunits known as *nucleotides*. Each nucleotide is in turn made up of a sugar molecule (deoxyribose), a phosphate group, and one of four different nitrogenous bases known as adenine, guanine, cytosine, and thymine (usually abbreviated by their first letters, A, C, G, and T). The entire structure is twisted like a spiral staircase, with the sugar-phosphate backbones along the inner and outer edges and the nitrogenous bases linking to the sugars. The helix is "doubled" because nucleotides are joined one to another at the midline by hydrogen bonds connecting nitrogenous bases, and it is the sequence of nitrogenous bases along the length of a gene that determines its function. While the sugar-phosphate backbone simply provides a structure or scaffolding for the molecule, the information for synthesizing individual proteins is coded in the sequence of the four nitrogenous bases along the length of the gene. The important principle of *complementary base pairing* is the key to this process. Due to the size and chemical configurations of the four nitrogenous bases, adenine bonds only with thymine and guanine bonds only with cytosine. Relatively weak hydrogen bonds can easily form and just as easily be broken between A and T and between G and C. The significance of complementary base pairing is that a single strand of the double helix can provide a template for the formation of the other matching strand.

Watson and Crick suggested that this aspect of DNA structure provides a simple explanation for the ability of chromosomes to replicate themselves in cell division. They noted that if the hydrogen bonds linking nucleotides across the midline of the DNA molecule were to be broken or "unzipped," each strand could then act as a template for the replication of the original

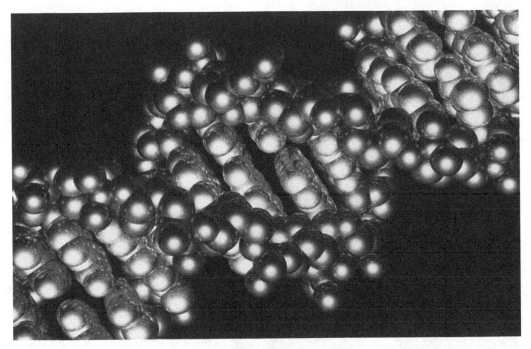

FIGURE 3.17 DNA, the double helix.
Credit: Kenneth Eward/Biografx/Science Photo Library.

double helix, assuming that free nucleotides were available in the cell nucleus. In the early 1960s, this suggestion was verified when the first very high-magnification images of chromosomal replication were obtained using electron microscopes. These images revealed a split or bifurcation moving down the midline along the length of the replicating chromosome, eventually resulting in the appearance of two identical daughter chromosomes where there was originally just one parent.

With the solution of the double helical structure and the nature of DNA replication worked out, scientists turned their attention to elucidating the code and the mechanism by which nucleic acid molecules directed the production of proteins. The *genetic code* provides the blueprint for the production of thousands of different proteins in the body's cells. As noted earlier, the proteins are an immensely diverse group of molecules that serve many purposes in living things, including catalysts for biochemical reactions, structural scaffolding for organs and other body parts, and molecular machines. Proteins are long chainlike molecules made up of smaller subunits known as *amino acids*, and biochemists in the 1950s were aware that all proteins were composed of different sequences of only 20 different amino acids. So how could the linear stream of information contained in sequences of four nitrogenous bases in a DNA double helix be translated into linear sequences of 20 different amino acids to make thousands of different proteins?

It was soon discovered that the genetic code is a triplet code in which a sequence of three bases along one strand of the DNA molecule codes for a single amino acid in a protein molecule. This three-to-one correspondence between nucleotides and amino acids makes sense because using fewer genetic "letters" (i.e., bases) to code for "words" (i.e., amino acids) would not provide the 20 codes required for 20 different amino acids. If a single base coded for a single amino acid, there could only be $4^1 = 4$, different signals, and if the genetic code were comprised of pairs of bases, there could only be $4^2 = 16$, different words. A triplet code provides $4^3 = 64$, different words, more than enough to allow this system to run. The genetic code thus has some built-in redundancy, with more than one triplet able to code for each amino acid. Understanding the workings of the genetic code also helps

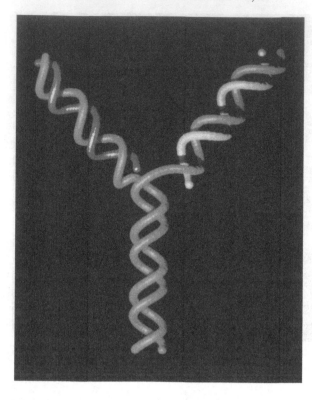

FIGURE 3.18 DNA replication occurs as a single double-helix molecule unzips and each strand acts as a template to copy itself through complementary base pairing (A-T and G-C). DNA replication occurs prior to every episode of cell division in all cells. Credit: Clive Freeman/The Royal Institution/Science Photo Library.

explain the nature of genetic mistakes or mutations, which can be seen as errors in the information processing of the DNA replication system. For example, if a TTT triplet were to be somehow changed to CTT, an amino acid substitution would occur in which the amino acid phenylalanine would be replaced by leucine, which might have serious effects on the functioning of the protein of which it was a part. If the function of the protein were to be seriously compromised, and if the protein was critical for life, a mutation like this could have lethal effects on the unlucky individual in whom it occurred. On the other hand, it could also improve the function of the protein and thus be favored by natural selection.

Now that we have a basic understanding of the structure of DNA and a working knowledge of the genetic code, the final aspect of the genetic puzzle concerns the actual cellular mechanisms of the synthesis of proteins. One stumbling block facing the early investigators was the fact that while DNA is restricted to the cell's nucleus, the site of protein synthesis was known to be in the cytoplasm outside of the nucleus, in the *ribosomes* lining the *endoplasmic reticulum* (ER). So how did the DNA message get from the cell's nucleus to the ribosomes, and once there, how is the information coded in nucleic acid translated into the amino acid language of proteins? Before scientists could fully understand these processes, several additional nucleic acid molecules had to be discovered: *messenger RNA* (mRNA) and *transfer RNA* (tRNA). The RNAs (*ribonucleic acids*) differ from DNA in four important ways: RNAs are single-stranded molecules, they use uracil (U) in place of thymine (T) as the complement of adenine (A), they have a slightly different sugar molecule known as ribose in place of deoxyribose, and they are found in both the cell's nucleus and in the cytoplasm. Messenger RNA is the molecule that carries the message from DNA in the nucleus to the site of protein synthesis, on the ER in the cell's cytoplasm.

This first step in *protein synthesis* is known as *transcription*, and it involves complementary base pairing between one of the DNA strands (the sense strand) and the single-stranded mRNA molecule. The gene that is being transcribed unzips down its midline (because the weak hydrogen bonds that connect complimentary bases in the DNA double helix are easily formed and broken), and free nucleotides of mRNA move into place to connect to complementary bases on the DNA (in RNA, U is complementary to A). When a gene is transcribed, the genetic message held by the sequence of bases in the DNA molecule is copied (through complementary base pairing) onto the mRNA molecule. When a stop sequence is encountered, the mRNA separates from the DNA and makes its way to the ER and ribosomes, where protein synthesis actually occurs. The second stage in this process is called *translation*, referring to a translation of the genetic information from the nucleic acid "language" into the "language" of amino acids, the constituents of proteins. At the ribosome, the mRNA encounters transfer RNA molecules, which carry the individual amino acids to the protein synthesis site. Amino acids are linked one to another by *peptide bonds*, and sometimes a protein molecule is referred to as a *polypeptide*. Messenger RNA base triplets are "read" by complementary triplets on one end of tRNA molecules (known as *anticodons*) that also carry the particular amino acid called for by the mRNA triplet (referred to as a *codon*). So the bases in the original DNA triplet are complementary to a particular mRNA codon, which is also complementary to a tRNA anticodon. The result is that a particular amino acid is brought in and connected to the growing chain of amino acids at the proper place, eventually forming the protein molecule coded for by the original sequence of DNA bases in the gene. After the protein is fully formed, it breaks free of the entire protein synthesis mechanism in the ribosome and travels to wherever it is destined to play a biochemical role in the life of the organism.

Finally, note that while all cells have a complete complement of chromosomes and genes typical of the species, particular genes are synthesized only in the cells that use their specific protein product. For example, the neurotransmitter *dopamine* is produced in several areas of the brain, in particular the *substantia nigra*, and therefore the gene for dopamine is transcribed and translated only in these particular cells of the brain. Similarly, the hormone *insulin* that facilitates the uptake of

First Base	Second Base				Third Base
	U	C	A	G	
U	UUU Phenylalanine UUC Phenylalanine UUA Leucine UUG Leucine	UCU Serine UCC Serine UCA Serine UCG Serine	UAU Tyrosine UAC Tyrosine UAA Stop UAG Stop	UGU Cysteine UGC Cysteine UGA Stop UGG Tryptophan	U C A G
C	CUU Leucine CUC Leucine CUA Leucine CUG Leucine	CCU Proline CCC Proline CCA Proline CCG Proline	CAU Histidine CAC Histidine CAA Glutamine CAG Glutamine	CGU Arginine CGC Arginine CGA Arginine CGG Arginine	U C A G
A	AUU Isoleucine AUC Isoleucine AUA Isoleucine AUG Start (Methionine)	ACU Threonine ACC Threonine ACA Threonine ACG Threonine	AAU Asparagine AAC Asparagine AAA Lysine AAG Lysine	AGU Serine AGC Serine AGA Arginine AGG Arginine	U C A G
G	GUU Valine GUC Valine GUA Valine GUG Valine	GCU Alanine GCC Alanine GCA Alanine GCG Alanine	GAU Aspartic Acid GAC Aspartic Acid GAA Glutamic Acid GAG Glutamic Acid	GGU Glycine GGC Glycine GGA Glycine GGG Glycine	U C A G

FIGURE 3.19 The genetic code is a redundant triplet code in which every three nitrogenous bases in DNA and RNA code for a single amino acid in a protein. Note that changing the base in the third position of each triplet usually has no effect on the amino acid that is selected.

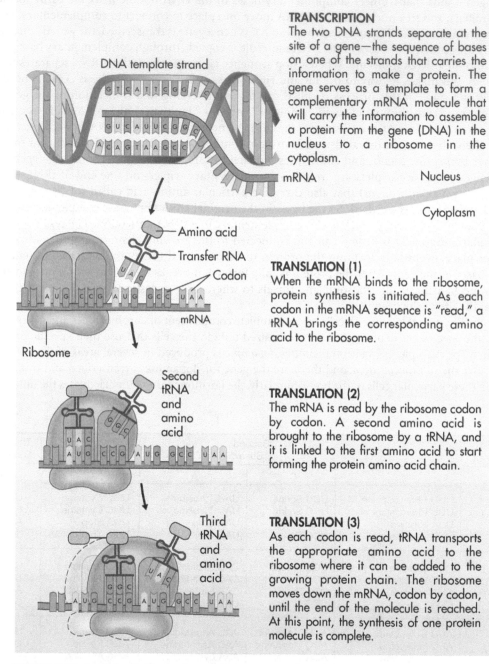

TRANSCRIPTION
The two DNA strands separate at the site of a gene—the sequence of bases on one of the strands that carries the information to make a protein. The gene serves as a template to form a complementary mRNA molecule that will carry the information to assemble a protein from the gene (DNA) in the nucleus to a ribosome in the cytoplasm.

TRANSLATION (1)
When the mRNA binds to the ribosome, protein synthesis is initiated. As each codon in the mRNA sequence is "read," a tRNA brings the corresponding amino acid to the ribosome.

TRANSLATION (2)
The mRNA is read by the ribosome codon by codon. A second amino acid is brought to the ribosome by a tRNA, and it is linked to the first amino acid to start forming the protein amino acid chain.

TRANSLATION (3)
As each codon is read, tRNA transports the appropriate amino acid to the ribosome where it can be added to the growing protein chain. The ribosome moves down the mRNA, codon by codon, until the end of the molecule is reached. At this point, the synthesis of one protein molecule is complete.

FIGURE 3.20 A schematic illustration of the two parts of protein synthesis, transcription and translation.

glucose from the blood and its storage as glycogen in the liver and muscle cells is produced only in the specialized *islets of Langerhans* cells in the pancreas. While these genes are present in skin cells, blood cells, and all other cells in the body, they are transcribed and translated only in the cells in which their protein products perform their function (substantia nigra for dopamine, islets of Langerhans for insulin).

THE MODERN SYNTHESIS AND THE FOUR FORCES OF EVOLUTION

With the rediscovery of Mendel's work at the start of the 20th century, one might suppose that the connections between the work of Darwin (on natural selection as a major mechanism of evolutionary change) and of Mendel (on the mechanics of inheritance) would have been obvious to biologists. In fact, nothing could be further from the truth. Mendel's theory of particulate inheritance explained how adaptive traits with a genetic basis could be passed on from parent to offspring, and Darwin's theory explained how the struggle for existence in nature could lead to the spread of adaptive traits throughout a population, but the connection between Mendel's genes and Darwin's selection was not yet clear. The followers of Darwin could not see how the particulate genetics of Mendel, with its focus on the inheritance of unit traits (e.g., short and tall pea plants) and of large mutations, could explain the small and gradual differences in many traits that ecologists had measured in the field and that seemed important in the struggle for existence. Humans, after all, don't come in just two sizes, short and tall. Human stature is a continuously variable trait, and it wasn't at all clear how Mendelian principles could explain the inheritance of continuous variables such as this one. It wasn't until the 1930s and 1940s that advances in several related branches of biology, including paleontology, ecology, and genetics, led to the reconciliation of Darwinism and Mendelism that has been called the *modern evolutionary synthesis*.

The modern synthesis made clear the intimate connections between Mendel's and Darwin's work and their complementary nature. It explained how discrete genes, acting in combination, with additive effects, and with modifications by the environment during development, could lead to the continuously variable traits that most biologists regarded as the raw material of evolutionary change. So Mendelism was relevant to how natural selection worked in the field: new traits arising as the result of modified genes could spread through populations as a result of natural selection, increasing the adaptation of their bearers and changing the population over time. The modern synthesis focused attention on the frequencies of genes within populations and suggested that evolutionary change within a population was synonymous with the changes in the relative frequencies of genes within that population. The study of evolution could then be seen as the study of the changes in gene frequencies within populations, and the mechanisms behind these changes in gene frequencies could be considered to be the causes of evolutionary change. Four different mechanisms were suggested to be the major forces of evolutionary change through their effects on changing gene frequencies within populations. Known as the *four forces of evolution*, they are natural selection, genetic drift, gene flow, and mutation. *Natural selection* can obviously change gene frequencies through the differential survival and differential reproduction of individuals carrying different genes. *Genetic drift* refers to random fluctuations in gene frequencies as a result of sampling error resulting from small population sizes. A particular type of genetic drift event, referred to as the *founder's effect*, occurs when a new population is founded by the migration or separation of a small number of individuals from a larger population. Often the new population can have quite different gene frequencies compared to the original population simply because of the small size of the founding population. *Gene flow* causes changes in gene frequencies when interbreeding occurs between individuals from different populations that already differ in certain gene frequencies. Finally, *mutation* is the ultimate source of genetic variation in populations, and it refers to the origins of new genetic variants as a result of mistakes in the genetic mechanisms involved in the copying of genes from one generation to the next.

With the insights provided by our understanding of Darwinian evolution, Mendelian genetics, and the molecular biology of Watson and Crick and their successors, we now have the biological tools to better understand the nature of human biological diversity and the meaning of race. This background provides a solid basis in biology with which we can critically examine the biological nature of race and explore the cultural dimensions of human variation.

BOX TWO

A Closer Look at James D. Watson

FIGURE B3.3 The discoverers of the structure of DNA, Francis Crick (left) and James Watson (right).
Credit: A. Barrington Brown/Science Photo Library.

Born in 1928 in Chicago, James D. Watson was one of the most successful and controversial scientists of the 20th century. He entered the University of Chicago at the age of 15, earned his Ph.D. from Indiana University at the age of 22, and was awarded the Nobel Prize for his work on the structure of DNA at the age of 34. After his work on DNA at the Cavendish Lab in Cambridge, England, in the early 1950s, Watson moved to Harvard University, where he taught from 1956 to 1976. Beginning in 1968, Watson also worked at the Cold Spring Harbor Laboratory on Long Island, New York, a biological research organization that under his leadership would become one of the most important biological research centers in the world and a leader in the search for a cure for cancer. Between 1988 and 1992, Watson played a key role in the U.S. government's establishment of the Human Genome Project under the aegis of the National Institutes of Health (NIH). Throughout his illustrious career, he has been the recipient of numerous honorary degrees and just about every major scientific award that a biologist could win. But all the accolades and honors he had earned through a long and productive life in science faded into the background as a result of the controversial comments he made in an article published in London's *Sunday Times Magazine* on October 14, 2007.

FIGURE B3.4 Francis Crick (left) and James Watson (right) in 1993.
© Pierre Perrin/Sygma/Corbis

In this biographical piece (Hunt-Grubbe 2007), written by a former student-assistant at Cold Spring Harbor, Watson speculated about a subject in which he had no real expertise: the supposed connection between race and intelligence. Here is a brief excerpt:

He says that he is "inherently gloomy about the prospect of Africa" because "all our social policies are based on the fact that their intelligence is the same as ours—whereas all the testing says not really," and I know that this "hot potato" is going to be difficult to address. His hope is that everyone is equal, but he counters that "people who have to deal with black employees find this not true." He says that you should not discriminate on the basis of colour, because "there are many people of colour who are very talented, but don't promote them when they haven't succeeded at the lower level." He writes that "there is no firm reason to anticipate that the intellectual capacities of peoples geographically separated in their evolution should prove to have evolved identically. Our wanting to reserve equal powers of reason as some universal heritage of humanity will not be enough to make it so."

We will return to the supposed link between race and intelligence in a later chapter of this book for a deeper critique, but suffice it to say at this point that there is no good scientific evidence to support Watson's stated position. The reaction of the scientific community to Watson's comments were swift and decisive. He was suspended from his administrative duties at Cold Spring Harbor, upcoming speaking engagements at universities and museums were cancelled, and he was forced to apologize publicly for the perceived racism of his remarks. Eleven days after the publication of the *Sunday Times* piece and as a result of the nearly unanimous condemnation of his remarks, Watson resigned from his position at Cold Spring Harbor, bringing an illustrious scientific career to a sad end.

THE HUMAN GENOME PROJECT

Perhaps the most exciting research accomplishment of modern molecular biology (as the field of genetics has come to be called) is the recent completion of the Human Genome Project (HGP). The HGP was formally begun in 1990 as a collaboration between two large U.S. government research agencies, the Department of Energy (DOE) and the National Institutes of Health (NIH). Originally planned for a duration of 15 years, the project was actually completed in 13 as a result of rapid technological advances in the field. The goals of the project were the following:

- *identify* all the approximately 20,000–25,000 genes in human DNA
- *determine* the sequences of the 3 billion chemical base pairs that make up human DNA
- *store* this information in databases
- *improve* tools for data analysis
- *transfer* related technologies to the private sector
- *address* the ethical, legal, and social issues (ELSI) that may arise from the project. [Human Genome Project 2008:1]

As a result of this work, we now have in hand a complete genetic map of the entire human genome, which should prove to be critically important in further advances in our understanding of the nature and treatment of a variety of human genetic ailments. Molecular biology is on the doorstep of a new era of personalized genomic medicine in which an individual's actual genome can be taken into account when considering medical treatments and in which genetic diseases can be treated at the level of individual genes, rather than treating the patient's symptoms. One of the curious results of the completion of the HGP was the publication of the complete genome sequence of none other than James Watson, the discoverer (with Francis Crick) of the double helix (Wheeler et al. 2008). Interested readers can access Watson's complete genome online at the Cold Spring Harbor Laboratory website.

BOX THREE

Rosalind Franklin and the Discovery of the Structure of DNA

FIGURE B3.5 Rosalind Franklin (1920–1958), British scientist and contributor to the discovery of the double helix structure of DNA. © World History Archive / Alamy.

While the names of James Watson and Francis Crick are well known as the discoverers of the double-helical structure of DNA, Rosalind Franklin's name is much less well known today, in spite of the fact that her data were absolutely critical to the successful solution of this scientific puzzle by her two Cambridge colleagues. The story of Rosalind Franklin and her role in the discovery of the structure of DNA is a revealing tale about the competitive nature of high-stakes scientific research and the damaging effects of sexism and personal animosity in the scientific world (Maddux, 2002). Franklin had earned her Ph.D. at Cambridge University in 1945 and in 1951 took a job as a researcher at Kings College in London. Her scientific background was in biophysics, and she was an expert in X-ray crystallography, in which high-powered X-rays are fired at crystallized molecules and the resulting pattern of diffracted X-rays is photographed and used to infer the three-dimensional structure of the material being examined. At Kings College, Franklin applied her X-ray crystallography skills on the structure of DNA with Maurice Wilkins, a close associate and friend of both Watson and Crick, who were at that time heavily involved in their race with Linus Pauling to determine the structure of DNA. Watson attended a seminar that Franklin gave on some of her preliminary work on DNA structure at Kings in November 1951, at Wilkins's invitation. In January 1953, Watson traveled to Kings College to talk with Wilkins and Franklin about joining forces in the race to determine DNA's structure. Franklin was uninterested in collaborating with the brash young American, and she and Watson apparently nearly came to blows when he suggested to her that she needed him to interpret her own data! Wilkins intervened and took Watson back to his own lab, where he shared with him the now famous photograph 51, taken by Franklin, of crystallized DNA. Significantly, Franklin was completely unaware of Wilkins's breach of scientific etiquette in sharing her data with a competitor without her knowledge or approval, and Franklin's work was barely acknowledged by Watson and Crick at the time. Writing many years later, Watson (1968:98) described his reaction in the following manner: "The instant I saw the picture my mouth fell open and my pulse began to race." This photograph convinced Watson that he and Crick were on the right path and that DNA's structure was indeed a double helix. This was the final piece in the puzzle that allowed Watson and Crick (1953) to finalize their model, which they published in a landmark paper in the leading British journal *Nature*.

When Watson's version of these discoveries was published in his 1968 book *The Double Helix*, it was impossible to ignore how poorly Rosalind Franklin had been treated by Wilkins and especially by Watson himself. Repeatedly referring to her as "Rosy," "as we called her from a distance" (Watson 1968:14), Watson denigrates her talents, patronizes her intelligence, and even criticizes her physical appearance in his best seller.

> By choice she did not emphasize her feminine qualities. Though her features were strong, she was not unattractive and might even have been quite stunning had she taken even a mild interest in clothes. This she did not. There was never lipstick to contrast with her straight black hair, while at the age of thirty-one her dresses showed all the imagination of English bluestocking adolescents. . . . Clearly Rosy had to go or be put in her place. [Watson 1968:14]

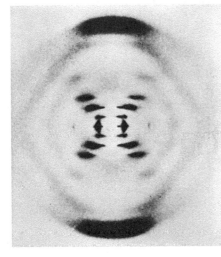

FIGURE B3.6 Rosalind Franklin's famous photograph 51, an X-ray diffraction picture of the "B" form of DNA taken in 1952. Seeing this photograph (without Franklin's knowledge or permission) provided Watson and Crick with the confidence to publish their double-helical model in 1953.
Credit: Science Photo Library.

Franklin left Kings College in March 1953, apparently due to her unhappiness at her working conditions there and in particular due to the personal friction between her and Wilkins. She moved to Birkbeck College, where she continued to use X-ray crystallography, notably to determine the structure of RNA within certain viruses, including polio and the tobacco mosaic virus. In the fall of 1956, she was diagnosed with cancer, and on April 16, 1958, she died in London at the age of 37. Six years later, her colleagues and competitors Wilkins, Crick, and Watson were awarded equal shares of the Nobel Prize in Physiology or Medicine in 1962 for the discovery of the structure of DNA. Many have wondered if Rosalind Franklin would have shared in that Nobel Prize had she been alive in 1962, but of course, the question is moot because Nobel Prizes are never granted posthumously.

In 1975, the first of several biographies of Rosalind Franklin was published, in part as a rebuttal of James Watson's portrayal of her in *The Double Helix*. In *Rosalind Franklin and DNA* (Sayre 1975), Franklin's friend Anne Sayre argued that Franklin was a victim of rampant sexism at Kings College and in many of her interactions with scientific colleagues and the scientific establishment of the 1950s in England. In recent decades, Rosalind Franklin has become a feminist hero to many—or perhaps more appropriately, a feminist martyr. In any event, her outstanding contribution to the unraveling of the structure of DNA has been underappreciated for far too long.

Discussion Questions

1. Explain the differences between Darwin's notion of blending inheritance and Mendel's theory that inheritance was a particulate process with respect to a trait such as human height. Which model of inheritance works better with Darwin's theory of evolution by natural selection? Explain your reasoning.

2. Provide short definitions for each of the following pairs of related terms:
   a. Genes and chromosomes
   b. Genotype and phenotype
   c. Zygote and gamete
   d. Haploid and diploid
   e. Amino acids and nucleotides
   f. Transcription and translation
   g. Somatic cells and germ line cells
   h. Meiosis and mitosis

3. Describe in your own words the meanings of Mendel's Law of Segregation and Law of Independent Assortment.

4. The function of genes is to synthesis proteins. Explain the two steps (transcription and translation) through which genes make proteins.

5. Explain the significance of complementary base pairing in DNA and RNA.

6. Name and briefly define the four forces of evolution.

CHAPTER 4

The History of the Race Concept

I am apt to suspect the negroes and in general all the other species of men (for there are four or five different kinds) to be naturally inferior to the whites. There never was a civilized nation of any other complexion than white, nor even any individual eminent either in action or speculation. No ingenious manufactures amongst them, no arts, no sciences. On the other hand, the most rude and barbarous of the whites, such as the ancient Germans, the present Tartars, have still something eminent about them, in their valour, form of government, or some other particular. Such a uniform and constant difference could not happen, in so many countries and ages, if nature had not made an original distinction betwixt these breeds of men.

HUME 1742

THE CONCEPT OF RACE

Since its beginnings, anthropology has sought to understand the nature and meaning of the biological variation characterizing human populations in different parts of the globe. Visible biological differences in skin and hair color, hair texture, body size, and body type have suggested to many the existence of a number of different groups or races, and biological anthropologists have played a leading role in scientific attempts to determine how many races exist among living *Homo sapiens*. In recent decades, anthropologists and other scientists have applied the tools and techniques of modern biology, including genetics and molecular biology, to the analysis of human biological diversity. These new approaches suggest that human diversity is much more than skin deep and that much variation exists between people and populations in blood types, enzymes, disease susceptibility, and other biochemical and genetic traits. Yet in spite of these powerful biological techniques, anthropologists are today no closer than they were in the 18th century to answering the straightforward question "How many races are there?" Why is this so, and what is it about the nature of biological variation in humans that makes this such a difficult question to answer? In this chapter, we will look at the history of racial classifications over the past 250 years and probe the different meanings associated with the notion of biological race. To determine why anthropologists have been unable to lay to rest this seemingly simple question concerning the number of races, we will take a closer look at the different ways in which race and human races have been defined, at the biology of human "racial" diversity, and finally at changes in theory and ideology that influence the ways in which scientists approach questions relating to human difference.

THE RECENT ORIGINS OF RACE

It is easy to assume today that the notion of dividing the peoples of the world into a series of biological races has always been with us and that the concept of human races has a great antiquity in human thought. But that would be wrong. Most historians argue that race as we know it in the Western world is a notion that arose during the Middle Ages, perhaps as recently as 500 years ago. While the ancient Greeks and Romans recognized that populations from different continents were physically and culturally diverse, this recognition of human diversity never led to the development of a racial ideology or worldview. In typically ethnocentric fashion, the ancient Greeks divided the world into Greeks and non-Greeks or barbarians, but they recognized that this was a purely cultural distinction. Barbarians were all foreigners who could not speak Greek, but it was acknowledged that barbarians could become Greek. They were not considered deeply or inherently different from Greeks; they were just unlucky enough to have been born and raised somewhere other than Greece. Later, the Roman Empire was built on the notion of making Romans out of foreigners, usually after military conquest. If you were conquered by Rome, you could become Roman by paying taxes to Rome, by becoming part of the Roman political system, and by learning to speak Latin. While it is true that slavery was common in the ancient Mediterranean world, slavery was never reserved for people of a particular racial or ethnic background: anyone could become a slave, and many slaves were able to eventually purchase or otherwise regain their freedom and become full citizens of Rome. As anyone who has seen the movie *Gladiator* knows, even former Roman generals could become enslaved. This was very unlike the enslavement of Africans in the Americas, which was based on a belief in the biological inferiority of Africans.

Rather, it appears that the notion of biological race began during the Age of Exploration in the late 15th century, when European ships were sailing the world's oceans and discovering new lands that were inhabited by new animals and plants and by new and different-looking people. Encounters between Europeans and the native inhabitants of the South Seas and the Orient, Africans, and Native Americans were to lead to the development of a set of *folk beliefs* about the nature of these people. These folk beliefs presumed European superiority and the inferiority of peoples of color, and they were supported by first religious and later scientific authority. Although in hindsight it is clear that these folk beliefs about racial difference had no real basis in science or biology, they quickly gained currency among Europeans and for whatever reasons became orthodox belief. Over the ensuing centuries, these beliefs became codified into what the anthropologist Audrey Smedley (2007) has called "the racial worldview," in which a particular set of beliefs or ideas about the meaning of racial difference influence the way we see the world. The North American racial worldview includes, according to Smedley (2007:28), the following components or core beliefs:

- Human populations form biologically distinct and discrete units that are inherently unequal in endowment.
- The superficial differences between human groups are the outer manifestations of deep and significant biological differences in intelligence, morality, and other psychological and behavioral features.
- All of these differences between populations can be inherited.
- The differences between human groups are permanent, were fashioned at creation (or later by evolution), and remain fixed and unchangeable.

The observant reader can perhaps see similarities between the ways in which race served in the Americas to structure society and to legitimize or naturalize social and economic inequality with the manner in which class performed these same functions in Old Europe. Class distinctions create a kind of horizontal divider between so-called upper- and lower-class people without reference to racial differences, while race provides a vertical separation linking socioeconomic classes but dividing them along racial lines. Discovery of a New World required a new world order, and the racial worldview helped pave the way.

RACE AND RACIAL CLASSIFICATIONS

Since racial classifications are, in one sense, taxonomic devices whose goal is to create order amid the enormous variation in the biological world, we can begin our inquiry into the origins of racial classification with the work of Carolus Linnaeus. Linnaeus was an 18th-century Swedish botanist who is famous for his development of the system of scientific nomenclature for living things that biologists still use today. Prior to Linnaeus, there was no standard and generally accepted approach used by all biologists to name the living things they studied. Linnaeus developed a system known as *binomial nomenclature*, in which each different kind of living thing was given two names (a binomen) in order to distinguish it from every other kind of living thing. These two names are the genus and species, and Linnaeus was the first to bestow on humans the somewhat flattering binomen *Homo sapiens* ("wise man"). Linnaeus built a hierarchical taxonomic system of seven levels, with genus and species at the bottom and ascending through family, order, class, phylum, and finally kingdom. In addition to these seven mandatory levels of classification for all living things, Linnaeus created an optional classificatory level for geographic variations within species. He called these subspecific taxa *varieties*, but today we refer to them as *races* or *subspecies*. Human races can then be said to be geographic variants

FIGURE 4.1 Carolus Linnaeus (1707–1778), who created the system of binomial nomenclature still used by biologists and botanists today. Linnaeus was also the first scientist to classify humans into races.
Courtesy of iStock by Getty Images.

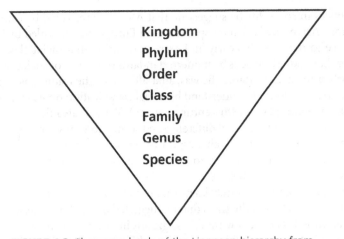

FIGURE 4.2 The seven levels of the Linnaean hierarchy from most inclusive at the top of the inverted pyramid (kingdom) to least inclusive at the bottom (genus and species). Subspecies or races would appear even lower, below the species.

within the species *Homo sapiens* or more formally defined as biologically distinct human populations from different parts of the globe that are classified at the subspecific level of the Linnaean hierarchy. That is to say, human races can be distinguished by some physical or morphological traits and are from different geographic regions of the world, but they are all members of the same species (*Homo sapiens*). Although there is nearly as much difference of opinion among biologists concerning a definition of species as there is among anthropologists on the definition of race, we will use Ernst Mayr's *biological species* concept (Mayr 1963). It states that species are comprised of populations that interbreed in nature and are reproductively isolated from other populations. It follows that since all humans are capable of interbreeding with other humans, we are all members of a single species, but the question of how many races or subspecies might exist within *Homo sapiens* has been highly contested since the 18th century. Linnaeus himself presented one of the first racial classifications of humans in his major work of 1758, *Systema Naturae*, and a close examination of this classification can explain much about certain attitudes toward race that still have some currency in the modern world.

Linnaeus suggested the existence of four different varieties of *Homo sapiens: Homo sapiens afer, H.s. asiaticus, H.s. europaeus,* and *H.s. americanus,* closely matching the four continental populations of humans that are still recognized today by many as major races (African, Asian, European, and Native American). With information culled from the mostly anecdotal reports of travelers, missionaries, soldiers, slave traders, and plantation owners, we would be well-advised to take Linnaeus's descriptions of the varieties of humans with a large grain of salt. Linnaeus himself spent nearly his entire life in Sweden, interrupted only by a three-year sojourn in the Netherlands during his university studies. He never traveled outside of Europe and certainly had no firsthand knowledge of the inhabitants of Asia, Africa, or the Americas. In his descriptions of these racial groups, Linnaeus relied on a curious combination of morphological, behavioral, psychological, and cultural traits. Morphological or anatomical features like skin and hair color, hair type, and facial features are described for each of his four races. Behavioral and psychological traits used by Linnaeus play a large and interesting role in Linnaeus's racial scheme, foreshadowing some racial stereotypes that may well be familiar to a modern reader. For example, Linnaeus proclaimed Europeans to be "active, very smart, inventive" while Africans were said to be "crafty, slow, foolish" and Asians were "melancholy" and "greedy." The cultural traits thought by Linnaeus to distinguish the human races include aspects of dress and body ornamentation and social or political organization. For example, while the African "anoints himself with grease" and the American "paints himself with red lines," the Asian is "covered by loose garments" and the European "covered by tight clothing." Finally, Linnaeus discussed differences in social life by suggesting that Africans are "ruled by caprice," Americans are "ruled by customs," Asians are "ruled by opinion," and Europeans are "ruled by laws."

What are we to make of this early and extremely influential racial classification devised by Linnaeus? Rather than judge Linnaeus by modern standards of science or society and to dismiss him as a racist or a poorly informed dilettante (he was, after all, one of the leading biological scientists of his day), it is more instructive to try to understand his racial classification on its own terms and as a product of a different time and place (18th-century Europe). We will also find it instructive to look for resonances between his notions of racial difference and some modern scientific and especially popular ideas about race. Perhaps the most striking aspect of this early attempt at racial classification is the incredibly broad brush that Linnaeus uses to characterize the inhabitants of Asia, Africa, Europe, and the Americas. Did Linnaeus really believe that all Asians were melancholy? Did he never encounter a dull or stupid European? Linnaeus surely knew that not all Europeans or members of any of his four races shared to the same extent in the traits that he suggested defined them as a group. But he ignored all the obvious variation that existed within these groups in order to define the essential or archetypal nature of each. In this way, he was following a long philosophical tradition known as *Platonism*, in which all things are thought to share an essential nature, irrespective of all the variation that existed around this essence. Let's take a closer look at Linnaeus's conception of the essential nature of each of his four human races, keeping uppermost in our minds the notion of racial stereotyping as we do.

Like many of his contemporaries, Linnaeus was convinced that members of different races could be distinguished by innate differences in intelligence, an idea that is still, unfortunately, very much with us. Linnaeus also believed that basic personality and character traits were racially determined, again a common component of many modern racial stereotypes. Furthermore, Linnaeus failed to distinguish between morphological traits that have a basis in biological and genetic processes (e.g., skin color, hair type, body size and shape) and aspects of culture, such as social organization and modes of dress or ornamentation. Since race is supposed to be a biological category, we recognize today that racial distinctions must be based on biological and not cultural differences between populations. If the discipline of anthropology has taught us anything over the past century, it is that cultural differences cannot be reduced to differences in biology or human nature, and hence these should not be used as the basis for biological (i.e., racial) classifications. For example, no modern anthropologist would expect genetic differences to underlie cultural differences in, for example, subsistence strategies (e.g., hunting and gathering versus horticulture) or marriage residence patterns (e.g., matrilocal versus patrilocal) between different societies. There is absolutely no evidence to support the notion that biology determines culture and much that contradicts it. Yet this confusion over the use of biological or cultural features to classify race is still a large problem in much public discourse about race today. Notions such as the existence of a Hispanic or Jewish race are clearly based on the *cultural* traits of language and religion, respectively, and only serve to muddle discussions of the *biological* validity of race. In spite of the two and a half centuries since Linnaeus first classified humans into four biological races, we are still grappling with many of the same issues and problems today. In fact, we can still see the remnants of 18th-century beliefs (that had no scientific basis then and even less today) in the racial stereotypes that persist, often in a subliminal or subconscious state, in American society today.

In 18th-century France, the Comte de Buffon popularized both the use of the term *race* for Linnaeus's varieties within a species and the notion that environmental differences in different parts of the world were responsible for the physical differences between human populations. Like Linnaeus, Buffon was a believer in a single origin of *Homo sapiens*, with racial differentiation occurring at some later time after human populations had multiplied and spread across the globe. The most common form of this argument was the notion that the hot sun of tropical Africa had burned the skin of Africans to a dark hue. Buffon thought that the climate, food, soil, air, and other aspects of the local environment had a direct effect on human morphology and physiology. While the idea that there is a causal link between environmental differences and morphological distinctions between groups is still supported by most biological anthropologists today, it should be noted that Buffon, who was writing roughly 100 years before Darwin, was not suggesting an evolutionary

FIGURE 4.3 Georges-Louis Leclerc, Comte de Buffon (1707–1788), was a pioneering French biologist. © Classic Image / Alamy.

mechanism for these changes. Indeed Buffon was, like Linnaeus, a firm believer in the notion of *special creation* of all the kinds or species of living things by a divine creator and in the *fixity of species*. They both envisioned biological change occurring only at the level of geographic races or subspecies, not at the level of the divinely created species.

Jonathan Marks (1995) has pointed out an interesting and important methodological difference in the approaches to the study of human race employed by Linnaeus and Buffon. It should come as no surprise that Linnaeus, the great pioneer of the classification of living things, was mostly interested in answering the primarily classificatory question of how many races existed. Linnaeus was convinced that human subspecific or racial variation could be cataloged and classified in the same way he had classified all known living species, and as we have seen, he suggested that the answer to this question was that there were just four human races. In his major work *Histoire Naturelle*, Buffon's concern was to explore the nature of the differences and similarities found among the peoples of the world in order to understand the historical and biological relationships of different peoples. Rather than naming or enumerating the human races, Buffon lavishly described the native peoples of many different parts of the globe, referring to them by their place of origin or by their own name for themselves. Marks suggests that while Linnaeus's purely classificatory approach was the dominant scientific approach to the study of human race until the 1960s, Buffon's descriptive and naturalistic approach (with the later addition of Darwinian evolutionary theory) has finally triumphed. Indeed, it is hard to disagree with Marks (1995:52) that the attempt to follow Linnaeus's example and focus on how many human races exist "has led anthropologists down one of the blindest alleys in the history of modern science." Most anthropologists today follow in the tradition laid down by Buffon: we are primarily interested in understanding the adaptive and evolutionary significance of polytypic or racial variation among human populations.

The German physician Johann Friedrich Blumenbach proposed a famous and influential racial classification that added a fifth race (Malayan) to the four recognized by Linnaeus—African, Mongolian (Asian), Caucasian (European), and American—and avoided the use of traits describing the personality, temperament, and morality of individuals or groups. In their place, Blumenbach added the size and shape of the skull to the list of exclusively morphological features used by racial classifiers and coined the term *Caucasian* for the white populations of Europe, North Africa, and the Middle East. The name was

FIGURE 4.4 Johann Friedrich Blumenbach (1752–1840) named the Caucasian race and created a classification of five major races that is still very popular today.
© Historical image collection by Bildagentur-online / Alamy.

based on what he considered a particularly representative skull from the Caucasus region near modern-day Armenia and Georgia. Blumenbach believed that the different races were the result of degeneration from a single ancestral human population that he identified (both geographically and morphologically) as the Caucasian. Like Buffon and many others, he argued that environmental and climatic differences across the globe caused the morphological differences seen in different races.

But unlike his predecessors, Blumenbach seems to have recognized the continuous nature of biological variation between the different races and the somewhat arbitrary nature of all racial classifications when he suggested that the "innumerable varieties of mankind run into one another by insensible degrees" in such a way "that it is very clear that they are all related, or only differ from each other in degree" (Blumenbach 1950:34). Many anthropologists today would agree with Blumenbach and argue that the continuous nature of racial variation is indeed a critical flaw in racial thinking. Blumenbach seems not to have been terribly troubled by his insight, however, since he persisted in naming and describing his five races. An examination of Blumenbach's actual descriptions of the races indicates that his approach to racial classification, like that of Linnaeus, was Platonic and that he was also describing what he considered to be the essential or average pattern for each race, ignoring the variation that exists in all populations. To the followers of Plato's philosophical approach, variation in a population was considered to be random and unimportant; what was important was the *archetype*, which demonstrated the essential nature of the thing itself. We will shortly examine how the Platonic approach to the study of variation was replaced by a Darwinian or evolutionary approach and the implications of this shift for the study of race.

How can we summarize the status of the race concept at the end of the 18th century? As race became an object of scientific study, the racial categories and the folk beliefs and stereotypes concerning non-Europeans on which they were based were regarded as legitimate scientific "facts." We will see that throughout the entire history of race, the prestige of objective science has been wrongly used to support dangerous social and political goals. In the 18th century, the support of

BOX ONE

Linnaeus's 1758 Classification of Human Races

FIGURE B4.1 *Homo sapiens americanus*: "red, ill-tempered, subjugated. Hair black, straight, thick. Nostrils wide. Face harsh. Beard scanty. Obstinate, contented, free. Paints himself with red lines. Ruled by custom."
Courtesy of Universal Images Group / Getty Images.

FIGURE B4.2 *Homo sapiens europaeus*: "white, serious, strong. Hair blond, flowing. Eyes blue. Active, very smart, inventive. Covered by tight clothing. Ruled by laws."
Courtesy of ullstein bild /Getty Images.

The 1758 classification of human races by Linnaeus is revealing and informative to a modern audience for a variety of reasons. The quotations accompanying the photos are translations of the entire descriptions provided by Linnaeus (Marks 1995), and we have already discussed how Linnaeus was attempting to provide a Platonic description of what he considered to be the essential or archetypal nature of each racial group. We have also noted that Linnaeus never traveled to these places to observe firsthand the morphology and behavior of their inhabitants. Instead he relied on anecdotal and obviously biased reports from the few Europeans who had traveled to Africa, Asia, and the Americas. Who were these people, and how reliable were their reports about the inhabitants of these distant lands? In general, they were sailors and soldiers, missionaries and merchants, explorers and adventurers, and slave traders. They were not anthropologists, and they were certainly not unbiased and objective students of human diversity.

(continued)

FIGURE B4.3 *Homo sapiens asiaticus*: "yellow, melancholy, greedy. Hair black. Eyes dark. Severe, haughty, desirous. Covered by loose garments. Ruled by opinion."
Courtesy of ullstein bild /Getty Images.

FIGURE B4.4 *Homo sapiens afer*: "black, impassive, lazy. Hair kinked. Skin silky. Nose flat. Lips thick. Women with genital flap; breasts large. Crafty, slow, foolish. Anoints himself with grease. Ruled by caprice."
Courtesy of The LIFE Picture Collection/Getty Images.

Perhaps the best indication of the unreliability of the reports on which Linnaeus based his classification scheme is provided by a consideration of the "fifth race" described by Linnaeus, which he called *Homo sapiens monstrosus*. This last race is essentially an imaginary group of "humans" from all over the world comprised of giants from Patagonia, dwarfs from the Alps, flat-headed Canadians, cone-headed Chinese, and other freakish and deformed creatures. Linnaeus was apparently as certain of the existence and nature of this fantastic grab bag as he was of his four geographic races. This tradition of monstrous races, devoid of any eyewitness accounts, can be traced back to the ancient Greek encyclopedist Pliny the Elder, who died in the eruption of Mount Vesuvius that covered Pompeii in 79 B.C.E. He populated unexplored territories, beyond the reaches of Greek civilization, with one-eyed, one-legged, dog-headed creatures. These descriptions continued in medieval travel literature and would have been well known and apparently credible sources for Linnaeus.

science for the existence of race suggested to many that race was a natural part of God's design of the world and of humanity. The basic set of four or five continental races that are still with us today had already been established on the basis of perceived differences in skin color and some other morphological features. Most Europeans and Americans accepted the biblical story of a single creation of humans and thought that the diversity seen between different races was the result of "degeneration" that had occurred as originally white human populations had spread around the globe into places with different climates and environments. In addition to their physical differences, racial groups were thought to differ with respect to their personality, morality, intelligence, behavior, and other cultural traits, and these characteristics were considered innate and not particularly subject to change. Finally, the inequality of the various human races was a critically important aspect of the 18th-century racial worldview. Races were usually portrayed in a linear hierarchical scheme with Europeans at the top and Africans at the bottom. Since the notion of racial inequality continues to be an influential (and dangerous) part of racial ideologies today, we need to take a closer look at the roots of this idea.

RACE, INEQUALITY, AND ETHNOCENTRISM

No one can read the racial descriptions of Linnaeus and not see that the European race is presented as the highest or best and that each of the other races fares poorly by comparison. By any judgment, being "ruled by law" is superior to being "ruled by caprice." This notion that the different races are inherently unequal and can be ranked in a linear sequence is related to an ancient idea that can be traced from the ancient Greeks to 18th-century biologists like Linnaeus, known as the *great chain of being*. In the pre-evolutionary 17th and 18th centuries, the great chain of being provided the key to understanding the patterns and relationships of all living things. It suggested that there was continuity in God's creation, with connections linking the simplest to the most complex life forms. Implicit in this continuous chain of life was an obvious hierarchy or rank order, with some creatures closer to the top and others at the bottom. Humans were considered to be near the very top of the chain, just below the angels and God. When the first comparative anatomies of other primates were published in the 17th century, it was realized that the great apes resembled "missing links" in the chain between humans and the lower primates, such as monkeys and lemurs. From there it was not a large step to designate certain human races as closer to the apes than the angels, and indeed the notion that Caucasians were the highest, most civilized, and in effect most godlike of the races, while the African race was the most primitive or apelike, was rarely questioned by most Europeans or Americans.

Why were Europeans so convinced of their superiority to other races? In general, we can attribute much of this sentiment to an attitude that anthropologists today refer to as *ethnocentrism*, in which people feel that their own culture or way of life is superior to that of other racial, ethnic, or cultural groups. In addition, the actual historical circumstances around which the notion of race first developed can explain much about the prejudices and biases that have always been an important part of European ideas about race. The early colonists considered Native Americans inferior to themselves for a variety of ethnocentric reasons based ultimately on cultural differences relating to religion (Native Americans were pagans rather than Christians) and to subsistence and residence practices (Native Americans were often nomadic hunters and gatherers or horticulturalists rather than farmers). In a word, Native Americans were considered an inherently "uncivilized" people, which clearly suggested that they were inferior to the "civilized" colonists. The fact that many Native American groups strongly opposed the loss of their own culture and resisted assimilation into Euro-American culture was seen as evidence of their inability to become civilized and a sure sign of their eventual, and to some minds deserved, extinction. These cultural differences were misinterpreted by the colonists as evidence of biological differences, and these differences were then used as proof of racial inferiority and the "savagery" of American Indians. This provided a rough-and-ready justification for genocidal attacks on Indian populations, taking of Indian lands with impunity (often in spite of legal treaties guaranteeing that land to the Natives), and eventually to the destruction of Native cultures. But the ethnocentrism of the early American colonists had deeper roots that can be traced back to the experiences of their English ancestors with "other" populations back in Europe.

In many respects, the experience of English colonialism in Ireland and the ethnocentrism associated with it prepared the English for the colonization of the New World (Smedley 2007). Historians have suggested that the attitudes of the English settlers toward Native Americans were strongly influenced by the historically hostile relations between the English and the Irish. For several hundred years, England had attempted to conquer Ireland and subjugate the Irish people and in so doing developed an extremely ethnocentric view of the "wild Irish" as lazy and savage nomadic pastoralists. The English were convinced that their own agricultural way of life was superior to that of the Irish and that rich Irish lands could be better used as agricultural plantations (owned and operated by English nobles, of course). The English ultimately used their greater military and political power to steal Irish lands for their own profit. Civilizing the Irish savages would be an added benefit, from the perspective of the English. Similar rationales would later be used in the occupation of Indian lands as the English colonies turned into the United States of America. The same ethnocentrism would color the relations between colonists and Native Americans and would play a large role in the development of early ideas of racial difference and inequality.

Africans were generally considered by most Europeans, based on many of the same ethnocentric reasons, to be an even lower race than American Indians or the Irish. Africans had an even greater burden of "evidence" supporting their inferiority in the fact that most Europeans knew Africans only as slaves. Some went so far as to suggest that slavery was the natural state of the Africans and that their childlike nature and lack of intelligence and initiative made Africans unable to thrive without the help of the superior races. With respect to European attitudes toward and experiences with Africans, we should make a clear distinction between the Iberians (Spanish and Portuguese) and the English (Smedley 2007). The former had a long history of relations with Africans, going back to the invasions of the Moors, who brought Islam to the Iberian peninsula in the 11th century and to even earlier North African Islamic settlers in the 8th century. Hispanicized Africans were members of the crews of most of the early Iberian explorers and conquistadores in the New World, including Columbus, Pizarro, Cortez, and Balboa. At the same time, the English were a much less cosmopolitan society who first interacted with Africans in the context of the West African slave trade in the mid-16th century, later becoming the major carriers of African slaves to the New World. Unlike the Spanish and Portuguese, the English explorers of the New World did not include Africans on their crews. As a result of their exposure to Africans in the context of the slave trade or as actual slaves in America, a very biased and one-sided view of Africans as the lowest of all human races came to be generally accepted in the English-speaking world.

Thus the origin of the racial worldview in the 18th-century Western world must be seen as the result of several hundred years of contact and interactions between Europeans, Africans, Asians, and Native Americans. During the period of European maritime exploration, imperial expansion, and conquest and colonization of the New World (including the development of the Atlantic slave trade), Europeans used their superior technology to destroy native societies, taking the people's land and wealth in the process. Convinced that their superior military technology, religion, and other cultural differences were evidence of biological superiority, Europeans developed a racial worldview, propped up by the prestige of both science and religion, that justified their often cruel and avaricious actions. In spite of the revolutionary zeal and noble words of the founders of the American republic and of the patriots storming the Bastille in Paris, even the most progressive members of European and American society did not truly believe that all men were created equal, and race was the main weapon in their attempts to dominate non-European peoples.

NINETEENTH-CENTURY VIEWS

The great racial debate of the first half of the 19th century concerned the question of whether the different races were in fact different species, the results of separate and different divine creations. Known as *polygenism*, the notion that Africans, Asians, and Native Americans were created separately from Europeans was a dangerously unorthodox position in the religious world of 16th- and 17th-century Europe: two prominent supporters of this heresy were burned at the stake by the Catholic Church. When Isaac de La Peyrère published an influential book, *Men before Adam*, in 1655 that suggested the existence of "pre-Adamite" races of mankind that were the ancestors of the natives of Africa, Asia, and the Americas, he was imprisoned for six months and forced to retract his heresy. In spite of its obvious deviation from the Judeo-Christian creation story told in the Bible's book of Genesis, polygenism came to the forefront of debates on race in the United States during the 19th century. The alternative notion of a single creation of all humankind, as described in the biblical account, became known as *monogenism*. It suggested that all peoples were the descendants of Adam but that different races or varieties had arisen as a result of degeneration, mostly due to the effects of the climate in different parts of the world. Although the debate between supporters of polygenism and of monogenism was ended at around midcentury by the publication of Darwin's *Origin of Species* in 1859, its history is instructive for what it tells us about one of the most important and divisive social and political issues of the day: slavery and the nature of Africans and African Americans.

The Catholic Church and the Spanish and Portuguese explorers had already dealt with the issue of the nature of Native Americans several hundred years earlier. In the early days of European maritime explorations, the question arose concerning whether Native Americans were humans or beasts. As they had done with Jews in the time of the Crusades, some Spaniards argued for a subhuman status for Native Americans or contended that if they were human, they were surely a people accursed by God, perhaps a remnant of the ten lost tribes of Israel. As a result of the work of Bartolomé de Las Casas, a Spanish conquistador turned priest and a tireless advocate of the rights of Native Americans, Pope Paul III proclaimed in 1537 that the native inhabitants of the New World were "truly men" and were entitled to the rights of men. Although this edict did not end slavery and the brutalization of Native Americans in colonial Latin America, it provided (at a very early date relative to the situation in the English colonies of North America) some degree of equality under the law for Native Americans and strong support for the monogenist position of a single creation of all peoples. European Catholics would disagree with this orthodox position of the church at their own risk during the 16th and 17th centuries, as exemplified by the burnings and imprisonings that occurred. But the question of the humanity of Native Americans and especially African Americans would not be so easily settled by religious authority in the mostly Protestant colonies of North America. In fact, the 19th-century debate on polygenism and monogenism in the United States would see the transition from the use of religion to that of science to explain and justify the inequality of the races.

Polygenism received its main scientific support from the work of a Harvard University professor of zoology, Louis Agassiz, and a Philadelphia physician, Samuel George Morton, two of the most

FIGURE 4.5 Samuel George Morton (1799–1851) and Louis Agassiz (1807–1873) were the two most prominent scientific supporters of polygenism in the early 19th century.
Credit: a) Courtesy of Hulton Archive/Getty Images b) Marine Biological Laboratory/Science Photo Library.

prominent and accomplished men of 19th-century American science. It is interesting to note that in one sense, polygenism did not come naturally to Agassiz who, as an intensely devout Christian and an opponent of slavery, would seem to have been a good candidate for monogenist beliefs. However, the historical record indicates that Agassiz's support for separate and unequal status for African Americans sprang not from any scientific evidence but from his deep sense of personal revulsion and disgust upon seeing African Americans for the first time in a Philadelphia hotel in 1846. Shortly after this pivotal experience, Agassiz described his feelings in a letter written to his mother:

> It was in Philadelphia that I first found myself in prolonged contact with negroes; all the domestics in my hotel were men of color. I can scarcely express to you the painful impression that I received, especially since the feeling that they inspired in me is contrary to all our ideas about the confraternity of the human type and the unique origin of our species. But truth before all. Nevertheless, I experienced pity at the sight of this degraded and degenerate race, and their lot inspired compassion in me in thinking that they are really men. Nonetheless, it is impossible for me to reprocess the feeling that they are not of the same blood as us. In seeing their black faces with their huge lips and grimacing teeth, the wool on their head, their bent knees, their elongated hands, their large curved nails, and especially the livid color of the palm of their hands, I could not take my eyes off their face in order to tell them to stay far away. And when they advanced their hideous hand towards my plate in order to serve me, I wished I were able to depart in order to eat a piece of bread elsewhere, rather than dine with such service. What unhappiness for the white race to have tied their existence so closely with that of negroes in certain countries. God preserve us from such a contact! [Gould 1996:76–77]

In his published work, Agassiz simply asserted the biological existence of race, the obvious and natural inequality of the races, and especially the clear superiority of Europeans and inferiority of Africans. He advocated social and educational policies to ensure that the training and education of each of the races take account of their innately different abilities. Hence blacks should be trained and educated for manual labor, while whites would be prepared for managerial, governmental, and other positions of authority. It is interesting to note that although Agassiz never relied on scientific evidence to argue for the inequality of the races, his work was accorded the respect due to a Harvard professor of science. In hindsight, it is clear that Agassiz's position was simply the dominant social and political notion of the time concerning the races and was in fact shared by most white Americans and Europeans. In spite of the lack of scientific support or argumentation for this position, it was presented (and received) with the seal of approval of the scientific community, an increasingly prestigious and powerful institution in American and European life.

The man who contributed most to the scientific argument in support of deep differences between the races was Samuel George Morton, whose measurements of the skulls of modern and ancient peoples of different races seemed to provide empirical and objective scientific support for the inequality of the races. The first practitioner of the new science of "craniometry" in America, Morton devised a method to measure the volume of the brain case by filling it with mustard seeds (later with BB-sized lead shot). His stated goal was to test the hypothesis of the inequality of the races by determining whether each race had a similar endowment of brain matter. Note the unstated (and unsupported) assumption of Morton's work that differences in the size of the brain are predictive of differences in intelligence among humans: modern neuroscience has proved this idea false. Morton published two major works (*Crania Americana* in 1839 and *Crania Aegyptiaca* in 1844) based on his measurements of nearly 1,000 skulls and thus provided the strongest scientific support for polygenism in the 19th century. In these two monographs, Morton built a strong case in support of a racial hierarchy of brain size and intelligence, not surprisingly with Africans having the smallest brains and northern Europeans having the largest. But a recent reanalysis of Morton's data (Gould 1978, 1996) demonstrates that Morton got it almost entirely wrong and that there is no evidence in his data of any significant racial disparities in brain size that cannot be accounted for by differences relating to sex, sampling, and body size. According to Gould, Morton probably unconsciously cooked his data in order to support his strongly held belief in the "obvious" inequality of the races. Apparently what Morton did was to bias his racial samples by including mostly large skulls for the "advanced" races (Caucasians) and mostly small skulls for the "inferior" races (Africans and Native Americans). As a result, his work validated the racial hierarchy that was accepted by most scientists and most citizens of the time, with Europeans at the top and Africans at the bottom.

During the 19th-century debates over polygenism and monogenism, most Americans of European descent would have supported the assertion that the races were not all equal and specifically that Native Americans and African Americans were inferior to Caucasians. The spectrum of belief ran from those who believed that the unequal status of the races was innate and unchangeable to those who thought that with proper care and training, even Africans could rise to the level of "civilized" societies like those of Europe. It is equally clear that a philosophy like polygenism, which asserted that the races were innately and deeply different and originated from different creations, could provide a powerful justification for the maintenance of slavery. Indeed, Josiah Clark Nott and George R. Glidden's 800-page polygenist tome of 1854, titled *Types of Mankind*, strongly supported the natural inferiority of African Americans and justified their enslaved status in the American South. This book was dedicated to Morton and helped popularize the polygenist doctrine. It must be noted, though, that polygenism was never very successful among the southern slaveholding class, who recognized that it contradicted the scriptural story of creation and could be considered heretical.

The publication of Darwin's *Origin of Species* in 1859, just eight years after Morton's death, provided closure to the debate between polygenists and monogenists by suggesting a single origin of

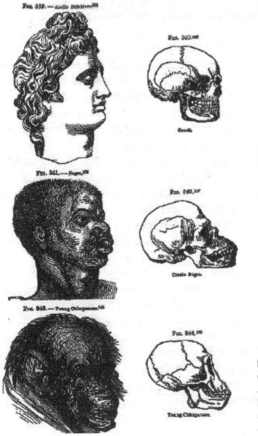

FIGURE 4.6 Images like these from Nott and Glidden's *Types of Mankind* (1854) were thinly veiled attempts to argue for deep racial differences and a hierarchy of the races, masquerading as scientific evidence for inequality.
Credit: Paul D. Stewart / Science Photo Library.

Homo sapiens in the context of a coherent evolutionary theory that applied to all living things. Although the development of evolutionary theory is a watershed in all biological analyses, including questions of the origins and differences between human populations, it is interesting to note that attitudes concerning the inequality and ranking of various races did not significantly change from pre- to post-Darwinian times. The social attitudes of Europeans and white Americans concerning racial superiority and inferiority were so well established that they were able to coexist as well with an evolutionary as with a creationist viewpoint. In a sense, science now provided the justification for racial inequality that was earlier supplied by a particular reading of the Judeo-Christian religious tradition. Where God's design of creation as seen in the great chain of being was once used to explain racial inequality, in the Darwinian world, one could (and many did) argue that nature had made Caucasians superior to the other races of the world. The result was the same either way, but now science was in the position of supporting slavery and its attendant brutalization of people based on their skin color and perceived inferiority. By the end of the 19th century and in spite of the end of slavery and the development of evolutionary theory, the idea of racial distinctions had acquired a scientific veneer of respectability, while the older folk beliefs of racial inequality and deep and innate differences between human populations continued to exert a strong hold on the American and European psyche.

TWENTIETH-CENTURY ANTHROPOLOGICAL VIEWS

As noted in chapter 3, recent advances in our knowledge of biological science, evolutionary theory, and genetics have been enormous. From the rediscovery of Mendel's laws in 1900 to the complete mapping of the human genome in 2003, anthropologists have sought to incorporate the latest biological findings in their attempts to understand the meaning and significance of race in *Homo sapiens*. In a somewhat ironic twist, the more that anthropologists have sought to clarify the meaning of race through scientific approaches, the more they have found that racial classifications are mostly social or cultural creations with little biological justification. In addition to scientific developments, some of the major social and historical events of the 20th century have influenced the ways in which anthropologists look at race today, including U.S. immigration restrictions based on race and national origins, the theory of eugenics and the racial genocide practiced by the Nazis in World War II, and the fight against the legacy of slavery, discrimination, and racial segregation in the United States. We will discuss the impact of each of these historical and sociopolitical events on American views of race in later chapters, but first let's review how the new advances in biological and especially genetic science influenced anthropological definitions of race throughout the 20th century.

The current split between the minority of anthropologists who continue to support a scientifically valid theory of biological race and the majority who are convinced that race makes little biological sense dates back to the beginnings of the field in early-20th-century America. One can make a strong case that the origin and central focus of anthropological inquiry in North America for at least the first half of the century was the race question, with the majority of anthropologists supporting the biological theory of race. However, early in the century, a new and critical strain of anthropological thought emerged that questioned the biological reality and usefulness of the concept of race in *Homo sapiens*. The roots of this dichotomy, which is still with us today, can be traced back to two of the most influential American anthropologists of the first half of the 20th century, Harvard University's Earnest A. Hooton and Franz Boas of Columbia University. Hooton's influence is still felt today as a result of his having trained most of the second generation of Ph.D.'s in biological anthropology, many of whom went on to teach at other American universities. Today most American biological anthropologists can trace their own educational lineage directly back to Hooton. For example, when I was a graduate student at the University of Washington in the 1980s, my major adviser was Gerald G. Eck, a student of F. Clark Howell, who was a student of Hooton's student, Sherwood Washburn. Boas trained both biological and cultural anthropologists at Columbia, although his influence on the development of attitudes toward race has been more strongly felt in cultural anthropology as a result of the work of his students, including Margaret Mead, Ruth Benedict, Melville Herskovits, Alfred Kroeber, and Robert Lowie.

FIGURE 4.7 Franz Boas (1858-1942) of Columbia. Through his training of the majority of the next generation of American anthropologists, he greatly influenced the anthropological understanding of race in the 20th century. © Bettmann/Corbis.

Hooton taught at Harvard for nearly 25 years beginning in 1930, and he can claim much of the credit (or blame) for the anthropological focus on race that characterized American biological anthropology for the first half of the 20th century. Hooton was a firm believer in the biological reality of race and a strong adherent of the newest methods of scientifically determining the racial differences that he claimed could lead to objective racial classifications. His approach to race was historical and descriptive in that he sought to understand the historical connections between different races or populations and to measure and describe the phenotypic differences that could be used to classify these populations. He believed in the original existence of "pure" races and suggested that much of the difficulty of distinguishing race in the modern world was a result of a long history of "race mixing." His interest in describing the essential racial characteristics or traits that could successfully define different races comes out of the Platonic tradition, a mainstay in Western thought first elaborated by the Greek philosopher Plato in the fourth century B.C.E. As mentioned earlier in this chapter, the Platonic idea, as applied to questions concerning the meaning and definition of race, is that one can define the true or essential and unchanging nature of different racial groups and that the variation that we see in the real world around these racial "types" is an illusion.

Hooton was following in the footsteps of Linnaeus and Blumenbach in his support for a Platonic notion of human race, but this notion would not hold up for long in the new and evolutionary 20th-century world of anthropology. The problem with typological notions of race is that they ignore what Darwin tells us is of critical importance to evolutionary theory. Darwin's theory of evolution by natural selection relies on the presence of inherited variation in all species; it is only through the existence of inherited variations that species can evolve new characteristics and become adapted to changing environmental conditions. Yet typological theories of race suggest that species and races are characterized by a permanent and unchanging essence and that the variation we see within species, populations, or races is illusory and unimportant. Only through the clouded lens of a Platonic notion of race could Hitler and other dark-haired, brown-eyed Nazis believe that they were members of a noble, blond, and blue-eyed Aryan race.

As the leading American biological anthropologist of his day, a professor at the leading American university, and a best-selling author of many popular books on the subject, Hooton was at the cutting edge of both popular opinion and scientific research on race. He advocated the latest scientific methods for measuring racial differences, including craniometry (the measuring of heads and skulls) and genetic measures of racial difference, such as blood group gene frequencies. Following in the craniometric tradition pioneered by Morton, Hooton was a strong supporter of the idea that races could be distinguished by the size and shape of their skulls, and he and his students measured thousands of skulls for the purpose of determining racial differences. For craniometry to be a true and reliable method for identifying racial affiliation, skull size and shape would have to be determined by biological or genetic factors, rather than by environmental or cultural differences. While Hooton and most other anthropologists of the day were convinced of the essential biological nature of racial differences in skull size and shape, this notion would be criticized in Boas's landmark study of head form in American immigrants.

Franz Boas was trained as a physicist in Germany but came to the United States as an aspiring anthropologist in 1884 after taking part in a German scientific expedition to Baffin Island to study Eskimo life. In 1896, he moved to New York City to work at both the American Museum of Natural History and Columbia University. As a German Jew from a family with a long history of involvement in liberal social causes, Boas was well placed to become involved in the anthropological debates concerning the meaning of race. Although at the time his voice was drowned out by the growing din of calls for race-based immigration restrictions, forced sterilizations, and "separate but equal" status for blacks and whites, history would eventually vindicate nearly all of Boas's positions on issues of race, racism, and inequality. At the beginning of Boas's American career as an anthropologist, he fought against the then prevailing notion that people of different cultures could somehow be ranked as superior or inferior. His work with Native American groups from the Northwest demonstrated that in language, art, social relations, and all other aspects of cultural life, people living at a so-called primitive level of technology had just as rich a cultural existence as members of technologically

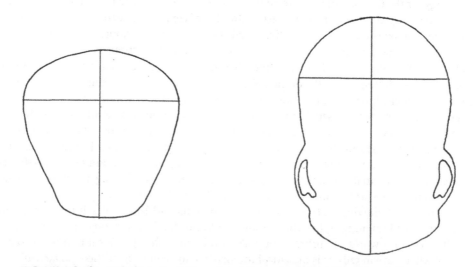

FIGURE 4.8 The cephalic index is the ratio of the maximum width of the skull to its maximum length, multiplied by 100. The skull on the left is *dolichocephalic*, or long and narrow, with a cephalic index of less than 76. The skull on the right is *brachycephalic*, short and broad, as determined by a cephalic index of greater than 80. Throughout much of the 19th and 20th centuries, many anthropologists thought that cephalic index was an excellent racial marker.

"advanced" Western societies. His work disproved the notion that biology determined cultural achievement and suggested that culture, rather than biological race, should be the central focus of anthropological inquiry. His concern for equality and social justice and his skepticism that biology could or should determine human potential or achievement made him the most important anthropological critic of the then-dominant typological view of race. Boas asserted that the environment played a more important role than biology in determining differences between people, races, and social classes. He decided to test his theory and to confront the central claim of the racial typologists, namely, that head form, as measured by the *cephalic index*, was an essential and unchangeable (i.e., biologically determined) trait that allowed one to distinguish between the races.

Between 1908 and 1911, Boas and his students measured skulls in order to test the central claim of the craniologists. This work was commissioned by the U.S. Congress as part of its efforts to learn more about the pool of mostly European immigrants who were at the time coming to America in large numbers. Boas calculated the cephalic index, a ratio of the head's width to its length, for nearly 18 thousand European immigrants and their children in the New York area. Most racial schemes of the day relied heavily on the cephalic index for distinguishing different European populations based on a typological scheme running from long-headed (*dolichocephalic*) to round-headed types (*brachycephalic*). Boas's results showed that the cephalic index of American-born children of immigrant parents was different than that of their parents or their older, European-born siblings. Apparently, assimilation into American society and the different environmental conditions under which these first-generation Americans were growing and developing could lead to changes in head form that racial typologists like Hooton had assumed were part of a racial heritage or biological essence. Anthropologists today refer to this kind of anatomical response of growing individuals to changed environmental conditions as *phenotypic plasticity* and consider it one of the defining traits of human growth and development. Boas's demonstration that human cranial shape was a plastic, environmentally modifiable trait was ignored by most anthropologists, politicians, and other supporters of racial typology and remained the minority opinion for decades.

Although most anthropologists today agree on the importance of Boas's work on plasticity in head form among American immigrants, a recent reanalysis of Boas's original data seriously questions the conclusions he drew from his study. Using modern statistical techniques to reanalyze a portion of the original data, Sparks and Jantz (2002) suggest that the differences in head form between parents and offspring in Boas's data were insignificant. They suggest that the plasticity argument is therefore not relevant in this context, and they support the usefulness of the cephalic index in distinguishing between different races. However, another recent reanalysis of Boas's data affirms that he did in fact get it right and suggests that modern statistical methods allow one to make an even stronger case for plasticity in human head form over the space of a single generation in Boas's immigrant data (Gravlee et al. 2003). Although the debate will doubtless continue, many anthropologists today support the conclusions reached by Boas 100 years ago that head form and skull shape are plastic characters that may vary in different environments and are not useful markers of racial difference.

Typological race theories based on morphological traits such as the cephalic index continued to be popular among anthropologists, but by the 1940s, genetic data and theory began to play a more important role in racial studies. To some extent, this work was a reaction to the problem posed by Boas's determination of the importance of environmental influences in the development of morphological traits such as head form. In particular, the study of population differences in the frequencies of genes for different blood types seemed to allow a scientific and objective approach to racial classification. Blood groups like the ABO, MN, and Rh systems were known to result from the action of individual genes with no significant environmental influence, and different populations were found to vary in the relative frequency of these genes. For example, with respect to the ABO blood group system, many Native American groups have little or no presence of the B gene, low levels of A, and very high frequencies of O. By contrast, western European populations have low levels of B with moderate to high levels of both A and O. William C. Boyd, one of the leading exponents of this approach to racial classification, used blood group gene frequencies to suggest the existence of six human races. In addition to the traditional Caucasian, African, and Asian races, Boyd (1950) named an American Indian and an Australian race and a "hypothetical" race that he referred to as "early Europeans" in which he included the modern Basque people of Spain as the only living representatives.

There are many problems with using gene frequencies of one or a few blood group systems as a criterion for racial classification. These mainly involve the problem of creating discrete categories (races) based on a continuously varying set of data points (gene frequencies). Since gene frequencies in a population can vary continuously from 0 to 100 percent, the researcher is required to make some arbitrary cutoff point between these continuous values in order to create different races. In addition, just about any populations examined will have different values for the frequency of particular genes, including, for example, neighboring villages in the Swiss Alps (Cavalli-Sforza and Bodmer 1971). The question arises, then, how different must gene frequencies be for a new race to be named? Answering this question can only lead to the arbitrary creation of different categories or races, because different scholars will necessarily locate the cutoff points at different places. It is similar to trying to define what it means to be tall or short in contemporary America: different people will often have very different definitions of how to describe the continuous variation seen in height into discrete categories labeled "tall" and "short." This problem with most racial schemes, earlier mentioned in chapter 1, exists for any racial classification based on traits that vary in a continuous fashion. While differences in the frequencies of blood types certainly characterize different human populations, these differences do not allow the creation of an objective and unambiguous set of races. Furthermore, it is obvious that knowing someone's blood type is of absolutely no help in determining that person's race: people with blood type A, for example, can be found in every population or race known on earth.

Another problem with the use of blood group or other gene frequency data for classifying races is the lack of concordance between genetic data and other racial traits. Race classifications based on one set of morphological features or gene frequencies are nearly always contradicted by classifications based on other traits. For example, while Eskimos and Australian aboriginals have nearly identical gene frequencies for the ABO blood group, they are very different in skin, hair, and eye color, body size, and just about any other racial trait imaginable. This lack of concordance between different racial traits is a general problem with all race classifications, all of which rely on the arbitrary process of choosing which racial traits to focus on. For example, one can identify European populations with low or high cephalic indices, different blood group frequencies, and darker or lighter skin color. There is no objective solution to the problem of how to classify these populations; in effect, one simply chooses to prioritize some racial trait, ignore the discordance with other traits, and classify the populations accordingly. But this approach will always lead to arbitrary and different racial classification schemes by different scholars.

Finally, the entire rationale of the gene frequency approach to racial classification is problematic as a result of the way in which genetic variation is distributed within (polymorphic) and between (polytypic) human populations. Genetic research beginning in the 1970s clearly demonstrated that polymorphic variation, the levels of genetic variation within human populations or races,— tends to be much higher than polytypic variation, the average differences between different populations or races. For example, there is greater gene frequency variation in blood groups on the African and Asian continents than the average difference between Africans and Asians. This somewhat counterintuitive result was first popularized by the Harvard geneticist Richard Lewontin (1974), who determined that roughly 85 percent of human genetic diversity is found among individuals within nations or tribes. The most genetically diverse people on the planet, according to Lewontin, are the inhabitants of Africa, who contain within their genome 93 percent of the entire pool of genetic diversity found in *Homo sapiens*. The approach of biologists like Lewontin suggests that a focus on polytypic racial differences is misleading because it ignores the majority of human genetic variation, which is polymorphic and can be found within, rather than between, human populations or races.

The 1960s was a tumultuous time of social change and evolving views concerning the biological, social, and political meanings of race in American society. The civil rights movement followed hard on the heels of the Supreme Court's 1954 *Brown* v. *Board of Education* decision, which outlawed school segregation and destroyed the fiction of "separate but equal" status of whites and blacks in the United States. The 1960s was also a time of rapid and momentous change in anthropological views of race as the majority opinion among professionals began to shift concerning the usefulness and biological justification of traditional views of race. Hooton's second Ph.D. student at Harvard, a man named Carlton S. Coon, was to play a leading, if unintended, role in this transformation as a result of the critical response to his controversial 1962 book *The Origin of Races*. Coon's views on race included an updated version of 19th-century polygenism in which he suggested a separate evolutionary origin for the five major living races (Asians, Australians, two African races, and Europeans). He hypothesized that modern *Homo sapiens* evolved at five different times in five different geographic locations from an ancestral species known as *Homo erectus*. The part of Coon's hypothesis that attracted the most criticism, including accusations of racism, was his suggestion that there was a direct connection between the time when these races crossed the threshold to modern *H. sapiens* and their cultural, intellectual, and biological status and achievements today. Coon argued that since Asians were the first to become modern (followed shortly by Europeans), they had the largest brains and the greatest intelligence—in effect, Asians had evolved further than the other races and were more advanced as a result of having reached the *Homo sapiens* stage of evolution first. Conversely, Africans and native Australians had evolved into *Homo sapiens* last, and their intelligence and cultural achievements similarly lagged behind those of the other races. In an unfortunate series of pictures demonstrating the different races, Coon (1962:xxxii) included a comparison of a Chinese and an Australian with the caption "The Alpha and Omega of *Homo sapiens*." Coon suggested that the Australian named Topsy had a brain size of under 1000 cc, well below the modern average for *Homo sapiens* and only about half that of the "Chinese sage," Dr. Li Chi. Coon's ranking and differential valuation of these individuals and, by implication, these two races was seen at the time by most anthropologists as racist, while his scenario of five separate speciation events leading from *Homo erectus* to *Homo sapiens* was unsupported by what was known at the time of evolutionary mechanisms and, as a result, thought to be unlikely in the extreme. Today most anthropologists share these critical views of Coon's ideas, and the response of the anthropological community to Coon's perceived racist scheme was an important episode in the changing views among anthropologists concerning the meaning of race.

One of the most influential responses to Coon's theories was a paper by University of Michigan anthropologist Frank Livingstone published in the journal *Current Anthropology* in 1962, titled "On the Non-Existence of Human Races." In this short article, Livingstone suggested that anthropologists should no longer engage in the classification of human races because the concept of races or subspecies was no longer justifiable in a biological sense. He argued that most variation in geographically distinct populations of *Homo sapiens* was continuous and that any discrete racial units created on this basis are necessarily arbitrary. He suggested that human biological diversity is better characterized as being clinal in nature. *Clinal variation* refers to a pattern of gradual change in morphological or genetic traits that occurs across the geographic range of a species. The best example of a racial trait that varies in a clinal pattern is the latitudinal (north-south) distribution of skin color in Old World human populations, but there are many other examples. Gene frequencies of blood groups vary clinally across Eurasia with, for example, decreasing frequency of the B gene as one moves from east to west. Arguing that much of the genetic variation between human populations was clinal, Livingstone (1962:279) suggested that "there are no races; there are only clines." Of particular interest was Livingstone's analysis of the evolutionary forces that might lead to a pattern of clinal variation in *Homo sapiens*. He clearly saw that human populations might vary genetically across geographic space as a result of one or more evolutionary processes, including natural selection, gene flow, or migration. The north-south clinal variation in skin color is best explained as a result of natural selection to different environments characterized by more or less intense ultraviolet radiation (see chapter 5), while the east-west cline in ABO blood groups across Eurasia is best explained as a result of genetic exchange resulting from westward migrations of Asian populations in historic times. Livingstone's critique suggested that racial classification could never be successful because the actual patterns of human diversity did not lend support to a discrete packaging of races.

C. Loring Brace was another major critic of the race concept in the early 1960s while at the University of California at Santa Barbara. Over the past 50 years, most of which he has spent at the University of Michigan, he has continued to be one of the most articulate critics of the biological race concept (Brace 2005). In 1964, Brace wrote a short but influential paper that clearly stated the scientific weakness of the race concept and supported Livingstone's work on clines. Brace suggested that the major problems with biological race theory were the completely arbitrary nature of the gradual boundaries between races and the lack of correlation between the distributions of different racial traits. Rather than name races and attempt to put bodies or populations into racial categories, Brace (1964:313) argued that "the first aim of the human biologist should be the attempt to correlate trait distribution with selective agency." Like Livingstone, Brace was advocating a dynamic and evolutionary processual approach to the study of human biological variation in relation to environment and habitat that would lead to an understanding of how and why traits (such as skin color and blood type) varied among different human populations. Brace clearly recognized the typological roots of the race concept in anthropology and argued strongly for its rejection and replacement with an evolutionary and adaptive approach to the study of human diversity, much like the one advocated by many anthropologists today.

Another longtime critic of biological theories of race and the anthropological obsession with describing and naming them was Ashley Montagu. After studying cultural anthropology at the London School of Economics with Bronislaw Malinowski, Montagu moved from his native England to the United States and obtained his Ph.D. in 1937 from Columbia University, where he studied with Franz Boas and Ruth Benedict. The author of more than 60 books and hundreds of articles (Sperling 2000), Montagu's most influential statement on race and racism was his 1942 book *Man's Most Dangerous Myth: The Fallacy of Race*, in which he critiqued the biological basis of human race, railed against the typological conception of races so prevalent at the time, and popularized the notion that human race functioned more as a social construction than a biological fact. He demonstrated that different societies often created unique kinds of racial categories, reflecting the social or cultural origins of racial difference. In this respect, as well as in his critique of typological race notions, Montagu was well ahead of his time. His outspoken and at times intemperate response to perceived racism among colleagues and in the larger culture led to an untimely end of his academic career at Rutgers University in the early 1950s. Moving to Princeton, New Jersey, Montagu became a beloved public intellectual and successful popularizer of the antiracial dogma, as well as other liberal social causes including feminism (Montagu 1953) and the importance of nurturing the development of children (Montagu 1955). His was one of the first and most critical voices raised in opposition to Coon's *Origin of Races* (Montagu 1963) and to the

FIGURE 4.9 British-born American anthropologist Ashley Montagu (1905–1999) was one of the first voices within anthropology to critique biological theories of race.
Courtesy of Hulton Archive/Getty Images.

scientific racism of the 1960s and 1970s, which suggested connections between race and intelligence (Montagu 1975). Montagu asserted that all race classifications were inherently racist because they all suggested false links between the individual's phenotype (or physical traits), the individual's intelligence or mental abilities, and the group's ability to develop higher levels of "civilization." Montagu clearly showed that there was no genetic or biological evidence to support these proposed links at a time when the majority professional and lay opinion on the subject was clearly against him. Today, of course, only the most committed racists among us would argue that the rise and fall of civilizations in the human past was determined by racial characteristics of the peoples involved, yet this was a common belief among both professional historians and the general public in the not-too-distant past. The suggested link between intelligence and race is still a much-debated point today, although the genetic evidence in support of it is no more substantial today than it was in the 1940s and 1950s when Montagu was writing.

BOX TWO

The UNESCO Statements on Race

In the aftermath of World War II, the United Nations was formed in 1945 to replace the League of Nations as a global organization of governments dedicated to fostering international cooperation, security, human rights, and economic development. The United Nations Educational, Scientific, and Cultural Organization (UNESCO) was also founded in 1945 as a specialized agency of the UN dedicated to international cooperation through educational, scientific, and cultural activities. Although the UN is headquartered in New York City, UNESCO is based in Paris, and in December 1949, the organization invited ten social scientists to UNESCO House to draft a statement on race. The goal of this gathering was to pose an alternative to the racial ideology of the Nazis that had led to the Holocaust. A draft statement was prepared, with much of the writing being done by Rutgers University anthropologist Ashley Montagu, and after further editing as a result of input from a number of prominent geneticists, UNESCO's First Statement on Race was published in July 1950. Further meetings attended by biologists, anthropologists, psychologists, and sociologists were held in Paris in June 1951, in Moscow in July 1964, and again in Paris in September 1967, resulting in the Second, Third and Fourth UNESCO Statements on Race (Montagu 1972). Taken as a whole, these documents provide a fascinating look into the scientific and social scientific debates on the nature of race and racism that have characterized the postwar years, and they form the basis for all modern anthropological and scientific discussions of the nature of race.

UNESCO's First Statement on Race included a list of 15 items that sought to characterize an emerging scientific consensus on the nature of race. The first four items sought to lay the foundation for a discussion of biological diversity in *Homo sapiens* by asserting a scientific consensus on the question of the unity of *Homo sapiens* as a single species, made up of a number of populations that differed in both phenotypic and genotypic traits and were considered to constitute separate races. Items 5 and 6 concerned some of the cultural aspects of race: namely, that different individuals and different societies have many different ideas as to what makes up a race. Linguistic (e.g., Hispanic) and religious (e.g., Jewish) groups were not the same as races, and the suggestion was made that the term *ethnic groups* should be used for national, religious, linguistic, and cultural groups. Points 7 and 8 suggested that although there might be some rationale behind classifying *Homo sapiens* into three major continental races (Asian, African, and European), there was absolutely no consensus among anthropologists or biologists on the question "How many races are there?" Item 9 spoke unequivocally to a very controversial point by asserting that there was no scientific evidence for differences in intelligence between the races. Item 10 stated that there was no evidence that genetics could explain cultural differences or differences in the level of cultural achievements between societies or races, and items 11 and 12 stated the same lack of evidence for genetic differences between human groups in temperament, personality, or character. Point 13 stated that there was no biological reason for prohibiting intermarriage or interbreeding between individuals of different races. In item 14, we find an early statement of the notion

(continued)

that race fails as a biological concept and is better considered a social construction. "For all practical purposes 'race' is not so much a biological phenomenon as a social myth" (Montagu 1972:10). Finally, in item 15, the authors assert the belief that human equality should be considered an ethical principle that stands regardless of any scientific finding concerning different endowments of different peoples. In other words, even if it were true that some populations were, for example, more intelligent than others, this fact should have no bearing on the ethical position of equality and human rights in equal measure to all humans.

In 1996, the American Association of Physical Anthropologists (AAPA), the leading international organization of professional biological anthropologists, published its official "Statement on Biological Aspects of Race." Appearing in the *American Journal of Physical Anthropology*, this statement was offered as an explicit revision of the UNESCO statements, and it reiterated in more modern form most of the same points made by the UNESCO participants 50 years earlier. (You may read this statement in its entirety at the AAPA website, http://physanth.org/positions/race.)

THE PRESENT AND FUTURE OF THE RACE CONCEPT IN ANTHROPOLOGY

Leonard Lieberman of Central Michigan University and several of his colleagues have attempted to determine what anthropologists currently think and teach about the biological race concept and how their ideas and opinions on this topic have changed over time. The researchers surveyed the opinions of biological anthropologists on race directly through a questionnaire (Lieberman and Reynolds 1978) and, as a means of gauging what is actually being taught about race, through an analysis of the content of biological anthropology textbooks on the subject of race (Littlefield et al. 1982; Lieberman et al. 1992). What they have discovered provides an interesting look at the present and future of the concept of biological race in American anthropology.

In a 1985 survey of nearly 900 anthropologists teaching at American universities, Lieberman and his colleagues discovered that 41 percent of the biological anthropologists and 53 percent of the cultural anthropologists disagreed with the statement "There are biological races in the species *Homo sapiens*" (Lieberman et al. 1992). When one considers that until the end of the 1930s, essentially all anthropologists would have agreed with this statement, this survey suggests that an enormous shift had taken place in anthropological opinions on the validity of the biological race concept in the latter part of the 20th century. When the researchers examined what biological anthropology textbooks were saying about race, they found a very similar picture of increasing rejection of the biological race concept in the more recently written textbooks. While only 7 out of 36 texts (19 percent) written from 1932 to 1974 rejected the concept of biological race in humans, 13 out of 33 (39 percent) written between 1975 and 1984 and 13 out of 19 (68 percent) written from 1985 to 1993 rejected this notion (Lieberman and Jackson 1995). A final piece of evidence in support of the idea that the biological race concept has been in decline among biological anthropologists is the almost complete absence of articles published in biological anthropology journals today that deal with matters of racial classification. This is a great contrast to the situation in the early decades of the 20th century, when articles on race were a common feature of the professional literature of biological anthropology. All of this evidence seems to suggest that at least among biological anthropologists, the notion of biological race is "approaching conceptual extinction" (Lieberman and Jackson 1995:233).

Another anthropologist who is a staunch opponent of the concept of biological race is not nearly as optimistic as Lieberman concerning the demise of the race concept in anthropology. Alan Goodman (1997b:222) suggests that the fact that half of all anthropologists still support the race concept for humans is "appalling" in light of the scientific weakness of biological race. Goodman argues that most anthropologists have been very slow to critique the biological race concept or to confront the long-standing connections between the history of our discipline and the racial world-view. Noting that with the exception of Franz Boas, essentially all anthropologists prior to World War II were supporters of race and racial classifications, Goodman states that early anthropology *was* the study of human race and that this legacy is still an important force today in some branches of anthropology and related disciplines, notably forensics, genetics, and medical studies.

Goodman (1997a, 1997b) has been very critical of the role played by forensic anthropologists in supporting or at least not questioning the biological nature of racial differences among humans. To demonstrate what seem like 19th-century typological definitions of race used by forensic anthropologists, Goodman (1997b) describes a popular catalog of reproduction casts of human skeletal remains designed for the teaching of skeletal biology and forensics. In this catalog, skulls are routinely labeled as "Negroid" or "Caucasoid" and are said to "illustrate racial traits very well." The message conveyed here is that individual skulls representing ideal morphological types can exemplify biological races and that variation between individuals within populations is unimportant. As Goodman (1997b:229) states, "This is solid typology. Plato would be proud."

The main problem with the well-meaning attempts by forensic anthropologists to assist law enforcement agencies in the identification of human remains is that they reflect antiquated models of human biological variation that rely on static, typological racial schemes and categories while ignoring the social, historical, and political dimensions of race in America today. Human variation is dynamic, fluid, and open-ended, with only arbitrary boundaries between socially constructed races. The actual terms we use to denote different races change over time and in different places: people with one-eighth or one-quarter "black" heritage are still known as *octoroons* or *quadroons*, respectively, in certain parts of Louisiana, as they were in much of the country in the 18th and 19th centuries. At other places or times in America, these people might be considered African American, mixed-race, or white. Since race is mostly a matter of self-identification today, there is much room for ambiguity, diversity, and difference of opinion concerning an individual's race. The golfer Tiger Woods even invented a new name to describe his own particular mixed-race background: Cablinasian (recognizing his *Caucasian*, *Black*, *Indian*, and *Asian* heritage). While this is not a problem as long as we recognize that race is socially constructed, it poses severe problems for any theory of race as a biologically validated concept. For many years in America, the "one-drop rule" was an informal racial identification system that ensured that the government would officially classify mixed-race children as belonging to whichever parental race was considered lower on the social scale. Marvin Harris (1964) has named this practice *hypodescent*. Thus having a single black great-grandparent would require that a child be classified as black, despite having seven white great-grandparents! When the algebra of genetic inheritance is so skewed, we are clearly in the realm of social rules and prejudice rather than objective science or anthropology.

The one-drop rule was clearly an attempt to penalize the mixed-race children for the sexual "transgression" of their parents and to maintain the "purity" of the "white gene pool." *Miscegenation*, or cross-racial breeding, was considered bad for the gene pool of the white race, and the one-drop rule was an attempt to ensure that "black genes" did not find their way into the "white gene pool." Indeed, in many U.S. states and until quite recent times, interracial marriage was a criminal offense. It is a sobering thought to realize the similarities between the antimiscegenation laws of 20th-century America, the Nuremburg laws of Nazi Germany (banning intermarriage between Jews and "Germans"), and the apartheid laws of South Africa (legislating legal separation between the races). All of these ideas about white and black genes, racial gene pools, and notions of genetic purity and pollution are a vestige of 19th-century ideas and prejudices and carry no weight among modern geneticists or anthropologists. No geneticist has ever identified a single gene that is found in all members of a single race and absent from all members of other races, so the entire notion of "racial genes" or "black blood" is a fiction. Miscegenation or indeed any social mixing of the races was thought to be a bad thing in a segregated America, and biology was used to provide a veneer of scientific respectability to this racist worldview. Today, siblings of mixed-race parentage can and do choose different racial labels for themselves in a system where self-identification is the norm and where mixed-race parentage is common. The inconsistency in the system of identifying race has been graphically demonstrated by a study in which more than a third of babies identified on their birth certificates as Native American were classified in some other race on their death certificates (Hahn et al. 1992). Clearly, forensic anthropologists are on dangerous ground when they naively use biology in their attempts to determine socially fluid categories such as racial affiliation.

While forensic anthropologists arguably do no harm by attempting to identify the race of human skeletal remains in legal settings (other than implicitly supporting outdated notions of race and racial classification), when race is used in the realm of medical care, real harm can be done to individual, usually minority, patients. Despite data suggesting that patterns of mortality, disease, and illness vary in America along racial lines, the meaning of these data are highly contested. What are we to make of the fact that African Americans suffer from much higher rates of hypertension (high blood pressure), heart attacks, and cancer than European Americans? Are these disparities caused by the genetic differences that are thought to distinguish the races, or might they be the result of environmental and behavioral (lived experience) differences between races or social classes? One approach is to assume that genetic differences between the races underlie these health inequalities and to consider them examples of racial or ethnic diseases. A hundred years ago, data like these were used to argue for an inherent inferiority of the "Negro" race that would eventually lead to its extinction. However, a more compelling explanation seeks to locate the cause of health disparities along racial lines in the complex interaction of genetic influences and environmental differences between the populations involved. African Americans tend to more frequently live in poverty, have access to poorer health coverage, are exposed to more environmental pollutants in their neighborhoods and places of work, and bear the legacy and burden of racial discrimination on a day-to-day basis. Each of these environmental influences is known to be stressful on the individual, and stress can have a powerful negative effect on health and wellness. Genetic arguments about racial differences in morbidity and mortality are a prescription for doing nothing to alleviate the socioeconomic inequalities in our society, and in so doing, they can only serve to perpetuate the medical disparities that they seek to explain. Until the obvious racial inequalities of life in American society are minimized, any hypothesis of genetically determined health disparities between blacks and whites must be seriously questioned.

As the technology of genetic analysis has advanced, culminating in the sequencing of the entire human genome in 2003, the complex interactions of race, genetics, and health in America have become the focus of much biomedical research. One of the often-stated goals of this genetic research is to improve human health through increased understanding of the genetic causes of or influences on human diseases. Medical scientists have vigorously debated whether using a patient's self-identified race or ethnicity will improve our ability to identify risk factors of different illnesses or if the ambiguity and arbitrariness of the biological race concept make it unsuited for studies of the real causes of health and illness. One of the leaders of the Human Genome Project, Francis Collins (2004) has recently made the case that the definitional problems with the biological race concept make it at best a very poor predictor of genetic patterns of illness. As presently construed, the concept of race is a "flawed surrogate" for a variety of environmental and genetic factors that may have a significant role in influencing patterns of illness. While admitting that genes certainly do play a large role in human health or illness, Collins argues that progress will not be made in identifying the underlying genetic influences on illness until we can move beyond loosely defined terms such as *race* or *ethnicity* and begin to understand individual patterns of genetic differences. Only then will we be able to probe the complex interactions of genetics and environment to understand how and why we stay healthy or become sick.

BOX THREE

BiDil and the Birth of Racial Medicine

In spite of much skepticism among geneticists and medical doctors about the biological basis of race, a new age of racial medicine may have begun in June 2005 when the U.S. Food and Drug Administration (FDA) gave its approval to "the first drug in the United States, and likely anywhere else, to be based on a patent formulated in terms of its benefit to a specific racial or ethnic group" (Sankar and Kahn 2005:556). The drug in question is known as BiDil, and it was approved for use by African Americans for congestive heart failure (CHF), a form of heart disease in which the heart is unable to pump enough blood to the body's organs. While people of all races may suffer from this and other forms of heart disease, African Americans are more likely to have CHF and are more likely to die from it than Americans of European descent, and cardiologists have for a long time wondered why this is so. The approval of BiDil for "self-identified black" patients provides "a striking example of how a treatment can benefit some patients even if it does not help others," according to a senior administrator at the FDA (Sankar and Kahn 2005:556). Some medical scientists suggest that BiDil signifies the beginnings of a new kind of medicine in which the effectiveness of our treatment options for a particular disease will vary, based on knowledge of individual genetic variations between patients. This new approach to medical practice, often referred to as *pharmacogenomics*, is the result of the enormous increases in our understanding of human genetic variation and in the recent sequencing of the complete human genome. Its supporters argue that self-identified race can serve as a proxy or stand-in for genetic differences between populations and that pharmacogenomics will eventually progress to using individual genetic variants in choosing the most effective treatment option for sick individuals. A closer look at the history behind the FDA's approval of BiDil in 2005 suggests a more complicated story (Brody and Hunt 2006).

BiDil is a combination of two drugs, both of which have been individually available for many years in inexpensive, generic form as approved heart disease drugs for all patients. The component drugs are known as hydralazine and isosorbide dinitrate, and they are both vasodilators. In 1987, a Minnesota cardiologist applied for a patent on the method of combining the two drugs (37.5 milligrams of hydralazine and 20 milligrams of isosorbide) in a single pill, and in 1996, he applied for FDA approval of BiDil. Although the FDA panel was apparently convinced that BiDil was a promising heart disease drug, it did not approve its use because the data in support of its beneficial effects was inconclusive. This might have been the end of the story of BiDil had not the cardiologist gone back to the original study of the effects of BiDil and reanalyzed the data by race. He discovered that blacks had responded to treatment with BiDil better than whites, although this result is suspect because it is based on a very small sample size of 49 blacks in the original study. In 2000, he was awarded a new patent for the use of BiDil to treat CFH in blacks alone, and "thus was BiDil reinvented as an ethnic drug" (Kahn 2007:42). The patent allowed him to undertake another clinical trial of the effects of BiDil on just over 1,000 black patients, and the results were again encouraging: the mortality rate in patients taking BiDil (as well as their regular medicine for heart disease) was 43 percent less than that for subjects taking a placebo in addition to their regular medicine. But this study involved only "self-identified black" patients, so it did not establish that BiDil worked *only* in blacks or better in black than other racial groups, in spite of many statements to the contrary, including that of the FDA administrator. In any event, with these new results in hand, the FDA approved BiDil for use only in black people in June 2005.

So much for the details of the drug itself and its history of regulation, but what can we say about the economic and other aspects of the BiDil story? It should be noted that as with all FDA-approved drugs, doctors are free to prescribe BiDil to any patient, in spite of the fact that FDA approval was explicitly for African American patients. Pharmaceutical companies and Wall Street investors recognized the substantial potential profitability of a newly patented and FDA-approved drug for heart disease, which remains the number one killer of Americans, with more than 900 thousand deaths annually (Carter 2006). Within a week of the FDA approval, the estimates of the potential market for BiDil were as high as $3 billion per year, with each pill priced at $1.80 (compared to 25 cents for the individual generics) and a recommended daily dose of six pills. The new patent awarded in 2000 allowed BiDil free reign in the marketplace with no legal generic equivalents for 20 years, and the particular dosage of 37.5 milligrams of hydralazine made it difficult for doctors to prescribe the generic versions of the two drugs individually because the generics come in 25- or 50-milligram sizes. With some insurance companies refusing to pay for this expensive new drug, the net effect on the health of African American patients with CHF could be said to have been negatively affected by the discovery and especially by the marketing of this new "racial drug." But the financial prospects for the pharmaceutical companies involved were very bright indeed.

One might reasonably argue that the pharmacogenomics vision of personalized medical treatments tailored to individuals based on their known genetic variations holds great promise, but it is clear that race is a poor proxy for individual genetic variation. We have seen that the levels of polymorphic variation within populations overwhelms the polytypic variation between populations, as Lewontin (1974) demonstrated decades ago. Therefore, using self-identified racial status to stand in for individual genetic variation between individuals makes no sense at all: two African Americans living in Los Angeles today

(continued)

can be very different from each other genetically, particularly if they trace their ancestry to, for example, Ethiopia and Nigeria. These two individuals would not necessarily be expected to react consistently in the same manner to a drug such as BiDil and differently from individuals of some other race or ethnicity. So the supporters of BiDil's status as a racial drug are clearly on shaky ground when they suggest that self-identified race can be a useful genetic marker for the way that individuals will react to particular medical treatments. In so doing, they are also supporting an antiquated and demonstrably incorrect notion of the validity of biological race, which assumes that the genetic differences between races are large and the genetic differences within races are small.

Whatever one's position on biological and social theories of race and their applicability to medicine, we can all agree that reducing the morbidity and mortality suffered by people with CHF is a very important social goal. Supporters of biological theories of race typically argue that significant differences in health and illness between "racial" groups are likely due to the biological or genetic differences between the groups, and they therefore seek different biological mechanisms that might explain these differing health outcomes. In the example of BiDil, the suggestion is that blacks and whites experience different "versions" of CHF that are best treated by different drugs. They tend to support the nature or biological and genetic side of the nature–nurture dichotomy. On the other hand, supporters of social construction theories of race are more prone to argue that different patterns of illness in different races or ethnicities are more likely the result of different environments, behaviors, and lifestyles of different people. This is the nurture side of the equation, and in the case of the variance in health status, life span, and patterns and rates of dying among Americans of African and European descent, there is much evidence in support of a strongly environmental position. African Americans may suffer to a greater extent and die more frequently and at younger ages than whites from heart disease as a result of their higher rates of poverty, hypertension, and obesity, mixed with their reduced access to health care and the fact that they remain the victims of the legacy of racism, discrimination, and slavery in America. Until the conditions of life in America are equal for people of all races, we should refrain from making definitive statements about the existence of genetic differences that explain health-related disparities between whites and blacks.

Discussion Questions

1. Describe the pre-Darwinian typological or Platonic approach to human variation that characterizes the work of Linnaeus and many of the other early racial classifiers. How is this approach different from the post-Darwinian evolutionary and adaptive approach favored by most modern anthropologists?

2. How did Morton's unconscious biases influence his work on the cranial capacity of different human groups?

3. When, where, and under what circumstances did the concept of human races first appear in the Western world?

4. Who was the first scientist to classify humans into different races? How would you describe the set of characteristics used by this scientist to classify races?

5. What is ethnocentrism, and what role did it play in the development of early ideas about human races?

6. Describe the 19th-century discussions and debates concerning a single origin (monogenism) or multiple origins (polygenism) of human races.

7. What is a cline or clinal variation? Explain the meaning of Frank Livingstone's statement that "there are no races; there are only clines."

8. Compare and contrast the ideas about race and craniometry espoused by Hooton and Boas in the early 20th century. Who were these two men, and why have they been so influential in anthropological discussions of race?

9. Do you agree or disagree with this statement: "Using genetic traits such as ABO blood group frequencies provides a completely objective and scientific method for determining how many races exist." Explain your answer.

10. What is meant by the "one-drop rule," and how does it complicate attempts to determine race based on, for example, forensic analysis of a human skeleton?

CHAPTER 5

Human Adaptation: Thermoregulation and Skin Color

"The appearance of the inhabitants is also not very different in India and Ethiopia: the southern Indians are rather more like Ethiopians as they are black to look on, and their hair is black; only they are not so snub-nosed or woolly-haired as the Ethiopians; the northern Indians are most like the Egyptians physically."

ARRIAN, *THE INDICA*, SECOND CENTURY C.E.

INTRODUCTION TO HUMAN ADAPTATION

From our humble beginnings in the African tropics during the Pleistocene, *Homo sapiens* has spread to all of the world's continents and today successfully colonizes a range of habitats and environments that is unprecedented among living mammals. From the Saharan desert to the rain forests of the Congo and the Amazon, from the highlands of the Himalayas and the Andes to the frozen Arctic, humans have proved to be among the most adaptable creatures on our planet. While we obviously owe much of this success to cultural variation and technological expertise, anthropologists are very interested in understanding how human biology contributes to our amazing ability to live and even to prosper in extreme habitats across the globe. Anthropologists are also keen to understand the ways in which life in different habitats has led to some of the morphological and physiological differences we see in human populations. These differences include such traits as the color of our skin, hair, and eyes; the size and shape of our bodies and limbs; the size of our lungs and hearts and the efficiency of our cardiovascular systems; and our ability to stay warm when it is cold and to cool down when it is hot. Morphological differences between people in different populations are known as *polytypic differences*, and they comprise the raw material that forms the basis of all racial classifications. From our evolutionary perspective, we seek to determine whether these traits contribute to the survival and reproduction of their bearers in the habitats in which they are found. In other words, we seek to understand the adaptive significance of the polytypic variations in human morphology that underlie racial classifications.

Several interesting questions immediately come to mind concerning the biological and anthropological meanings of polytypic human variation. Which racial traits found in human populations are adaptations to the stress of life in particular habitats? Have human populations been shaped by the forces of evolution in relation to the habitats they live in, or are racial traits random and nonadaptive features with no particular relevance to human survival? Does the existence and distribution of these between-population differences support a racial worldview, or do they undermine the race concept? These are some of the questions that we will pursue in this and the next two chapters. After an introduction to the study of human adaptation, we will explore the evidence of human difference and biological adaptations to life in hot and cold environments and at high altitude. Then we will explore how patterns of health and sickness in different human populations can contribute to our understanding of human diversity and adaptation. Although cultural adaptations to different environments will be noted where appropriate, the emphasis in these chapters will be on biological differences in human morphology and physiology in relation to life in extreme environments and the relevance of this information to the race concept.

Known as *physiological anthropology* or *human adaptability*, the study of human diversity in and adaptation to different habitats is an exciting area of research in anthropology. Like all work in modern biological anthropology, research in the field of human adaptability is based on evolutionary theory, and its goals are to understand the origin and significance of biological features in individuals and populations of *Homo sapiens*. We will need to define a set of terms and introduce some new concepts in order to proceed. Let's start with a consideration of a term that we have already used in some related contexts, the notion of *adaptation*. In human adaptability studies, *adaptation* is an important term that can be used in several ways. *Adaptation* sometimes refers to an organism's state of being well suited to a particular environment. Thus we might say that polar bears are well adapted to life in the Arctic. Another sense of *adaptation* refers to a particular trait or characteristic possessed by an individual or population that is thought to be of survival or reproductive value to that organism. In this sense, we might suggest that the white color of the polar bear's fur is an adaptation for life in the Arctic because it functions as camouflage, allowing the animal to stalk and surprise its

FIGURE 5.1 The polar bear is a well-adapted Arctic predator. Some of its adaptations include its large size and ferocity, white fur, large claws, and sharp teeth.
Courtesy of iStock by Getty Images.

prey. Darwin himself used both of these senses of the term *adaptation*, and their meanings are in the mainstream of evolutionary thought. In both senses, *adaptation* refers to a feature (or a set of features) in an organism or population that is favored by natural selection in the struggle for existence. While organisms are generally assumed to be well adapted to their environments (if they were not, they would be expected to be replaced by other, better-adapted organisms), one can never simply assume that a feature found in some organism or population is necessarily an adaptation. Arguments for features being adaptations must be explicitly made in the context of natural selection on a population in a given environment. The question that must be answered is "How does this feature improve the survival or reproduction of its possessors in the environment in which they are found?" Thus the epicanthal eye fold of many Asian human populations may be an adaptation, or it may be a nonadaptive feature with absolutely no effect on survival or reproduction, perhaps the result of random genetic drift. The burden of proof in all arguments concerning the adaptive significance of human features falls on theorists who would argue for a trait's being an adaptation. Later in this chapter, you will encounter an argument for the adaptive significance of dark and light skin color in humans, and you may judge for yourself if our adaptive scenario is convincing or not.

Central to the entire field of human adaptability and environmental physiology are the related notions of stress, strain, and homeostasis. *Homeostasis* refers to the dynamic process whereby individual organisms seek to maintain internal physiological functions within a normal range, in spite of external disruptions. Humans are at thermoregulatory homeostasis when our internal temperature is maintained within a narrow range centered about 37°C (98.6°F). Homeostasis can also be defined for other physiological functions such as blood sugar level, blood pressure, heart rate, and testosterone or estrogen level. An important aspect of the concept of homeostasis is that living organisms actively seek to maintain physiological homeostasis through a variety of nervous, hormonal, and behavioral means. For example, the healthy pancreas makes available copious amounts of the hormone insulin after we eat a sugary meal or snack in order to stimulate the metabolism of sugar and hence to maintain blood sugar levels within the homeostatic range. After strenuous exercise, we seek water (or other liquids) in order to quench our thirst and in this way maintain homeostasis in our fluid and ion concentrations in our bloodstream and our muscle cells. When we feel cold, we add layers of insulative clothing in order to maintain our internal body temperature within the homeostatic range.

Homeostasis is clearly something of value to living organisms, and we know that it can be disrupted by a wide variety of causes. Pathogenic organisms such as bacteria or viruses can infect us and lead to a rise in our internal body temperature, something that we refer to as "having a fever." Drinking lots of caffeine-containing drinks can lead to an increased heart rate; a diet heavy in salt may lead to increased blood pressure. Internal or external factors like these that tend to disrupt our

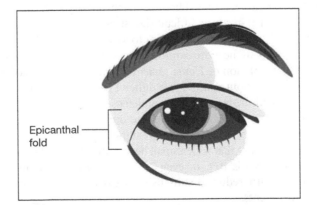

FIGURE 5.2 The epicanthal eye fold is a common feature of individuals from many Asian populations that has no known adaptive function.

physiological homeostasis can be referred to as stress. We can define *stress* as anything that causes potentially injurious changes to an organism's normal homeostatic functioning. All stresses are not created equal, and they do not all affect us to the same extent. The notion of *strain* can be used to describe the intensity of a particular stress, providing a measure of the magnitude of the deviation from homeostasis that a stress can cause. An example of how these concepts are used in human adaptability studies might involve a laboratory study of the effects of hand immersion in ice water. Homeostasis might be defined by the normal internal temperature and superficial finger temperature of the individual prior to immersion of the person's hand in a bucket of ice water. The stress is obviously presented by immersion of the subject's hand in the ice water, and we can measure the intensity of the stress (i.e., the strain) by the drop in internal or finger temperature over time. As you will see shortly, studies using this experimental design have indicated that different human populations actually respond to this stress in very different ways, some in a much more obviously adaptive manner than others.

Summarizing, we can say that adaptations are physical or physiological features or behaviors of organisms that allow them to minimize the strain involved in exposures to particular stresses. As a result, adaptations allow organisms to maintain or regain homeostasis when exposed to stress. An evolutionary biologist who is seeking to identify adaptations in an animal species is often required to determine the fitness effect of possible adaptive features. This requires demonstrating that the possession of a particular feature improves an organism's ability to survive and leave descendants. In human adaptability studies, the bar is set a bit lower for determining the presence of adaptations. Here we must simply determine that a trait, feature, or behavior minimizes the strain associated with a particular stress. Typically, we can assume that dealing successfully with the stresses of life should increase the fitness of an individual or population, and if we are correct, the kinds of adaptations that we study in environmental physiology will meet the more demanding criteria of the evolutionary biologist.

A CLASSIFICATION OF ADAPTATIONS

Adaptations come in many different sizes and shapes, and it will be instructive to create a classification of the different types of adaptations that we find in the study of human environmental physiology. A primary distinction to make is between *biological* and *cultural adaptations*. Sometimes cultural behavior and technology provide the main buffer between people and the stresses of their environment. For example, all cultures create some kinds of shelter as a means of minimizing the strain produced by life in inclement weather. Peoples of the arctic and subarctic regions obviously rely on a very well developed set of technological adaptations in order to survive the chilling temperatures to which they are routinely subjected. These include insulated houses, warm and dry clothing, and the tools and know-how to find food and stay warm in a very difficult (i.e., stressful) environment. These kinds of cultural adaptations—housing, clothing, and technology for food acquisition and preparation—are present in every culture, even those living in the more comfortable and less stressful environments found closer to the equator. The cultural adaptation of *Homo sapiens* is generally recognized as one of the real hallmarks of being human, for without culture, it is difficult to imagine humans successfully occupying any environment on earth. Culture is the first line of defense against the stresses of the environments in which people live. It serves as a buffer between us and our environments, allowing people to inhabit more hospitable "microenvironments" of our own making. For example, a well-constructed igloo is an insulated and windproof structure that with a small heat source provided by an oil or blubber lamp can create a microenvironment that is 10°C or even 20°C warmer than the outside environment. Thus cultural adaptations can greatly reduce the intensity of environmental stresses, allowing humans to survive in extreme environments.

Biological adaptations come in several forms. *Genetic adaptations* are those that are said to be "hard-wired" in the genetic material of a population or an entire species. The ability to sweat in response to heat or exertion is a universal human genetic adaptation: sweating is adaptive in the

FIGURE 5.3 The igloo creates a warm microenvironment by reducing convective heat loss as a result of wind chill. Courtesy of iStock by Getty Images.

functional, human adaptability sense of acting to preserve thermoregulatory homeostasis by dissipating excess heat. The ability to sweat is a genetic adaptation common to all members of the species *Homo sapiens* since all normal humans possess millions of functioning sweat glands as a result of genetic inheritance. However, the possibility exists that some populations may be better or worse at sweating than others, possessing genetic adaptations that are unique to that group. Another interesting set of biological adaptations are those that fall into the category of *phenotypic plasticity*. These adaptations are caused by exposure to environmental stresses and result in observable biological changes to the organism's phenotype. The most common example of phenotypic plasticity is known as *acclimatization*, which refers to adaptive biological changes in an organism's phenotype that occur over a short time scale of exposure to an environmental stress, typically on the order of days to weeks. Examples of acclimatization include the tanning response seen in light-skinned individuals after a few days of sunbathing and the cardiovascular changes that occur when low-altitude natives travel to areas of high altitude. Note that acclimatization is always a reversible process: when the environmental stress is no longer present, the physiological changes that occurred on exposure will disappear, again over a time scale of days to weeks. Sadly, the tans that some light-skinned individuals spend their summers "working on" disappear every autumn. With respect to our sweating example, it is noteworthy that after exposure to extreme heat, most individuals will become acclimatized and begin to sweat more effectively. Another example of phenotypic plasticity is *developmental acclimatization*. This refers to nonreversible adaptive changes to the phenotype that occur as a result of exposure to some types of stress during growth and development of the individual. In chapter 6, we will discuss the best example of developmental acclimatization known to human adaptation scientists: the cardiovascular adaptations seen in populations native to high altitude environments.

PRINCIPLES OF THERMOREGULATION

Humans and other mammals are *homeothermic* or warm-blooded creatures who seek to maintain a relatively constant internal temperature in spite of the ambient temperature. All homeotherms need to regulate internal body temperature within narrow, homeostatic limits because a deviation of more than a few degrees from 37°C can result in hypothermia or heat stroke, and either can potentially lead to death. As a result, all humans have a series of genetic adaptations designed to maintain homeostasis in body temperature. In addition to this basic human thermoregulatory ability, all healthy humans have the ability to become acclimatized to cold or hot environmental conditions after a period of exposure to temperature extremes. Finally, some populations with a long history of living in cold or hot habitats show a series of physiological traits that may be evidence of genetic adaptation to life at climatic extremes. After a discussion of the basic human physiology and physics of thermoregulation, we will examine the evidence for acclimatization and for genetic adaptations to hot and cold climates. This discussion will lead to a consideration of human variation in body size and shape and of differences in skin color. Since skin color has played such a large role in definitions of race in American society, a consideration of the scientific basis of worldwide skin color variation in *Homo sapiens* is essential to a critical evaluation of the validity of the race concept.

Maintaining homeostasis with respect to body temperature is essentially the process of regulating an organism's inputs and outputs of heat. When inputs and outputs are equal, an individual's body temperature will be maintained within the homeostatic range, and we can describe such an individual as being at *thermal equilibrium. Thermoregulation* is a dynamic process in which the amount of heat gained or lost by an individual is regulated in order to maintain thermal equilibrium. Excess heat must be lost when an individual is under heat stress, and extra heat must be produced and conserved when an individual is under cold stress. Physiologists typically distinguish between two different parts or zones of the organism with respect to maintaining thermal homeostasis. The *core* refers to the central axis of the body, including all the vital organs within the head, chest, and abdomen. The *shell* refers to the body's extremities or limbs. This distinction is important because whenever an organism is subjected to thermal stress (i.e., either too much or too little heat), it is imperative that thermal homeostasis be maintained in the core, even if that means sacrificing parts of the shell. While one can survive

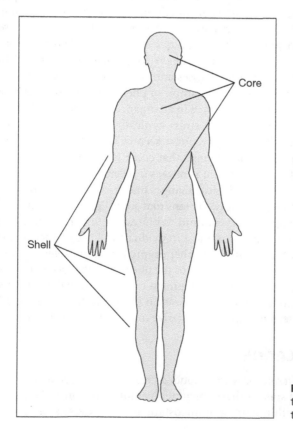

FIGURE 5.4 The core refers to the head, thorax, and abdomen. The shell refers to the body's extremities.

frostbite of the toes or fingers, a deep freeze of any of the internal organs in the body's core is not compatible with life. Skin temperatures can be safely allowed to rise or fall to a much greater extent than the body's core temperature. We will see that the human adaptive response to cold exposure recognizes this basic distinction between core and shell and that under extreme thermal stress, the shell is often "sacrificed" in order to preserve homeostasis in the core for as long as possible.

Living things exchange heat with their environment through four basic physical processes or mechanisms: radiation, convection, conduction, and evaporation. For heat to be transferred between an individual and some other object, a temperature difference must exist between the objects exchanging heat, and the actual heat transfer always occurs at the surface area of the objects involved. *Radiation* refers to the transmission of electromagnetic energy through space between two objects that are in direct line of sight of each other. All solid objects that are warmer than absolute zero (−273°C) radiate heat. The direction of heat transfer is from the hotter object to the cooler one, and it is proportional to the amount of surface area involved and to the reflectance properties of the object on the receiving end. Our most common experience with heat transfer via radiation is when we sunbathe: solar infrared radiation warms us as it travels from the sun across space to strike our bodies. Since dark bodies absorb more (i.e., reflect less) radiation than lighter bodies, individuals with dark skin can absorb more heat than those with light skin, all other things being equal (e.g., the amount of radiation, the amount of insulation, and the surface area exposed to the radiation). *Conduction* refers to heat transfer between two solid objects or organisms through direct contact. The amount of heat transferred by conduction is proportional to the surface areas in contact, the difference in temperature between the two objects or organisms, and the thermal conductivity of the materials. Touching a block of ice with one hand would lead to some heat loss due to conduction, but lying flat on a large block of ice would cause an individual to lose much more heat as a result of the greater amount of surface area in contact with the ice. Touching a hot piece of metal leads to a transfer of heat from the metal to the hand, since the direction of energy transfer is always from the hotter to the colder object. *Convection* is the process of heat transfer between a solid object and a fluid, typically a gas such as air or a liquid such as water. It occurs when there is a difference in temperature between the solid and the fluid and as a result of the fact that hot fluids tend to rise while cold ones sink. When a warm body is exposed to cold air or water, the air or water molecules in contact with the body are heated, rise, and are replaced by cold molecules, which are again heated, rise, and are replaced once again with more cold molecules. As this cycle continues, more and more heat is lost by convection from the warm body to the moving cold air or fluid. Convection also takes place within the tissues of our bodies, notably in the transfer of heat by the bloodstream from the internal organs of the body's core to the body's surface, where it can be dissipated to the environment. Since convection (like radiation and conduction) is a bidirectional process, a body can be made colder by contact with a cold fluid or warmer by contact with a warm fluid (think of yourself in a hot tub or exposed to a hot wind on an already hot summer day). In any case, the direction of heat transfer is always from hotter to cooler, and the amount of heat transferred is proportional to the amount of surface area exposed and the temperature differential between air or fluid and solid. *Evaporation* is the process whereby heat or energy is used to convert a liquid to a gas. In humans, it occurs on our skin when we sweat, while in some other mammals, evaporation occurs along the respiratory tract, resulting in the characteristic panting that dogs use to cool themselves off. Human sweat glands produce copious amounts of salty sweat that, when evaporated on our skin, can dissipate enormous quantities of body heat. Consequently, sweating is the most effective method that humans have for shedding excess heat. One unique feature concerning the role of sweating and evaporation in heat transfer is that it can only result in heat loss, unlike the other three methods of heat transfer, which can cool or heat an organism. This is because evaporation requires an input of energy in order to change the state of liquid to gas. The amount of energy required to evaporate a liquid is known as the liquid's *latent heat of vaporization*, and this quantity varies for different liquids. Some liquids such as rubbing alcohol have a very low latent heat of vaporization, which means that little energy is required to evaporate a given quantity of the liquid. The amount of energy required to evaporate water is substantial, so when we evaporate our sweat, we dissipate enormous amounts of excess heat and thus significantly reduce our heat load. You can test this by putting equal amounts of water on one arm and rubbing alcohol on the other and seeing which liquid evaporates quicker. If humans were to sweat alcohol rather than water, our sweat would evaporate faster and more easily, but it would dissipate much less excess heat, due to the much lower latent heat of vaporization of alcohol compared to water.

In addition to the heat that organisms gain or lose through radiation, conduction, convection, and evaporation, individual bodies also generate their own internal heat through the normal processes of metabolism and muscular activity. We can refer to two different kinds of metabolic heat that living organisms routinely generate: resting or basal metabolism and active metabolism. *Basal metabolism* is equal to the minimum caloric requirements needed to sustain life in a resting individual for a day. In a sense, it refers to the amount of heat produced by a resting body as a result of all the normal physiological functions that are required to maintain life. *Active metabolism* is the additional energy generated by an organism during daily life, mostly as a by-product of muscular activity. We can determine the amount of energy an individual produces at rest if we measure the amount of oxygen he or she consumes, since metabolic heat is the by-product of the oxidation of food. On an average diet, an individual at rest will generate roughly 4.83 kilocalories for every liter of oxygen consumed. Oxygen consumption at rest is on average about 250 milliliters per minute, leading to the consumption over 24 hours of 360 liters of oxygen and generating 1,739 kilocalories of resting metabolism. Obviously, this is only a minimum estimate of the energy required for life; the true

BOX ONE

How Much Heat Is Lost through Evaporation of Sweat?

To understand the effectiveness of sweating as a means of dissipating excess heat, we can do a simple calculation involving real experimental data based on the performance of Australian Aborigines on a standardized heat stress test involving a set of stair-stepping exercises performed at a room temperature of 34°C (93°F) for four hours. The average amount of sweat produced over the four hours of the test for the entire sample of 31 Australians was just over 1,600 milliliters. If we assume that all this sweat was evaporated on the skin of the subjects (and not dripped off their bodies in the liquid state), how much energy would have been required for the transformation of 1,600 milliliters of liquid water into water vapor? The scientific units of heat include calories, kilocalories, and joules. A calorie is defined as the amount of heat required to raise the temperature of 1 milliliter of water by 1°C, from 14.5°C to 15.5°C. A more useful standard is the kilocalorie, which is equivalent to 1,000 calories and is defined as the heat required to raise the temperature of 1 liter of water by 1°C, from 14.5°C to 15.5°C. The generally accepted international standard for energy is known as the joule, and kilocalories can be converted to joules by multiplying by 4,184. Finally, the amount of heat required to evaporate 1 milliliter of a liquid is known as the liquid's latent heat of vaporization. We know that 580 calories of heat is the latent heat of vaporization of water per milliliter, so if we multiply this by 1,600 milliliters of sweat, we determine that 928 kilocalories (or 3,882,752 joules) of excess body heat were dissipated in this four-hour experiment through the mechanism of sweating. Let's assume that only 3.6 million joules of body heat were actually dissipated, assuming that not all sweat is always evaporated (and to make the math a little simpler). To get a better sense of how much energy this represents, we can ask how long this much energy could run a 100-watt light bulb. One hundred watts represents an energy usage of 100 joules per second, or 6,000 joules per minute. A simple calculation then reveals that 3.6 million joules would suffice to power a 100-watt light bulb for 600 minutes, or ten hours (3.6 million joules divided by 6,000 joules per minute). Pretty impressive!

value will be affected by variables such as the ambient temperature and the amount of physical activity performed, which can raise the metabolic rate significantly over the resting value.

Putting together our four heat transfer methods and our two internally generated heat sources, we can come up with an equation that will help us understand thermal equilibrium and our body's homeostatic thermoregulatory response. The *heat-balance equation* tells us that an organism is at thermal equilibrium ($\Delta S = 0$) when the amounts of heat inputs and outputs are equal and the internal temperature is within the homeostatic range of plus or minus 1°C of 37°C:

$$\Delta S = M_b + M_a \pm K \pm C \pm R - E$$

In English, this equation tells us that the change in energy in a body (ΔS) is equal to the amount of resting metabolic heat (M_b) plus the amount of heat generated by active metabolism (M_a), plus or minus the amount of heat gained or lost due to conduction (K), convection (C), and radiation (R), minus the amount of heat lost due to evaporation (E). All warm-blooded individuals must, over the long term, maintain thermal equilibrium ($\Delta S = 0$).

ADAPTATION TO COLD ENVIRONMENTS

We can distinguish between at least three different kinds of cold environments to which humans have demonstrated some level of successful adaptation. Each of these types of habitats presents a different kind and intensity of cold stress to human populations attempting to survive there. For humans living in tropical and semitropical habitats, cold stresses are moderate at worst, typically occurring in the form of cool nighttime temperatures. These cold stresses are a concern only for populations that sleep in the open air without much protection from the elements. The extremely long record of human habitation of the African tropics (several million years) reflected in the archaeological record suggests that the mild cold stresses of the tropical and subtropical regions have never posed a serious threat to human survival. Another area of human habitation where cold

FIGURE 5.5 Cold stress is severe in high mountains and at high latitudes.
Courtesy of iStock by Getty Images.

stresses can be quite severe is in mountainous regions, where temperatures vary inversely with altitude and where daily variations in temperature can be extreme. Evidence of successful human habitation in the highlands regions of the world has been quite recent (perhaps only a few thousand years), suggesting that specialized adaptations are necessary for humans to survive the stresses of life at high altitude. Finally, the most extreme cold stresses associated with severe winter temperatures are found in the world's temperate and especially arctic zones. The intense and prolonged cold temperatures that are found in these regions present serious difficulties for human habitation and adaptation. Whereas humans have successfully colonized the temperate zones of the Old World for nearly a half a million years, successful habitation in the Arctic is a much more recent phenomenon (on the order of a few tens of thousands of years at most).

Wherever and to whatever extent humans experience the stresses of life in the cold, culture and technology play a large role in mediating our actual exposure to the cold. Some of the earliest evidence of the use of fire by fossil humans dates to more than 100 thousand years ago in the temperate zones of Europe and Asia. Campfires were used to cook food and to create warm occupation and sleeping zones, often in sheltered caves. As long as humans have lived in the temperate zones, they have also relied on the use of animal skins and furs for clothing. Clothing keeps its wearer warm by creating an insulative "dead space" of air around our bodies. This reduces heat loss due to convection, because the air in this dead space is warmed by our body heat but cannot escape (by convectively rising). Insulation is very important in bedding, as nighttime temperatures are often the coldest in the temperate zones. Shared sleeping (the "family bed") is another cultural adaptation to cold stresses at night, allowing the members of a family or group to share, and thus better conserve, their body heat through the night. Housing or some form of shelter that can keep out the wind contributes greatly to the reduction of convective heat loss and provides insulation from outside temperatures. The fact that humans have successfully lived in temperate zones for only a few hundred thousand years suggests the importance of these cultural adaptations. Without shelter, clothing, and fire, it would be difficult or impossible to conceive of human survival in the face of the severe cold stresses associated with these environments. On the other hand, a basic adaptive pattern of physiological responses to cold exposure clearly characterizes all healthy humans. This set of biological responses must be considered a genetic adaptation, for it is universal among *Homo sapiens* and appears to be hard-wired into our DNA.

How, then, do humans typically respond physiologically to cold stress? In general, all homeotherms need to limit the loss of heat that occurs at their surface areas and to maximize the amount of internal, metabolic heat they produce. Heat loss can be limited in three ways: minimizing surface area by changing the shape or size of the body, increasing insulation with more subcutaneous fat, and relying on vascular adaptations, mainly vasoconstriction. Heat production can be boosted by increasing the volume of the body, increasing the basal metabolic rate, and engaging in shivering and nonshivering thermogenesis. Let's look at each of these adaptive responses to cold stress among humans, starting with the ways in which we limit heat loss and then discussing the methods for increasing heat production.

Vascular adaptations for cold stress serve as an important means for reducing heat loss in cold environments. *Vasoconstriction* is a shrinking of the diameter of the superficial and peripheral blood vessels that serves to reduce blood flow to the body's shell and surface and acts to reduce heat loss in several ways. When the peripheral blood vessels constrict, a greater proportion of the body's blood remains in the core, serving to keep the body core warmer (because arterial blood carries much of the body's metabolic heat) and to reduce the amount of heat lost at the body's surface. Skin temperature drops when superficial blood vessels constrict, which further reduces heat loss at the surface by reducing the temperature difference between the skin and the environment (remember that heat transfer by radiation, conduction, and convection is proportional to the temperature difference between the organism and whatever solid or fluid it is exchanging heat with). Vasoconstriction of the blood vessels in our hands and feet is responsible for the painful stinging sensation we endure in our fingers and toes during cold stress. In the long run, it makes much more adaptive sense to endure this pain and even to risk losing digits to frostbite than to risk a serious drop in core temperature, which could result in hypothermia and death. Another aspect of cardiovascular adaptation to cold stress is reflected in the anatomical design of our arteries and veins and works in a coordinated fashion with vasoconstriction. Most arteries bringing warm blood from the core are surrounded by two veins returning cooler blood from the shell. This results in some degree of heat exchange between the cooler blood returning from the body's shell and superficial regions in veins and the warmer arterial blood being pumped by the heart. This *countercurrent heat exchange* results in warming of the cool venous blood before it reaches the body core and cooling of the arterial blood before it reaches the shell and periphery. The amount of heat lost at the body's surface is thereby reduced in this efficient plumbing scheme. The other ways in which humans can limit the amount of heat they lose in cold environments are by increasing the amount of insulation they possess and by limiting their surface areas. Insulation obviously decreases the amount of heat lost to the environment, so a greater amount of subcutaneous adipose (fat) tissue is of adaptive value to cold-stressed populations. Because all transfers of heat or energy occur at the body's surface, decreasing an individual's surface area should also reduce the amount of heat lost to the environment. As you will see, changing body size and shape in certain ways will have a predictable effect on an individual's surface area–to–volume ratio. These considerations will help explain some of the population variation we see in body size and shape around the world.

Increasing the amount of metabolically generated heat is the second way in which homeothermic creatures like *Homo sapiens* respond to cold stress. Having a higher basal metabolic rate (BMR) would seem to be a good adaptation for cold-stressed populations, and there is some evidence suggesting that native populations of Alaska and northern Canada have generally higher BMRs than most peoples of European descent and other non-cold-adapted populations. Because metabolic heat production occurs mostly as a result of muscular activity, changing body size and shape to maximize muscle mass would seem to be a good adaptation for dealing with cold stress. Again, body size and shape would be expected to reflect the fact that metabolic heat is produced in proportion to an individual's mass or volume, and so cold-adapted populations would be expected to have large volumes in order to generate more metabolic heat.

At some point during exposure to cold stress, individuals will often begin to shiver. *Shivering* is involuntary muscular activity that can result in a significant increase in an individual's metabolic production of heat, sometimes by as much as three times the rate of basal metabolism. While this kind of increased heat production sounds highly adaptive for life in the cold, it should be recognized that shivering leads to a greatly increased rate of heat loss to the environment. It can be a very dangerous strategy for an individual with limited insulation or fuel (i.e., food) and can lead to a rapid drop in core temperature and, eventually, hypothermia. Another metabolic adaptation to cold stress is known as *nonshivering thermogenesis*. Although nonshivering thermogenesis is known to be an important adaptation among hibernating and other cold-adapted mammals, its significance in human adaptation to cold is still debatable. It involves the metabolism of a special fatty substance in the body known as *brown adipose tissue* (BAT) to generate heat without shivering. Among human infants, whose thermoregulatory systems are still imperfectly developed, BAT makes up as much as 5 percent of body weight, but by adulthood, it has virtually disappeared, replaced by white adipose tissue. Nonshivering thermogenesis due to the metabolism of BAT plays an important role in thermoregulation of human infants but is probably insignificant among adults.

What is the evidence for adaptive features in the physiology of cold-stressed human populations that do not occur in non-cold-stressed populations? It turns out that different patterns of acclimatization and genetic adaptation seem to exist between moderately cold-stressed populations and populations that live under conditions of extreme cold. Among moderately cold-stressed populations such as Australian Aboriginals and Kalahari San, the basic strategy is one of energy conservation. When exposed to moderate, typically overnight cold stress (involving temperatures slightly above 0°C), these populations generally reduce their metabolic heat production, resulting in a decrease in their internal and skin temperatures. In spite of body temperatures that would keep an unacclimatized European awake all night shivering, these acclimatized individuals are able to sleep comfortably without shivering. The ability to sleep comfortably under cold conditions with very little clothing or shelter and with greatly reduced core and extremity temperatures may be the result of the process known as *habituation*, in which the nervous system's response is reduced as a result of repeated and long-term exposure to some stress. The logic of heat conservation under moderate cold stress may have something to do with the quality or quantity of nutritional resources available to these populations. It has been suggested that desert- or savanna-dwelling foragers such as Australian Aboriginals and the San may have limited nutritional resources at least during some parts of the year, and this may limit their ability to increase their metabolic heat production when subjected to cold stress.

The situation seems to be quite different for some New World populations living under extremely cold conditions, including the Inuit of Greenland and Alaska and Athabascan- and Algonquian-speaking Native American populations of northern Canada. Here, where the diet is mostly comprised of the meat of land and sea mammals and the cold stress is extreme, well-adapted human populations respond to cold stress by increasing their metabolic heat production by as much as 45 percent compared to Europeans. Higher heat production leads to a greater ability to maintain warm extremities and higher skin temperatures than seen among nonacclimatized populations. Extremities are kept warm during occasional long periods of cold exposure by a novel vascular response known as *cold-induced vasodilation* (CIVD). Whereas the typical vascular response of most humans when their hands or feet are immersed in ice-cold water involves vasoconstriction, a rapid drop in skin temperature, and intense pain, something different happens among Inuit and northern Canadian Native peoples. In these individuals, vasoconstriction and vasodilation alternate in the cold-immersed extremities, resulting in a rhythmic alternation between cooling and rewarming of the extremities and a much slower drop in finger and toe temperatures. The overall result of the CIVD response is a much longer period of time in which manual dexterity is maintained during exposure of the extremities to extreme cold. In fact, the technological adaptation to life in the Arctic that is such an important part of the culture of all successful dwellers in this environment suggests that these people rarely experience whole-body cooling of an extreme nature. Rather, they experience extreme cold

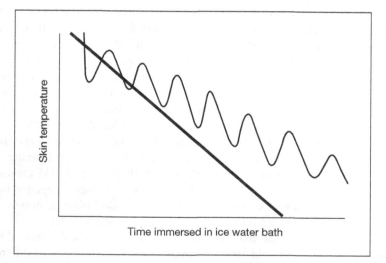

FIGURE 5.6 The straight line shows a gradual decrease in skin temperature due to continual vasoconstriction when an extremity is immersed in an ice-water bath: this is the normal human response. Some Native Americans from northern Canada show the CIVD response, marked by the curved line. Here vasoconstriction and vasodilation occur in a rhythmic pattern that serves to maintain higher skin temperatures for a longer time.

stress on their extremities primarily while performing outdoor activities that require the kind of manual dexterity that can be accomplished only with the bare hands. CIVD is such an obviously adaptive response to this common and essential occurrence among hunters and gatherers of the New World Arctic that it is also known as the "hunting response."

One of the most interesting and most extreme cases of cold stress known to anthropologists occurs among a group of Koreans known as the Ama. Among the Ama, a group of women have traditionally worked year-round as divers for plant and animal food in the cold ocean waters. In spite of winter water temperatures that fall to 10°C, until recently the divers have used only cotton swimsuits while diving to depths of as much as 20 m for periods of several hours a day. As might be expected, this extreme cold stress has elicited some major adaptive responses in these women. They resemble Inuit and other extremely cold-stressed populations by responding with an enormous increase in their metabolic heat production by as much as 35 percent above that of nondivers during the winter. Ama divers also begin to shiver at a lower water temperature than nondivers, suggesting that they can deal with cold stress without shivering to generate extra heat for a longer period of exposure than nondivers. In 1977, the divers began to wear wet suits instead of cotton swimsuits. When they were restudied under these changed conditions, many of the extraordinary adaptations seen in the earlier studies (performed in 1960 and 1961) had disappeared. Metabolic heat production and shivering threshold were no longer significantly different between Ama divers and nondivers. The rapid reversibility of these adaptive responses clearly indicates that they should be considered the result of acclimatization rather than evidence of genetic adaptation.

In summary, we have seen that all humans share a basic, genetic adaptation for dealing with moderate cold stress by reducing heat loss through peripheral vasoconstriction and aspects of vascular design (e.g., countercurrent heat exchange). Populations that have been exposed to moderate to severe cold stress for long periods of time show a range of adaptive responses, from heat conservation and habituation to lowered body temperatures during moderate cold exposure at night among Australian Aboriginals and Kalahari San and the increased heat production and CIVD found among both New and Old World populations exposed to severe and chronic cold stress. Natural selection also seems to have modified the size and shape of different human populations in response to climatic stress, a topic that will be explored later in this chapter. Ultimately, for humans to survive the severe cold stresses present in the temperate and polar regions, culture and technology must be available to allow the creation of warmer "microhabitats" because our physiology alone is insufficient to allow us to survive extreme cold stress. As you will soon see, *Homo sapiens* is a tropical species shaped and formed by the stresses of life in the tropics.

ADAPTATION TO HOT ENVIRONMENTS

In the tropical and semitropical parts of the earth, hot environments come in two types: either hot and dry or warm and humid. Habitats such as the Sonoran Desert in the American Southwest and the Sahara in North Africa are classic *hot and dry* environments. In these environments, heat stress is severe as a result of the extremely high air temperatures—often above 49°C (120°F)—caused by intense solar radiation and the lack of available shade. Strong winds can increase the heat load on individuals through convective heating because the air temperature is often much hotter than the skin temperature. Furthermore, the ground is often as hot as or hotter than the air and radiates and conducts additional heat to individuals. Daily temperature ranges are extreme because much of the heat absorbed by the earth during the day is radiated out to space during the clear, cloudless nights. The most efficient way that humans can dissipate excess heat in hot and dry environments is by sweating and the resultant evaporative cooling. The availability of water is thus an important limiting resource in hot and dry environments.

Air temperatures that are warm but typically cooler than body temperature, cooling winds, little solar radiation, abundant shade, and lots of moisture characterize *warm and humid* environments. Conduction, convection, and radiation can often contribute to the dissipation of excess heat in warm

FIGURE 5.7 Death Valley National Park in California is a classic hot and dry environment.
Courtesy of iStock by Getty Images.

and humid environments, but the efficiency of sweating is reduced in very humid conditions because the air may already be saturated with moisture, leading the sweat to drip off the body without evaporating. Cultural adaptations to life in hot and dry habitats include behavioral and technological responses such as scheduling activities so as to avoid exertion in the midday heat, wearing light-colored and lightweight clothing to protect the skin from solar radiation and to create an insulative layer of cool air, and building housing with insulative properties. Warm and humid environments are particularly resistant to cultural solutions: clothing and shelter tend to be very simple here, and activity scheduling is not particularly useful because daily temperature changes tend to be minimal. Unlike the situation with respect to human adaptation to cold stress, the bulk of our adaptation to heat comes in the form of biological adaptations. In adapting to the stress of heat, culture takes a back seat to biology. As a result, it is our biological adaptations that allow humans to thrive in deserts and savannas: these are the mark of a species with a long and successful history of life in the hot and dry tropics.

But what exactly is the nature of the human biological adaptation to life in the hot and dry regions of the world? When subjected to heat stress, all humans react in the same basic physiological fashion as a result of a set of genetic adaptations. The initial response is vascular, involving peripheral vasodilation in order to bring more of the body's warm blood close to the surface. *Vasodilation* leads to a major increase in the amount of heat present at the body's surface, thus raising the skin temperature and decreasing its insulative properties. This is an essential step in dissipating this excess heat at the interface between the organism and the environment. The heart must pump harder to move the blood through these enlarged vessels, and this fact contributes to the increased mortality among older individuals and those with weak or diseased hearts during prolonged heat waves. Excess heat can be lost at the body's surface through the processes of radiation (if cooler objects are in direct line of sight), conductance (by direct contact with cooler objects), or convection (if the air temperature is lower than skin temperature). However, by far the most important mechanism of heat loss among

FIGURE 5.8 This tropical rain forest in Costa Rica is a classic warm and humid environment.
Courtesy of iStock by Getty Images.

FIGURE 5.9 A thatched-roof hut on the tropical Pacific island of Fiji is part of the cultural response to life in the tropics. Courtesy of Education Images/Getty Images.

humans is evaporation of the slightly salty, watery secretions known as sweat. Sweat is secreted by the 2 to 3 million active *eccrine sweat glands* that are distributed throughout the skin over most of our bodies. The enormous amount of heat required to evaporate water (known as the *latent heat of vaporization*) is provided by the excess heat that the cardiovascular system brings to the body's surface through vasodilation. As sweat is evaporated and enters the air as water vapor, the body's excess heat is used up, and cooling results. However, when the air is nearly or completely saturated with moisture, as it is under very humid conditions, sweating becomes a very inefficient means of cooling because most of our sweat fails to evaporate and instead simply drips off our bodies. Without the evaporation of this moisture, no excess heat is dissipated. This is why many people typically prefer hot and dry climates to warm and humid ones and often extol the virtues of "dry heat."

Whereas an unacclimatized individual can sweat more than 1.5 liters per hour, an acclimatized and fit athlete can nearly double that rate, approaching an hourly rate of 2.5 liters. In several other respects, the difference in level of adaptation and physiological functioning in the heat between acclimatized and unacclimatized individuals and populations is very significant. For example, acclimatized individuals have a lower skin temperature threshold for the initiation of sweating. As a result, they begin to sweat and to lose excess heat earlier in the process of heat exposure and maintain a lower core temperature as a result. The sweat of acclimatized individuals also tends to have a lower electrolyte concentration, to be distributed more evenly around the body, and to evaporate more efficiently. Acclimatized individuals are also much more efficient in vasodilation and as a result can conduct more heat from the body's core to the periphery with less cardiovascular strain. All these differences lead to the inescapable conclusion that acclimatized individuals and populations are better adapted for life in a hot and dry climate because they are all associated with increased work capacity in heat for a longer time and at lower core temperatures, suggesting lower strain in the face of similar stress.

With respect to these kinds of traits, there is some suggestive evidence for real population differences in genetic adaptation to life in the heat. Although much evidence suggests that exposure and training under hot conditions can lead to greater adaptive ability and less strain in any healthy individual, comparative studies indicate that populations native to the hot tropics show significantly higher levels of performance than acclimatized individuals from nonnative populations. One of the best studies involved a comparison between 20 acclimatized male Bantu agriculturalists of southern Africa and an equal number of acclimatized male Caucasian medical students. This study involved four hours on a stair-climbing simulator at 34°C (93°F). The results suggest a much higher level of adaptive functioning in the heat among the Bantus. All of the Bantu subjects successfully completed the four-hour experiment, while only half of the Caucasians were able to finish. The Bantus all had a lower heart rate and sweated less than the Caucasians but still maintained a lower core temperature throughout the experiment. Clearly, the Bantus were functioning at a much more adaptive level in spite of the fact that age, physical conditioning, and acclimatization status had been controlled for. These results suggest a genetic difference in adaptation to heat between these populations, one of which has a long history of life in the hot and dry tropics of Africa while the other hails from the temperate zone.

THERMOREGULATION AND BODY SIZE AND SHAPE

Let's take a closer look at how climate affects the body size and shape of warm-blooded mammals such as humans. Might there be patterns of geographic or clinal variation in body size and shape between human populations that have lived for long periods of times in different climatic regions? In the 19th century, two biologists noticed certain patterns of geographic variation in body size and shape in closely related warm-blooded animals from different parts of the globe. Karl Bergmann was a German medical doctor and anatomist who noticed a consistent relationship between the body weight and size of animals and the climate in which they lived. *Bergmann's rule* states that in closely related warm-blooded animals, body size and weight tend to be larger when the animals live in cold climates and smaller when they live in warm climates. Note that Bergmann was not saying that all tropical animals were small and all arctic animals were big: elephants and arctic fox would seem to

FIGURE 5.10 A North American black bear in the snow. The comparison of skulls demonstrates Bergmann's rule relating body size in warm-blooded mammals to climate. For instance, a black bear skull from northern Canada has been found to be larger than one from Washington. Courtesy of iStock by Getty Images.

disprove that notion. What he was saying was that, for example, bears that live in the tropics tend to be smaller than bears that live in colder climates. J. A. Allen was a 19th-century American biologist who was also interested in geographic and climate-related variation among birds and mammals. Allen's observation that tropical-dwelling animals tended to have longer limbs and other protruding body parts (e.g., noses and ears) than their relatives living in cold climates has been called *Allen's rule*.

What is the physiological basis for these ecological rules? While much evidence supports Bergmann's and Allen's rules today for many different kinds of mammals, is there evidence supporting their application to humans? Let's begin by exploring the physical and physiological basis for the relationships between body size, extremity length, and temperature that are formalized in Bergmann's and Allen's rules. To understand the basis of these ecological relationships, we need to discuss the surface area and volume of organisms in the context of heat generation and heat transfer. The *volume* of an organism is reflected in its mass and is proportional to the amount of metabolic

FIGURE 5.11 Allen's rule suggests that long extremities and appendages (such as ears) are advantageous to tropical animals because they provide greater surface area and maximize heat loss. Courtesy of DEA Picture Library/Getty Images.

heat an individual can generate. Larger organisms, by virtue of their greater muscle mass, can generate absolutely greater amounts of metabolic heat than smaller organisms. The *surface area* of an organism, by contrast, determines how much heat the organism can exchange with the environment, because heat exchange occurs where the body meets the environment, at the body's surface. An organism that maximizes its volume will have the potential to generate lots of body heat, a useful adaptation for animals that live in cold climates. Cold climates would also seem to select for organisms with relatively small surface areas, since less heat would be lost to the environment with a reduced surface area. Conversely, an individual that maximizes its surface area would seem to be well adapted for losing excess heat in a hot environment. A small volume would lead to less buildup of excess heat, another useful feature for life in hot environments. So it seems that nature should prefer heavy animals with relatively small surface areas in cold climates and light animals with relatively large surface areas in the tropics. This is exactly what our two ecological rules predict: Bergmann's rule is about maximizing volume in the cold and minimizing it in the heat, and Allen's rule concerns maximizing surface area in the heat and minimizing it in the cold.

What about human populations? Bergmann's and Allen's rules would predict that body size and shape of inhabitants of the arctic should be heavy, thick, and stocky (lots of mass), with short limbs (little surface area). We might also expect arctic individuals to be muscular and with some superficial fat distributed around the body. The muscle helps generate metabolic heat, and the fat is a good insulator. On the other hand, optimal design of the human body for life in the tropics might involve a long and lean body type. Long arms and legs create lots of surface area for losing excess heat, while a lean build (e.g., light musculature and little fat) minimizes the chances of generating too much metabolic heat and facilitates heat loss. In many respects, the kinds of body types predicted are very close to what we actually see. The long, lean, and linear body build of many East Africans seems well designed for the tropics, while the short and stocky Inuit (as well as the tall and stocky Scandinavians) seem well adapted for the rigors of intense cold stress.

Another approach to testing the notion that human variation in body size and build reflects adaptations to temperature can be achieved through an analysis of data collected from many different

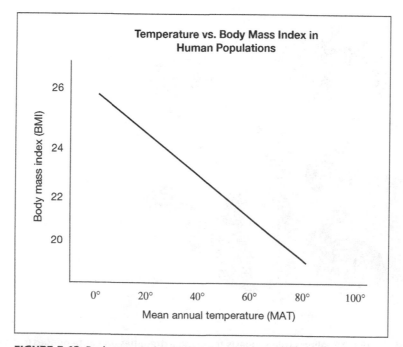

FIGURE 5.12 Body mass index (BMI) is inversely correlated with mean annual temperature (MAT), which means that as environmental temperature rises, average body size decreases.

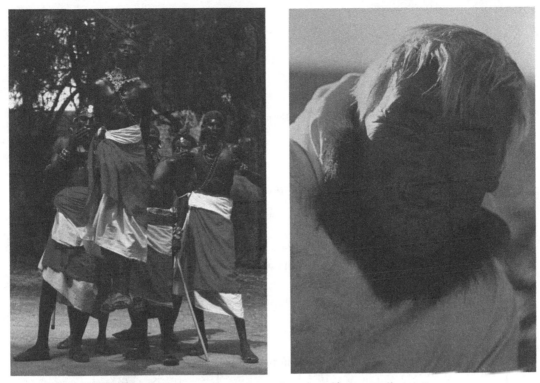

FIGURE 5.13 The different body types of Kenyan Samburu and Alaskan Inuit reveal Bergmann's and Allen's rules at work in human populations. a) Courtesy of Chris Jackson/Thinkstock by Getty Images b) Courtesy of National Geographic/Getty Images.

populations in different parts of the world. The *body mass index* (BMI) is one standard measure of the relationship of weight to height that is often used by medical practitioners. BMI is calculated as the weight in kilograms divided by the square of height in meters. BMI can also be calculated as weight in pounds divided by squared height in inches times 703. For adults, the overweight range is considered to be a BMI of 25.0–29.9; 30.0 or above is considered obese. The normal range for BMI is 18.5–24.9; below 18.5 is considered underweight. When we plot a data set of average BMI values for a variety of Old World populations against *mean annual temperature* (MAT) in the places where they live, we find that BMI correlates nicely with temperature in exactly the direction that Bergmann's rule predicts. That is, the hotter the MAT, the lower the BMI, and vice versa. The relationship between these two variables is not perfect, nor should we expect it to be. After all, populations have migrated across the continents, climates have changed over the course of human evolution, and changing diets and activity levels in many populations also strongly affect body mass. In the New World, Bergman's and Allen's rules don't work well at all, perhaps due to the relatively recent migrations of groups of Asians across the Bering Straits to populate the Americas (some 20 thousand years ago). But in general, the two ecological rules fit the human data for Old World populations quite nicely. In general, we can say that much population variation in body size and build is a result of natural selection to life in different climatic regimes. Climate explains body size and shape in humans to a large degree, and we gain nothing by attempting to classify populations into large and small or fat and thin "races" in order to explain these differences.

SKIN COLOR AND SOLAR RADIATION

In the United States, race is and always has been synonymous with skin color. Since the earliest days of racial classification, skin color has played an important role in determining racial classification. One of the most interesting biological features about skin color is its pattern of geographic variation.

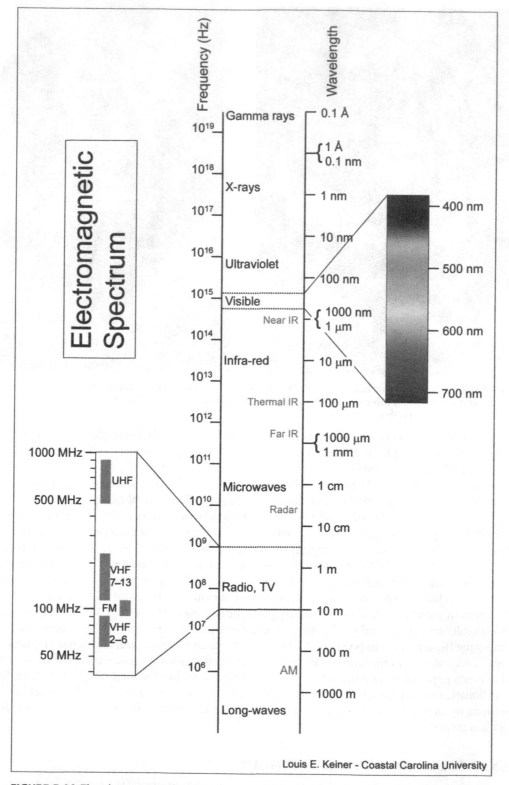

Louis E. Keiner - Coastal Carolina University

FIGURE 5.14 The electromagnet spectrum ranges from very short wavelength forms of radiation (e.g., gamma rays and X-rays) to those with very long wavelengths (e.g., radio waves).

Linnaeus, Blumenbach, and nearly all other would-be classifiers of human race have emphasized the association of black skin color with Africans, white with Europeans, and yellow with Asians. But the actual geographic variation of skin color across the globe is more interesting than this. In all continents, populations with dark skin color tend to be found nearer to the equator at lower latitudes, while populations that inhabit the more temperate zones farther from the equator and at higher latitudes tend to be lighter in skin color. While this relationship is most obvious in the Old World, it also describes to some extent the distribution of New World populations. This kind of variation in which some morphological trait changes gradually over geographic space is called *clinal variation* or a *cline*, and skin color can be said to form a latitudinal or north-to-south cline in *Homo sapiens*.

In seeking to explain why a biological trait might vary with geography, we need to determine the kinds of environmental changes that occur over the same geographic space that may influence human physiology. A latitudinal gradient in skin color might be controlled by temperature changes, seeing that temperature gradually drops as one moves away from the equator toward the poles, or it might be controlled by some other variable related to latitude. It turns out that the best explanation for the north–south gradient in skin color is not temperature but rather the amount of solar radiation that reaches the earth's surface. Solar radiation comes in many forms that can be characterized by their wavelength, ranging from the very short-wavelength gamma rays and X-rays to the very long-wavelength radio waves. Near the middle of the electromagnetic spectrum lie three types of radiation with significant biological effects: the ultraviolet (UV), visible, and infrared (IR) parts of the spectrum. The infrared wavelengths are the warming rays of the sun that we feel as heat, while the visible part of the spectrum is what allows us to see objects in the world. The ultraviolet wavelengths are the particular parts of the electromagnetic spectrum of solar radiation whose biological effects are most important for the discussion of skin color. The shorter-wavelength X-rays and gamma rays that are also emitted from the sun are screened out by ozone in the atmosphere and never reach the earth's surface. New satellite-based remote-sensing technologies

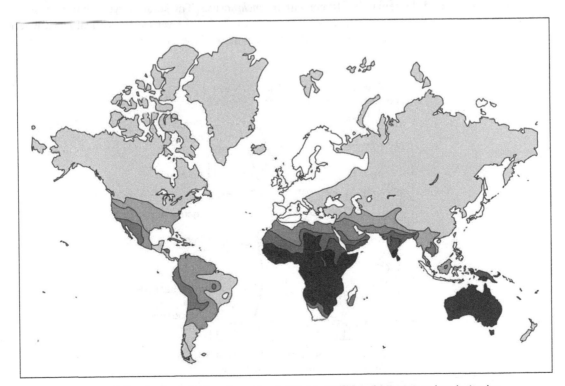

FIGURE 5.15 Clinal distribution of skin color across latitudes. Darker colors occur at low latitudes and signify darker pigmentations. Lighter colors at higher latitudes represent lighter skin colors.

have allowed the precise measurement of annual levels of UV radiation all across the globe. This new knowledge has verified the geographic relationship between skin color and UV radiation exposure: where skin color is darkest, UV radiation is most intense (i.e., near the equator), and as UV radiation levels become reduced (at greater distances from the equator), skin color lightens. Before we explore the biological effects of UV radiation on human skin and population differences in the degree of pigmentation, we will need to first discuss the structure of skin and the biology of the skin pigment known as melanin.

THE STRUCTURE OF SKIN

A basic knowledge of the structure of the skin is a prerequisite to understanding the function of melanin and the evolutionary significance of skin color among humans. Rather than being a mere outer covering for the body, "the skin is not only the largest and most versatile organ of the body but also, with the possible exception of the brain, the most complex" (Robbins 1991:1). Consisting of two components known as the dermis and the epidermis, the skin is a complex structure made up of different cell types with a rich nervous and vascular supply. The *dermis* is the deeper of the two layers, a complex connective tissue that includes structures such as the eccrine sweat glands and oily sebaceous glands, the hair follicles as well as the tiny smooth muscles that at times lift our body hair into "goose bumps," and numerous blood and lymphatic vessels. The *epidermis* lies superficial to the dermis and contains no blood vessels or nerves. Its outermost layer, the *corneal layer* or *stratum corneum*, is a layer of dead keratinized cells forming a thick and strong protective membrane around the entire body. The individual cells of the corneal layer are eventually sloughed off at the surface and replaced by more cells growing and pushing up from the lowest level of the epidermis, known as the *basal* or *germinative layer* (*stratum germinativum*). The basal layer is where new skin cells form through the process of cell division known as mitosis. Approximately 90 percent of these skin cells are *keratinocytes*, and the remaining 10 percent are *melanocytes*. The keratinocytes change in shape and composition and eventually die as they move from the basal layer to the corneal layer, where they are sloughed off: the entire process takes from four to six weeks for an individual skin cell.

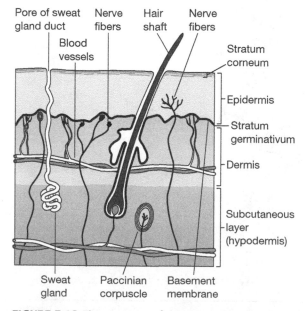

FIGURE 5.16 The structure of skin in cross section.

The melanocytes are found only in the basal layer of the epidermis, near the junction between the dermis and epidermis. These specialized skin cells are the cellular factories where the skin pigment *melanin* is manufactured and packaged into granules known as *melanosomes*, which are distributed to the rest of the epidermal cells. Melanosomes develop through four stages with characteristic changes in shape (from spherical to ellipsoid) and intensity of pigmentation (light or translucent to dark or opaque). There are no significant differences between human populations in the number or density of melanocytes in human skin. Rather, skin color differences between individuals and populations are to a large extent the result of three other factors: the number and size of the melanosomes, the rate of melanosome formation and development, and the rate of melanosome transfer to keratinocytes (Robbins 1991). The skin of darkly pigmented Africans, for example, has larger melanosomes that tend to be aggregated throughout the epidermis and that are mostly of the darker, stage 4 variety. Lightly pigmented Europeans tend to have small melanosomes distributed individually throughout the epidermis, almost none of which are at stages 3 or 4. If skin color really is a valid biological marker of race, then race, like beauty, is truly "only skin deep," localized in the basal layer of the skin's epidermis.

BIOLOGICAL EFFECTS OF SOLAR RADIATION

The subject of tanning provides an excellent opportunity to bring to bear the tools of biocultural analysis. From the biological perspective, tanning is an adaptive process of increased melanization that occurs in response to exposure of the skin to the ultraviolet spectrum of solar radiation. Because tanning is a short-term, reversible adaptive response, it is an example of acclimatization, a form of phenotypic plasticity. Upon exposure to the sun, the activity of the melanocytes in the basal layer of the epidermis of the exposed skin increases, leading to increased production of melanin and gradually, over a period of hours to days, to a darker, tanned skin tone. Tanning is considered an adaptive response because the increased melanin in the epidermis acts as a filter of UV radiation and

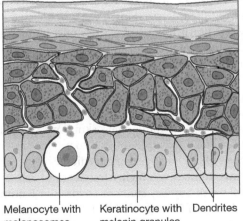

Melanocyte with melanosomes   Keratinocyte with melanin granules over the nucleus   Dendrites

FIGURE 5.17 Melanin is produced in melanocytes in the basal layer of the epidermis. Packets of melanin known as melanosomes then move into the keratinocytes, where they help shield the nucleus and its genetic machinery from the damaging effects of ultraviolet radiation.

thus protects the dermal layer of the skin from the damaging effects of this radiation. In modern American society, a tan is regarded as a marker of health, vigor, affluence, and general well-being, and countless people spend many hours each summer in pursuit of the perfect tan. But in other cultures and at other times, the meaning of a tanned complexion can be very different. For example, in Japan and much of Asia, a tan signifies working-class status, because only working-class individuals spend enough time in the sun to acquire a tan. Since the wealthy have the luxury of staying out of the hot midday sun, light skin is associated with beauty, wealth, and leisure in Japanese society. Clearly, we are no longer in the world of scientific or biological interpretation but are now standing firmly in the realm of cultural interpretation, where arbitrary cultural meanings or statuses can be attributed to biological or purely phenotypic differences between people or groups. Is one culture correct in its interpretation of the meaning of a tan and the other incorrect? While one might argue that the Japanese have the healthier outlook concerning the value of a tan in light of modern discoveries concerning the causes of skin cancer, the anthropological approach does not seek "truth" or "falsehood" in the cultural meanings or beliefs held by various social groups. Different societies create an integrated set of cultural beliefs that may or not be biologically adaptive or scientifically valid or even healthy but need to be understood from the perspective of each particular society because different cultures create different meanings for the same phenomena. We can, however, observe the biomedical results of different cultural beliefs concerning tanning and compare the individual costs and benefits of the different behaviors that flow from these cultural beliefs.

What, then, are the biological effects of exposure to ultraviolet radiation? We can begin with an entirely positive result: exposure of the skin to UV radiation stimulates the production in the epidermis of vitamin D. An essential component of the physiological processes of calcium absorption from the intestine and vital for the mineralization of tooth and bone, vitamin D has until recent times been almost entirely absent from most human diets. Prior to the age of vitamin D–enriched milk and nutritional supplements, humans have always relied on the production of vitamin D in our skin to ensure normal formation of bones and teeth. Insufficient amounts of vitamin D during childhood can lead to a disease known as rickets, characterized by the formation of soft and misshapen bones. Having soft and permanently bent limb bones would seriously limit an individual's ability to travel and thereby impair the ability to forage for food. In addition, rickets often leads to a misshapen pelvis and a seriously undersized birth canal in affected females. These factors would make a successful vaginal birth nearly impossible for a women suffering from rickets and would lead to high mortality of both mother and baby during birth, especially during the many years of human existence before the availability of cesarean sections (C-sections). As a result of these considerations, any condition leading to an individual's inability to synthesize adequate quantities of vitamin D would have been very strongly selected against during much of human evolution. Insufficient vitamin D production will result from inadequate exposure of the skin to the sun's radiation, but one complicating factor is the color of the individual's skin. One study determined that six times as much UV radiation is required for a "Negroid subject" to produce an equal amount of vitamin D as a "Caucasoid" (Clemens et al. 1982). Finally, strong medical evidence from the United States during the early 20th century points to the much higher frequency of rickets among black children than among whites. One example is an autopsy study of children in Baltimore who died between 1926 and 1942 before reaching the age of 2. It revealed that 45 percent of the white children and 72 percent of the black children showed evidence of bone deformities resulting from rickets (Robbins 1991:201). Another study of 2,500 white and 1,500 black women found that the black women were three times as likely to have a deformed pelvis as the white women (13 percent versus 40 percent; Robbins 1991:201). Since vitamin D is formed in the deeper layers of the epidermis (below most of the melanin), it seems that darkly pigmented skin acts as a sunscreen and reduces the amount of UV radiation that penetrates the epidermis to stimulate vitamin D production. All the medical evidence seems to agree that compared to light skin, darkly pigmented skin requires significantly more exposure to UV radiation in order to synthesize enough vitamin D to ensure proper bone formation and mineralization.

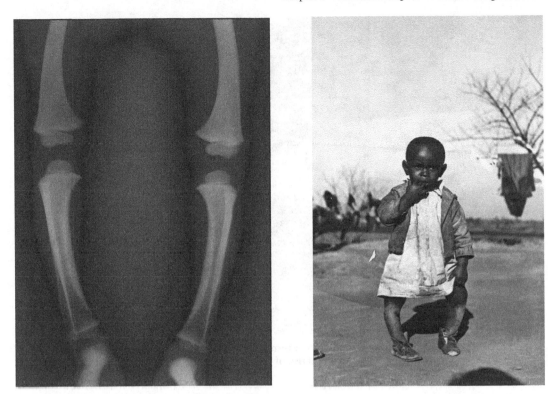

FIGURE 5.18 A radiograph of the lower limbs of a child with rickets demonstrates the bowed legs that result from this bone disease. This Indian child exhibits additional signs of rickets, including a distended abdomen, large forehead, and swelling in the wrists.
a) Credit: Biophoto Associates/Science Photo Library b) © CORBIS

Excessive and repeated exposure to the sun also leads to premature aging of the skin, a condition known as *photoaging*. In photoaged skin, the elastic fibers of the skin become thickened and degraded, resulting in loose and sagging skin. The epidermis becomes thickened and takes on a leathery texture, and the sebaceous or oily glands of the face become enlarged, leading to an acnelike condition. A variety of benign and sometimes precancerous lesions may occur as a result of cellular damage caused by years of exposure to ultraviolet radiation. Sunburn is an acute and painful effect of UV exposure; symptoms include redness, swelling, and sometimes blistering of the skin. In severe cases, chills and fever and even nausea can result. Severe sunburn can damage sweat glands and seriously limit an individual's ability to keep cool while working or traveling in the heat.

The most dangerous medical condition arising from chronic sunburn is of course skin cancer, and the most dangerous form of skin cancer is cancer of the melanocytes known as *melanoma*. Often lethal and usually affecting adults, it can also occur among young people. Recent research has pinpointed, for at least one kind of sometimes fatal skin cancer known as squamous cell carcinoma, the actual genetic defect that leads to the cancer. Furthermore, this research has proved that the cancer-causing genetic mutation in a gene known as p53 can be caused only by exposure to ultraviolet radiation. Two important facts should be considered concerning the incidence of skin cancer: all forms of skin cancer are much more common among light-skinned individuals, and rates of skin cancer are much higher in low-latitude zones of high solar radiation (i.e., near the equator). Both of these facts stem from melanin's ability to act as a natural sunscreen and to protect skin cells from the deleterious effects of solar radiation. Skin cancer is very rare among very darkly pigmented individuals and races, and it is most common among light-skinned people living in the tropical zones of high solar radiation. For example, American whites

FIGURE 5.19 The damaging effects of long-term overexposure to solar radiation include dry and leathery skin and a greatly increased risk of skin cancer.
Courtesy of iStock by Getty Images.

have a death rate from skin cancer that is three times as high as American blacks, and among whites, skin cancer is much more common in the South than in the North. At the level of the individual, skin cancer is most common among blue-eyed, red- or blonde-haired, fair-skinned individuals. Among albinos who live in regions of high solar radiation, cancer rates are extremely high and typically occur during adolescence or in early adulthood. All of this epidemiological evidence suggests that natural selection has strongly favored darker skin and the ability to tan among human populations that live in the tropics.

Finally, recent evidence suggests another important selective agent that favors the presence of darkly pigmented skin in the tropics. Exposure to high levels of solar radiation is now known to result in *photolysis* (destruction by light) of folate, one of the B vitamins. *Folate* is an essential nutrient for pregnant mothers because it is required for the proper formation of the embryonic neural tube, the developmental precursor to the bony spine and the nervous tissue of the spinal cord. Insufficiency of folate during the first trimester of pregnancy can result in a class of birth defects known as *neural tube defects* (NTDs). The most common NTD is *spina bifida*, which is characterized by the presence of an open neural canal due to failure of the developing spine to fully enclose the spinal cord. Anencephaly is the most extreme NTD and is always fatal, with death typically occurring shortly after birth. It involves developmental malformation of the cranial vault of the skull resulting in either missing or severely reduced cerebral hemispheres. The biological anthropologist Nina Jablonski (2006) has cogently argued that photolysis of folate is one of the most important biological effects of exposure to UV radiation. She suggests that light-skinned women living in tropical zones of high ultraviolet radiation are at increased risk of giving birth to children born with neural tube defects, as a result of the high levels of folate damage they would experience. Melanin would again act as a natural sunscreen in protecting women from the photolytic effects of solar radiation, leading to the prevalence of dark skin in the tropics due to the workings of natural selection over the millennia.

BOX TWO

Albinos and Albinism

Albinism is a genetic condition caused by an autosomal recessive gene that interferes with the production of melanin in the skin, hair, and eyes. The resulting phenotype includes pale white skin and hair and a light blue or red iris in the eye. In the United States, about one child in every 20 thousand births is an albino (homozygous recessive), but a much higher number of heterozygous carriers exists in the population, on the

FIGURE B5.1 Albinism is not restricted to humans, as the wallaby and alligator demonstrate. An albino child is held by her mother in Angola, West Africa. a) © ERIC LAFFORGUE / Alamy b) Courtesy of iStock by Getty Images c) Courtesy of iStock by Getty Images

(continued)

order of one in 70. In other populations, the rates of albinism vary enormously, including an estimated one in 3,000 births in East Africa. Albinos are typically born to parents of normally pigmented phenotype who happen to be heterozygous carriers of the genetic condition. A quick Punnett square reveals that such parents would be expected to have a 25 percent chance of having an albino child for each pregnancy, along with a 25 percent chance of having a normal homozygote and a 50 percent chance of having heterozygous carrier children. A national support organization exists for people with albinism and for parents of children with albinism, known as NOAH, the National Organization for Albinism and Hypopigmentation (http://www.albinism.org). Because they produce little or no melanin, albinos are highly susceptible to sunburn and skin cancer when they live in regions of high ultraviolet radiation. They often have a number of visual problems that seem to be associated with the lack of melanin in the iris, including extreme sensitivity to light, "crossed" or "lazy" eye (strabismus), myopia (nearsightedness), and astigmatism. Albinos are found on every continent and in people of every race or ethnicity, as well as among many different kinds of animals including deer, alligators, kangaroos, and mice.

While there is no cure for albinism, most albinos in America are able to live normal and fulfilling lives; they are not victims of outward discrimination, and despite a variety of medical concerns and susceptibilities that many normally pigmented people do not, they can and do live long and happy lives. In parts of East Africa, however, albinos are feared and reviled and sometimes killed, simply on account of their lack of pigmentation and the superstitious beliefs surrounding this condition. Beginning in 2007, disturbing reports came from Tanzania about albinos being killed and their bodies mutilated. Apparently, local practitioners of witchcraft have been encouraging gangs of men to attack and kill albinos or to dig up the graves of recently deceased albinos in order to use their body parts in potions that are said to guarantee riches. An undercover BBC reporter who posed as a businesswoman was told that for $2,000, she could have an albino corpse. Despite the Tanzanian government's efforts to halt these grisly and superstitious activities, the *New York Times* reports that more than 40 albinos have been murdered for their body parts since 2007 (McNeil 2009). Perhaps a hopeful sign is the recent appointment of Tanzania's first albino member of parliament. Al-Shymaa Kwaa-Geer hopes to improve the medical and social conditions of life for Tanzania's estimated 17 thousand albinos. International pressure is beginning to come from the United Nations to encourage Tanzania's government to appoint a special prosecutor to investigate the albino murders. While more than 170 individuals have been arrested, none has yet been brought to trial.

THE EVOLUTION OF SKIN COLOR

What evolutionary conclusions can we draw from all this information about geography, skin color, melanin, vitamin D and folate, cancer, and solar radiation? The basic story is simple: the degree of skin pigmentation in different human populations is an adaptive trait for mediating the effects of ultraviolet radiation on human health. Skin color is clearly a plastic or labile trait, one that has changed at several times in different human populations of the past and that presumably can change in the future. The details of this evolutionary scenario are illustrative of how environmental change can lead to morphological change in populations according to the principles of Darwin's theory of evolution by natural selection.

Our starting assumptions are that the skin color of the last common ancestor of the human and ape lineage was hairy and perhaps light-skinned and that this ancestor would have lived in Africa perhaps 6 to 8 million years ago. Our closest cousins among the primates are the African chimpanzees, some of whom typically have light skin color (due to a lack of melanocytes in most of their skin) covered by a dense coat of dark fur. Chimpanzees are mostly inhabitants of forests and woodlands, habitats that have a much lower level of ultraviolet radiation than the more open grasslands and savannas where early human ancestors presumably spent much of their time. When upright and bipedal (two-legged) human ancestors began to spend significant amounts of time walking or running through the open country of the hot and dry African tropics in search of food, they greatly increased their need to thermoregulate (keep cool) and to cope with the extremely high amounts of solar radiation they would have experienced on the open savanna. This is probably when our ancestors became darkly pigmented, naked, and sweaty. Losing the heavy coat of dense fur in favor of a dense coverage of sweat glands would have increased their ability to evaporate away the excess heat generated by an active lifestyle in the hot and dry African grasslands. But retaining light skin color would have seriously compromised their ability to survive with the high ultraviolet radiation to which they were exposed every day. A photoprotective layer of melanin would have greatly increased their ability to survive and reproduce in their new environment in several ways. As noted earlier, there are several selective benefits to decreasing one's susceptibility to acute and debilitating sunburn. Excessive or severe sunburns can damage sweat glands and impair thermoregulation in the heat, greatly increase one's lifetime risk of skin cancer and increase the risk of neural tube defects through the destruction of folate in pregnant women. For all these reasons, dark skin color is favored by natural selection in the tropics, both today and millions of years ago.

If the earliest human ancestors evolved dark skin as a protective sunscreen in the open country of the hot and dry African tropics by 6 million years ago, where and when and under what environmental conditions did some human populations evolve white skin? As we already know, most modern light-skinned populations are found at high latitudes in the temperate zones, where solar radiation is much less intense than it is in the tropics. Retaining a very dark pigmentation in these latitudes predisposes individuals to suffering from vitamin D deficiency, and we can be sure that weak and deformed bones would have been strongly selected against in these hunting-and-gathering populations of the distant past. Lighter skin would have allowed the production of sufficient vitamin D to ensure proper bone calcification and normal bone development. Furthermore, since the levels of harmful ultraviolet radiation are much reduced in the temperate zones, the threat of dangerous sunburns would have been greatly reduced. As a result, natural selection would no longer have strongly favored darkly pigmented individuals. Perhaps light skin with the ability to tan after exposure to solar radiation first appeared when ancestral human populations spread out of the tropics to regions such as southern Europe, where summers are hot with substantial solar radiation. As higher latitudes were colonized, where summers are cool and cloudy and ultraviolet radiation levels are low (think of Scotland), even the ability to tan was lost in certain populations, as in many red-haired, fair-skinned, and freckled individuals. This very fair skin would have allowed sufficient vitamin D to be produced in these regions of very low solar radiation. The evolution of white skin, then, appears to be related to the colonization of cooler and cloudier, more temperate latitudes with lower levels of solar radiation. Once the threat of skin damage due to sunburn was reduced, there was no longer any need for the natural sunscreen effects of heavy melanin in the epidermis. Instead, selection now would have favored fairer skin in order to ensure sufficient epidermal production of vitamin D and proper bone and tooth mineralization.

This scenario makes excellent sense in explaining the cline in skin color that we can observe among living populations except for one often mentioned exception. One of the world's most northerly dwelling populations, the Greenland Inuit, are also quite dark in skin color, certainly much darker than one would have predicted based on their geographic location. Our evolutionary scenario explains quite nicely why their skin color never lightened up as much as other high-latitude populations. The traditional diet of the Greenland Inuit included such marine resources as fish, seals, and whales and would have provided them with more than adequate levels of vitamin D, since fish oils are the single largest dietary source of vitamin D. Thus they would never have faced the same kind of selective pressure to lighten up the skin in order to ensure adequate vitamin D production in their epidermis: unlike most human populations, Eskimos eat their vitamin D!

Recent genetic research has further elucidated the origins of the hypothesized change in human skin color from black to white. First found in the zebrafish and later in *Homo sapiens*, the gene SLC24A5 appears to be the key gene that causes pale skin in Europeans but, interestingly, not in Asians. Further study of this gene suggests that the genetic change that produces pale skin color in Europeans occurred much more recently than expected, perhaps only 6 to 12 thousand years ago. This suggests that the earliest hunters and gatherers who left Africa for the temperate zones of Europe would have retained their dark skin pigmentation for perhaps 100 thousand years. Only when their descendants began farming in Europe (at about 6 thousand years ago) did the lightening in skin color occur. Perhaps the early European hunters and gatherers had ready access to vitamin D in their diet of meat and fish.

Discussion Questions

1. The terms *stress, strain,* and *homeostasis* come from the engineering world. Explain their uses and meanings to the physiological anthropologist.

2. What are the different kinds of adaptation that humans rely on to adjust to life in stressful environments?

3. Describe the clinal variation seen in skin color in the Old World, and discuss the role that vitamin D, skin cancer, rickets, and folate play in explaining this cline.

4. If you had the power to design a human being perfectly adapted to an extremely hot and dry environment with high levels of UV radiation, what would you come up with? What would a perfectly adapted human to an arctic climate look like?

5. What are Bergmann's and Allen's rules? Provide some examples of how they might explain some of the polytypic variation in the body size and shape of some human populations.

6. Explain the significance of volume and surface area in climatic adaptation among warm-blooded mammals such as humans.

7. Is the report on albinism in Tanzania a reflection of racism? Explain your reasoning.

CHAPTER 6

Human Adaptation: Life at High Altitude

"Great things happen when man meets the mountains."

REINHOLD MESSNER, THE FIRST CLIMBER TO SUMMIT MOUNT EVEREST
WITHOUT SUPPLEMENTARY OXYGEN, IN WETZLER 2002:2

HIGH ALTITUDE AS A HUMAN STRESSOR

Chapter 5 explained that humans have been able to adapt to the stress of life in extreme heat and cold as a result of a combination of cultural and biological adaptations. Two of our major conclusions can be restated here. First, it was noted that the human adaptation to the extreme seasonal cold experienced in the Arctic relies primarily on a superb cultural adaptation in this harsh and difficult environment. With the exception of a few small biological differences, the major way in which people such as the Inuit are able to cope with life in the cold is a combination of technology, cultural knowledge, and experience. Second, it was noted that all humans show the mark of millions of years of tropical heritage; in other words, we all bear the basic biology of tropical dwellers regardless of where we live today. Arctic as well as tropical dwellers share the same basic physiology of efficient sweating and peripheral vasodilation in order to maintain thermoregulatory homeostasis in the heat. By contrast, humans have lived in the world's high-altitude zones for only a relatively short period of time, measured in thousands of years. Furthermore, the major stress of life at high altitude is *hypoxia* or low availability of oxygen, which cannot be coped with by cultural adaptations alone, short of wearing oxygen tanks on a daily basis! You will see that the stress of life at high altitude has led to some interesting biological differences between highlands and lowlands dwellers in both the Old World and the New. In this chapter, we will explore the stresses involved in life at high altitude and the mainly biological ways in which people and populations have coped with the low oxygen availability that is the hallmark and major stress of life at high altitude.

Let's begin this discussion by answering some basic questions about human adaptation to the stress of life at high altitude. What do we mean by high altitude, and what exactly are the stresses that humans experience there? Somewhat arbitrarily, anthropologists refer to elevations above 3,000 meters (10 thousand feet) as high altitude, although this definition implies no real physiological threshold between high and low altitude. Life at 2,900 meters is only slightly less stressful than life at 3,000 meters; the stresses are essentially the same at both elevations. Although there are many places in the world where the land lies above 3,000 meters, many of these places have few inhabitants due to the rugged

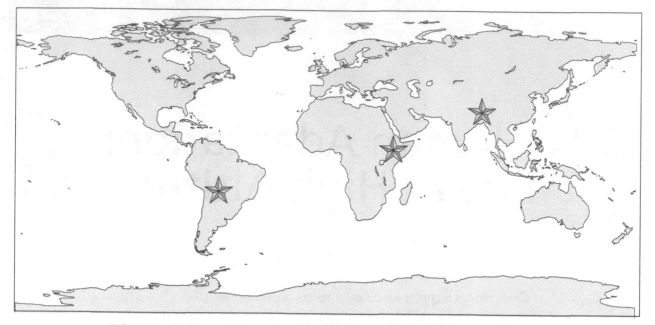

FIGURE 6.1 The three high-altitude areas with significant populations are in the Andes of South America, the Ethiopian highlands of Africa, and the Himalayas of Asia.

terrain and cold weather. There are perhaps 15 million high-altitude inhabitants in today's world, and the great majority of these people live in one of three different regions: the Andes Mountains and Altiplano of South America, the Himalaya Mountains and Tibetan plateau of Asia, and the Ethiopian highlands of Africa. Wherever people live at high altitude, they must cope with a series of stressful environmental conditions that can pose very serious problems for human comfort, reproduction, and survival. Stresses encountered by people living at high altitude include high solar radiation, low temperatures and high winds, poor nutrition due to low natural productivity and a short growing season, rugged terrain that limits travel, and hypoxia. While any of these stresses can be a significant factor in limiting human occupation at high altitude in a particular location, by far the most significant human stressor at high altitude all over the world is hypoxia. Hypoxia is perhaps unique among all human environmental stressors in that it requires a biological adaptation: culture is simply inadequate for coping with the stress of hypoxia. Accordingly, we will devote most of our attention in this chapter to hypoxia and to the ways in which high-altitude populations have biologically adapted to this very difficult stress.

Simply put, hypoxia is the physiological condition of oxygen deficiency that leads to impairment of a variety of bodily functions. Since all of the body's tissues require oxygen for basic metabolic and cellular functions, a lack of sufficient oxygen can quickly result in a wide range of serious medical problems and functional impairments. A discussion of the relationship between altitude, air pressure, and oxygen availability in the atmosphere should clarify why hypoxia is such an important human stressor for people living at or visiting the world's high-altitude areas.

AIR PRESSURE, OXYGEN AVAILABILITY, AND ALTITUDE

Air pressure can be defined as the force per unit area that is exerted against a surface by the weight of the air molecules above that surface. As you increase the number of air molecules pressing down on an object, you increase the pressure exerted by the air on that object. At the earth's surface, air pressure is determined by the weight of the overlying column of air. Furthermore, the density of air is greater at low elevations because air molecules are compressed by the weight of the overlying air. This explains why air pressure is greater at lower elevations on the earth's surface, since the air column above an object at sea level is taller than one at the top of a mountain. So where air pressure is greater (i.e., at low elevations), more molecules of air (and hence of oxygen) are available. Conversely, less air and less oxygen are available at high altitudes, due to the low air pressure found there because there is less air pressing down from above. This is the physical basis behind high-altitude hypoxia.

Air pressure is measured by an instrument called a *barometer*, and so another name for air pressure is *barometric pressure*. The Italian scientist Evangelista Torricelli invented the mercury barometer in the 17th century and was the first scientist to understand that air had weight. Torricelli's mercury barometer was a simple instrument in which a glass vacuum tube was inserted upside down into a dish of liquid mercury. He determined that the weight of the air pushes the mercury partway up the tube through the vacuum and that the height to which the mercury rises is a measure of the weight (or pressure) of the air. Barometric pressure is still measured in millimeters (or inches) of mercury. At sea level, the mercury in a barometer rises 760 millimeters, so we say the barometric pressure at sea level is 760 millimeters (29.92 inches) of mercury. How much force is generated by this kind of atmospheric pressure? Probably a lot more than you would have guessed! The actual force exerted by air pressure at sea level is 14.7 pounds per square inch, or 1 kilogram per square centimeter. The force exerted by air pressure at sea level on a surface area of 1,000 square centimeters (only slightly larger than a square foot) is 1,000 kilograms, or more than a ton! The reason we are not ordinarily aware of that much weight pressing down on us is that the insides of our bodies are filled with air too, and thus the pressure outside and inside our bodies is equalized.

As we climb to higher elevations, the number of air molecules above us becomes smaller, thereby reducing the density of the air that we breathe and the weight of the atmosphere pressing down. Barometric pressure thus decreases as altitude increases, and as it decreases, less oxygen is available in the air. We can calculate the contributions of the different gaseous constituents of air to the measured barometric pressure at different altitudes. We know that oxygen makes up 21 percent of the air that we breathe and that the barometric pressure at sea level is equal to 760 millimeters of mercury. Thus 21 percent of the 760 millimeters of air pressure is contributed by oxygen: this is known as the *partial pressure* of oxygen, and at sea level it is equivalent to 160 millimeters of mercury (21 percent of 760). Since 78 percent of air is composed of nitrogen, its partial pressure at sea level is 593 millimeters of mercury (78 percent of 760). At an elevation of 3,000 meters, the relative proportions of the gaseous components of air remain the same: 21 percent for oxygen and 78 percent for nitrogen. But since the barometric pressure is so much lower at 3,000 meters (522 millimeters of mercury), the partial pressure of each constituent gas in air is also significantly less than at sea level. For oxygen, 110 millimeters of mercury are available at 3,000 meters (21 percent of 522), and for nitrogen, 407 millimeters of mercury (78 percent of 522). The lower partial pressure of oxygen reflects the scarcity of oxygen molecules in the air at 3,000 meters compared to sea level. Thus every breath we take at 3,000 meters delivers nearly a third less oxygen to our lungs than at sea level (160 minus 110 divided by 160 equals 31 percent). Anyone who has experienced life at 3,000 meters will remember the constant shortness of breath, the burning lungs, and the exertion required for the simplest acts all as a result of this oxygen deficit.

Before we focus on the stress of hypoxia, a few words about the other stresses that typically occur at high altitude are warranted. Several of these other stresses are, like hypoxia, related to the thinness of the atmosphere. For example, cold temperatures are a common feature of high-altitude environments because less heat is retained in the atmosphere at altitude than at sea level. Cold stress can be quite extreme in many high-altitude zones as a result of the inverse relationship between altitude and temperature. Mountainous areas also tend to have very windy conditions, increasing the wind chill factor and exacerbating cold stress. Solar radiation can be substantial at high altitude because the thin atmosphere is less effective at screening out or absorbing the rays of the sun. This is especially true near the equator, where the sun's rays strike the earth more directly than at higher latitudes. Nutrition is often limited as a result of the short growing season, low humidity, and low overall productivity of high-altitude environments. Finally, the rough terrain makes travel difficult and minimizes the amount of arable land available for agriculture. The combination of cold

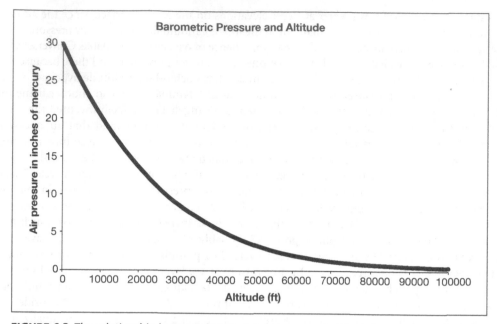

FIGURE 6.2 The relationship between barometric pressure and altitude is negative or inverse. That is, as altitude increases, barometric pressure decreases.

temperatures and rough terrain combine to limit the productivity of high-altitude lands, limiting both the quality and the quantity of nutrients available for human consumption. By themselves, none of these stresses would suffice to make high-altitude environments particularly difficult for human occupation, and human populations that live at high altitude have devised a variety of cultural adaptations to deal with them. Terraced agriculture, often concentrating on cold-adapted crops (e.g., the many varieties of potato grown at high altitude in the Andes), warm and wind-resistant clothing, and airtight houses are just a few of the cultural solutions to some of the stressful features of life at high altitude. But the combination of these stresses, added to that of hypoxia, makes the high-altitude environment one of the most difficult for human habitation.

ANATOMY AND PHYSIOLOGY OF THE CARDIOVASCULAR AND RESPIRATORY SYSTEMS

Coping with the stress of hypoxia places extraordinary demands on the body's cardiovascular and respiratory systems. The *cardiovascular system* consists of the heart, blood, and the blood vessels and can be considered the pump (heart) and pipes (blood vessels) through which the blood travels. The *respiratory system* consists of the lungs and the various pathways through which air enters and leaves the body. The connection between these two systems is, of course, the blood, which carries the respiratory gases, mainly oxygen (O_2) and carbon dioxide (CO_2), throughout the body. Gas exchange occurs in the lungs, where the blood picks up oxygen molecules and drops off carbon dioxide. Blood becomes oxygenated for delivery of this essential gas to the various cells and tissues of the body. Carbon dioxide is also exchanged in the lungs, from where it can be exhaled. A brief illustration of the anatomy and physiology of these two systems will prepare us for a discussion of how the human body adapts to the difficulties of life at altitude.

The mammalian heart is a four-chambered pump (two ventricles and two atria) that moves blood in two different paths throughout the body. The *pulmonary circulation* involves the movement of deoxygenated blood from the heart's right ventricle to the lungs via the pulmonary artery. From here, oxygenated blood is returned to the left atrium via the pulmonary vein. The returning oxygenated blood of the pulmonary circulation moves from the left atrium to the left ventricle through the heart's mitral valve. The *systemic circulation* begins with the left ventricle, which pumps oxygenated (arterial) blood through the aorta to all parts of the body. Deoxygenated (venous) blood arrives back at the heart at the right atrium via the inferior and superior *vena cavae*. In the heart itself, deoxygenated blood from the returning systemic circulation flows from the right atrium to the right ventricle through the heart's tricuspid valve. In general, the arteries are the vessels that carry oxygenated blood away from the heart to the cells and tissues of the body, whose mitochondria require oxygen for most cellular reactions. Arteries are large vessels that branch into smaller arterioles, eventually ending in very small-diameter vessels known as capillaries. Capillaries are the actual sites of gas exchange between the cells and the molecules of oxygen and carbon dioxide carried by the blood. In the capillaries, oxygen is diffused to the cells while carbon dioxide moves from cells to the bloodstream, to be returned to the lungs, where the carbon dioxide is exhaled, and more air (with 21 percent oxygen) is inhaled. Capillaries can be viewed as the end of the line for arterial blood and the beginning of the voyage of deoxygenated, venous blood on its way back to the heart and lungs. Venules and veins are to the venous system what arterioles and arteries are to the arterial blood supply, and they are built up from the same capillaries where gas exchange occurs. These capillaries gradually increase in diameter to become venules and veins that ultimately bring the deoxygenated blood back to the right atrium of the heart. The blood is composed of red blood cells, white blood cells, and the noncellular fluid matrix in which the cells reside, known as the plasma. Red blood cells are concerned primarily with carrying gases between the lungs and the tissues; white blood cells form an important part of the immune system, fighting off infection from microbes, bacteria, or other foreign invaders that enter the organism.

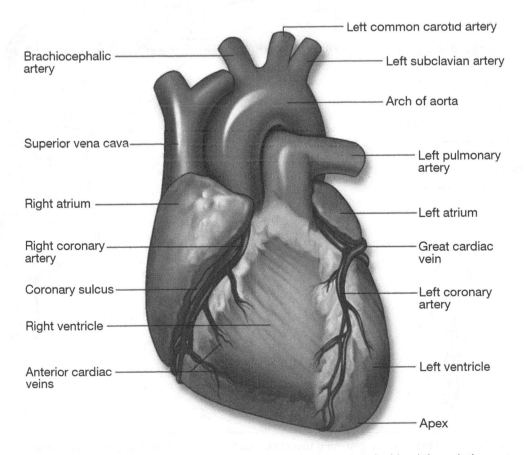

Left common carotid artery

Brachiocephalic artery

Left subclavian artery

Arch of aorta

Superior vena cava

Left pulmonary artery

Right atrium

Left atrium

Right coronary artery

Great cardiac vein

Coronary sulcus

Left coronary artery

Right ventricle

Anterior cardiac veins

Left ventricle

Apex

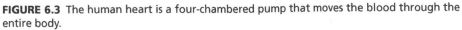

FIGURE 6.3 The human heart is a four-chambered pump that moves the blood through the entire body.

The *lungs* are paired air sacs that serve as the body's organs of respiration. Inspired air enters the lungs through the *trachea*, which divides into left and right *bronchi*. The lungs are divided into lobes (the right lung has three; the left, two) within which the bronchi branch segmentally into smaller and smaller branches known as bronchioles. *Bronchioles* end in a series of alveolar ducts and sacs, which are the sites of gas exchange between air and blood by diffusion across their thin membranes. The branching and segmentation of these functional units within the lungs provide an enormous surface area for gas exchange.

A similar exchange occurs between the blood and the body's oxygen-hungry cells, tissues, and organs. Oxygen is carried through the bloodstream in the red blood cells by a specialized protein molecule known as *hemoglobin*. Some carbon dioxide is also carried by hemoglobin back to the lungs, but most CO_2 is transported as bicarbonate ions, with a small amount carried in solution in the blood plasma. Hemoglobin is a complex protein made up of four polypeptide chains (two alpha chains and two beta chains). Each polypeptide chain in a hemoglobin molecule carries an iron-bearing heme group, which is the part of the protein that actually binds to oxygen. As a result, a single molecule of hemoglobin can carry four oxygen molecules. Since hemoglobin has the ability to

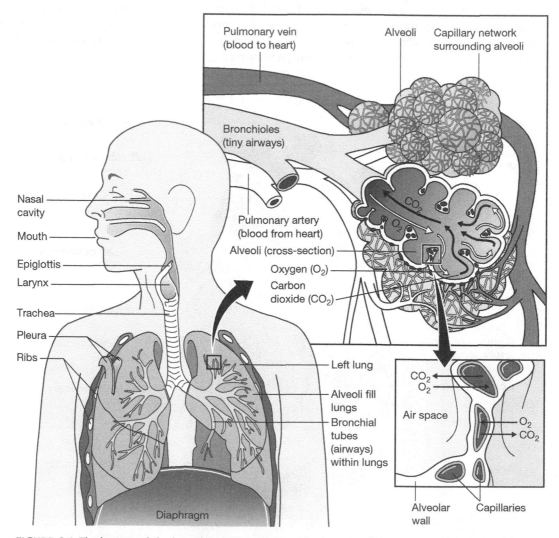

FIGURE 6.4 The lungs and the branching tubes that lead to them (trachea, bronchi, and bronchioles) make up the respiratory system, where gas exchange occurs between the blood and the air breathed in.

bind oxygen molecules in areas of high oxygen pressure and to release them in zones of low oxygen pressure, red blood cells naturally pick up oxygen in the lungs (where the air we breathe in provides high levels of oxygen) and drop them off in capillaries (where oxygen levels are low) throughout the body's tissues and cells where oxygen is used in a wide variety of cellular metabolic functions.

A series of important terms that pertain to the physiological functioning of the heart and lungs can now be defined. The work of the heart can be measured in a variety of ways. The *heart rate* is the number of heartbeats per minute. *Stroke volume* refers to the volume of blood moved by the heart through the systemic circulation with each contraction of the left ventricle. *Cardiac output* can be determined by multiplying the heart rate by the stroke volume: it refers to the volume of blood moved per minute through the systemic circulation. *Blood pressure* comprises two separate measurements of the amount of pressure within the systemic arteries. *Systolic pressure* is the peak pressure exerted by the blood on the walls of the arteries. It occurs each time the left ventricle pumps blood into the arteries and is the larger of the two numbers yielded by a blood pressure measurement. *Diastolic pressure* is a measure of blood pressure when the heart is at rest (i.e., between left ventricular beats) and is the lower of the two numbers in a typical blood pressure measurement. Like barometric pressure, blood pressure is measured in units of millimeters of mercury; normal blood pressure is generally expressed as "120 over 80" (120 millimeters of mercury systolic pressure and 80 millimeters diastolic pressure). With respect to the function of the lungs, the amount of gas exhaled in a normal breath is known as the *tidal volume*. *Forced vital capacity* refers to the amount of gas exhaled during a maximal exhalation, and the lungs' *residual volume* is the amount of gas remaining in the lungs after a maximal exhalation. The *total lung volume* can obviously be determined by summing forced vital capacity and residual volume. Finally, *respiration rate* refers to the number of breaths taken per minute.

ACCLIMATIZATION AND THE EFFECTS OF HYPOXIA

When the Spanish conquistadores confronted the Inca Empire in the highlands of 16th-century Peru, these European soldiers and adventurers first experienced the difficulties of life at high altitude and the stress of hypoxia. In 1590, a Spanish missionary named Father José de Acosta provided the first written description of what is today known as acute mountain sickness, experienced by Father Acosta himself while crossing an Andean mountain pass at an elevation of 4,800 meters. After establishing a settlement at 4,000 meters (the city of Potosí), the Spanish quickly learned to send their pregnant women (and livestock!) to the coast to give birth due to the incredibly high rates of miscarriage and infant mortality that these Spanish women were experiencing at high altitude. The fact that the fertility of highland native women was not impaired at altitude suggested to the Spaniards something that was well known to the highland Inca. The Inca understood that highland natives were already acclimatized to the rigors of life at high altitude while lowland natives (like the Spanish and natives of lowland areas of South America) were not. As a result, the Inca routinely maintained two standing armies, one of which was kept in the highlands at all times in order to ensure that the soldiers were acclimatized for fighting at altitude.

Europeans learned about the medical risks of rapidly ascending to high altitude during the 19th century in the first hot-air and hydrogen aerial balloons, and this message was later relearned by the pioneering mountaineers of the 20th century. In 1862, James Glaischer and Henry Coxwell ascended in a hydrogen balloon to an elevation of at least 8,800 meters. At this point, their barometer read 247 millimeters of mercury, and as they continued to ascend, Glaischer gradually lost all ability to function. His arms and legs became paralyzed, he could neither see nor speak, and he eventually lost consciousness. Coxwell somehow managed to release hydrogen from the balloon to enable their descent by pulling on the rope securing the valve with his teeth: his hands were effectively paralyzed. Both men survived this near-death experience and regained all their faculties as they descended to lower altitudes. By 1953, when the Sherpa guide Tenzing Norgay and New Zealand mountaineer Edmund Hillary first successfully summited Mount Everest (at 8,848 meters the highest point on earth), the importance of gradually ascending to high altitude was well understood. The expedition spent several weeks at 4,000 meters before attempting to set up high camps in preparation for the summit attempt. In spite of the fact that the climbers used bottled oxygen above 6,500 meters, the excruciating difficulties of climbing above 7,900 meters (what climbers call the "death zone") have been noted in much of the writing about this first ascent and many others. Bottled oxygen was long thought by physiologists and climbers to be absolutely essential for a successful ascent of the highest Himalayan peaks, but in 1978, this dogma was proved incorrect when Peter Habbeler and Reinhold Messner climbed to the summit of Everest without oxygen. Weakened by the lack of oxygen and the enormous exertion of reaching their final camp at 7,800 meters, it took the climbers two hours to get dressed after waking on the morning of their summit attempt! The final climb of several hundred meters to the summit had the climbers falling to their knees in the snow and gasping for breath after every couple of steps. Messner later famously described the feeling of extreme oxygen deprivation he experienced on that day as follows: "I am nothing more than a single narrow gasping lung, floating over the mists and summits"(Messner 1999:180).

High-altitude physiologists and doctors recognize three medical conditions that result from a failure to cope with the lack of oxygen at high altitude. *Acute mountain sickness* (AMS) is a common pathological response experienced by many nonacclimatized individuals during the first few days of exposure to high altitude and is often but not always the result of a too rapid ascent. The symptoms include shortness of breath, lack of appetite, nausea and vomiting, fatigue, headache, and difficulty sleeping. These symptoms can be relieved by descending to lower altitudes and by administering oxygen; they can be exacerbated by drinking alcohol and physical exertion. There is much individual variation in susceptibility to AMS, with some individuals falling victim at relatively low elevations (e.g., 1,500 to 2,000 meters) and others being immune at very high elevations (e.g., 4,000 to 4,500 meters). In general, women are less susceptible to AMS than men, but the reason for this is

BOX ONE

Athletic Competition and Training at High Altitude

The 1968 Summer Olympics in Mexico City were, for a variety of reasons, one of the most controversial games of the modern Olympics. Less than two weeks before the beginning of the competition, more than 250 university students were killed by army troops after a riot on the Mexico City campus turned violent. The 1968 Olympics were also marked by the famous "Black Power" protest salute against American racism by U.S. sprinters Tommy Smith and John Carlos during the playing of the U.S. national anthem as they received their gold and bronze medals in the 200-meter race. But the Mexico City Olympics were also controversial because they were held in a city at more than 2,300 meters (7,500 feet)—the highest elevation in Olympics history—where the reduced atmospheric pressure played a large role in the outcome of many of the events. Did the "thin air" help or hinder the performances of track and field athletes at Mexico City in 1968? An examination of the competitive results suggests that the answer to this question would have to be "It depends on the event." Record-breaking performances were turned in by the winning athletes in every men's and women's race up to 1,500 meters, suggesting that the sprinters greatly benefited from the reduced air resistance that accompanies lowered barometric pressure at high altitude. Lee Evans's gold medal performance in the 400 meters set a new world record (43.86 seconds) that would stand for 20 years, and James Hines's 100-meters world record time of 9.95 seconds would last for 15 years. The performance of sprinters did not suffer from the reduced availability of oxygen at high altitude because of the short duration of their events. In the distance events (5,000 meters, 10,000 meters, and marathon), the medal-winning times of 1968 were all significantly slower than the winning times of the several previous and succeeding Olympics. This result should not surprise anyone who has traveled from low to high altitude and gone for a long jog in the "thin air." Distance events in Olympic track and field require enormous aerobic effort for long periods of time, and this is where we would expect to see the most detrimental effects of a lack of oxygen. Perhaps the most surprising result of all was the outcome of the men's long jump competition, where the American Bob Beamon won the gold medal with an incredible jump of 8.90 meters (29 feet 2.5 inches), nearly two feet longer than the existing world record, and this new record lasted for more than two decades until Mike Powell's jump of 29 feet 4.5 inches at the World Championships in Tokyo in 1991. Like the sprinters, the long jumpers clearly benefited from the reduced wind resistance in the depleted air of Mexico City. The longevity of some of these track and field records was unprecedented and suggests the magnitude of the effect of the high-altitude conditions on the results of the Mexico City Olympics of 1968.

The results of the 1968 Olympics took many track and field athletes, fans, and commentators by surprise. Today, however, we have a much better sense of the role of altitude and atmospheric pressure in athletic performance. For many years now, world-class endurance athletes in a variety of sports have known that to compete successfully at altitude, they had to train at altitude. Today, no serious athlete would dream of running a marathon at high altitude without spending some time at altitude prior to the competition in order to become acclimatized. Many athletes have also believed for a long time that the best way to prepare for competing in endurance events at sea level is to train at altitude. The logic is that training at altitude will result in acclimatization with an increase in red blood cell and hemoglobin concentration (i.e., erythrocytosis) that will increase the athlete's oxygen transport capabilities and result in faster times in competition at any altitude. The logic of this argument seems unassailable, but recent research suggests that there is a better way for endurance athletes to train for low-altitude competitions.

The new approach is sometimes referred to as "living high and training low," and its logic is based on another well-known fact among exercise physiologists and high-altitude biologists. It is well known that humans are not able to exercise at their maximum levels in a hypoxic environment because the relative lack of oxygen limits the maximum heart rate that can be attained, even by world-class athletes. This limitation on the intensity of workouts at altitude seems to outweigh the benefits provided by erythrocytosis, yielding a net deficit for athletes who are training for distance events at low altitudes. The idea behind "living high and training low" is that an athlete can benefit from erythrocytosis by simply living and sleeping at high altitude and from workouts of maximum intensity (i.e., maximum heart rate) allowed by training at low altitude. The newest results indicate that a world-class endurance athlete can improve his or her performance by 1 or 2 percent through this kind of regime. While a 1 or 2 percent improvement may seem small or even insignificant to most amateurs, at the highest levels of Olympic competition, it can make the difference between a gold medal winner and an also-ran. "Living high and training low" thus provides the best of both worlds and seems to be the optimum training regime for endurance athletes, allowing for both erythrocytosis and maximum-intensity workouts.

---

unknown. A much more serious pathological condition resulting from a failure to cope with altitude is known as *pulmonary edema* (PE). Pulmonary edema is a condition most commonly found among acclimatized individuals (including both natives and experienced mountain climbers) who return to the highlands after stays of a week or two at lower elevations. The first signs of PE often occur in the first two to three days after return to high altitude, often associated with increased physical activity or exertion. It is again more common among males than females, in particular among young males, and most frequently occurs at elevations of 3,500 to 4,500 meters. Individuals with PE experience fluid accumulation and swelling in the alveoli of the lungs as a result of increased blood pressure in the pulmonary vessels. Gas exchange in the lungs is compromised, and the victim experiences shortness of breath and difficulty breathing. Although PE is readily treated (with oxygen, steroids, bed rest, and return to low altitude), it can be a life-threatening condition if unrecognized or untreated. Finally, *chronic mountain sickness* (CMS) is a rare pathological condition found only among fully acclimatized Andean natives who have lived at altitude for long periods without symptoms. Symptoms include cyanosis or blackening of the skin of the lips, ear lobes, and face due to lack of oxygen; fatigue; and right-ventricle hypertrophy. The physiological basis of CMS involves an exaggeration of the normally adaptive increases in *hematocrit* (red cell count) and hemoglobin levels in the blood that are found in acclimatized individuals. Increased red blood cell concentration in CMS increases the viscosity of the blood to such an extent that it cannot pass through the tiny capillaries and deliver oxygen. Individuals with CMS have lost their adaptation to high altitude, and the only successful treatment is to move to a lower altitude where, over a period of months, their symptoms will eventually disappear. The cause of this rare condition is unknown, although it again is more common among (young to middle-aged) men than women.

ADAPTIVE RESPONSES TO HYPOXIA

It is clear that life at extreme altitude poses significant difficulties for human physiology. But what are the physiological changes that occur when individuals experience hypoxia at high altitude? What exactly does hypoxia do to the human body, and how do people adapt to its demands? Much of what we know about the physiology of high-altitude adaptation comes from a series of anthropological investigations in the 1960s and 1970s of Quechua-speaking peoples living on the Andean Altiplano of Peru. Led by a Pennsylvania State University biological anthropologist named Paul Baker, these studies of Andean peoples set the modern standard for the study of high-altitude adaptation. More recent studies of Aymara speakers in Bolivia and Tibetan and Ethiopian high-altitude populations by Cynthia Beall of Case Western Reserve University, a former student of Paul Baker's, have led to a new understanding of the diverse ways in which human populations have adapted to life at high altitude.

The main difficulty for humans living at high altitude is obtaining enough oxygen for normal metabolism, for as you have seen, the amount of oxygen available (i.e., the partial pressure of oxygen) is much lower than at sea level. Each breath inhaled at altitude brings in many fewer molecules of oxygen, the exact number being a function of the altitude and barometric pressure. It should come as no surprise, then, to learn that one of the immediate responses among low-altitude natives when exposed to hypoxic environments is an increased depth of pulmonary ventilation (i.e., people breath more deeply at high altitude). This is accomplished by an increase in tidal volume of the lungs with no significant change in respiration rate. While average tidal volume at sea level is about 500 milliliters, it increases to about 700 milliliters at 4,000 meters. High altitude also affects heart rate, with an average rate of 70 beats per minute at sea level rising to an average of 105 at 4,500 meters. Blood pressure remains unchanged or can even decrease at altitude. Important changes occur in the blood at high altitude involving the red blood cells and the oxygen carrier molecule, hemoglobin. The production of red blood cells increases significantly, as does the amount of hemoglobin. The increase in red blood cells or hematocrit is coupled with a decrease in blood plasma to yield a net effect of increased viscosity of the blood, which may explain the increased resting heart rate seen at altitude. In any event, it is clear that by pumping thicker or more viscous blood, the heart muscle is under greater stress at high altitude. Another circulatory system response that occurs with exposure to high-altitude hypoxia is an increased degree of capillarization in the muscles and other tissues of the body. Many other bodily systems are negatively affected by the hypoxic conditions found at high altitude, including muscle weakness and loss of motor coordination, anorexia and weight loss, dehydration, loss of memory and cognitive function, and increased production of stress-related hormones.

What are we to make of the physiological changes associated with exposure to hypoxia? It is important to distinguish between the ill effects of oxygen insufficiency at high altitude (muscle weakness, memory loss, anorexia, etc.) and adaptive responses to this stress. Three responses in particular are considered adaptive responses to hypoxia among visitors or migrants to high altitude. These are the increased rate of pulmonary ventilation that occurs as a result of an increase in tidal volume, the increased oxygen-carrying capacity of the blood as a result of increased red blood cell count or hematocrit, and the increased degree of capillarization. These responses are considered adaptations because they increase the amount of oxygen available to the organism. Increased pulmonary ventilation increases the partial pressure of oxygen in the lungs, increased hematocrit allows the blood to carry more of this oxygen to the tissues, and increased capillarization allows greater diffusion of oxygen from the bloodstream to the body's oxygen-hungry cells. These physiological responses to the stress of hypoxia are short-term, reversible, and adaptive and thus suggest some degree of acclimatization among migrants to the highlands. However, the long list of clearly deleterious effects indicates that lowland natives routinely experience strain at high altitude, suggesting that their acclimatization is only partial. How does the response of low-altitude migrants to the highlands compare to that of high-altitude natives in South America?

ADAPTATION TO HIGH ALTITUDE IN SOUTH AMERICA

Our prediction would certainly be that highland native populations should have a more successful adaptation to hypoxia as a result of the long-term effects of natural selection experienced by these populations. We would expect to see more effective oxygen delivery to the cells and tissues, as well as fewer deleterious or pathological effects of hypoxia among native populations that have lived for long periods of time in the highlands. Let's look at some of the details of the adaptive response to the problems posed by life at high altitude found among the Quechua of Peru and the Aymara of Bolivia. In particular, we will compare the physiology of highland native populations with that of lowland migrants to the highlands. The historic pattern of migration between the coastal and interior lowlands of South America and the Andean highlands provides the physiological anthropologist with a kind of natural experiment to test hypotheses concerning evolution and adaptation to the stresses of life at high altitude.

Andean populations of Peru and Bolivia are the high-altitude groups that have been studied by anthropologists and physiologists for the longest period of time and the most thoroughly. They are typically short of stature with very large, "barrel-shaped" chests and with an extraordinary work capacity at high altitude, unlike low-altitude adult migrants to the highlands, who tend to be taller, with smaller chests and much reduced work capacities at high altitude. The large, barrel chests found among high-altitude natives of South America enclose a large pair of lungs and a heart that is heavier and differently proportioned than among lowland populations. Among highland natives, the right ventricle is larger than the left, while the "normal" condition for all other human populations is for the left ventricle to be significantly larger than the right. Since the right ventricle only pumps deoxygenated blood to the nearby lungs, it would seem to do less work than the left ventricle, which moves oxygenated blood through the entire systemic circulation. Among highland natives, the larger right ventricle is most likely an adaptive feature designed to increase oxygen transport and delivery by increasing blood pressure in the pulmonary circulation, thus leading to more efficient oxygenation of the blood in the lungs. Highland natives in South America also have significantly larger lung volumes than lowlanders or adult migrants to the highlands, as measured by forced vital capacity and total lung volume. While the heart of Andean natives is larger than that found among lowland inhabitants of South America or Europeans, highlanders attain roughly the same cardiac output (stroke volume times heart rate) in the highlands as they do at sea level. Contrast this with the fact that upon initial exposure to hypoxia, lowland migrants greatly increase both heart rate and stroke volume in order to increase oxygen delivery by increasing blood flow to the lungs and cells. Highland natives obviously solve the problems posed by hypoxia by increasing the extraction of oxygen from the blood rather than by increasing the amount of blood flow. Interestingly, blood pressure among high-altitude natives of South America is typically low, suggesting that chronic hypoxia aids in arterial vasodilation by relaxing the smooth muscle found in the walls of the arteries.

With respect to the actual composition of the blood, among high-altitude natives of the Andes we find a major increase in the proportion of red blood cells (RBCs) coupled with higher levels of hemoglobin. More RBCs and more hemoglobin allow for a greater oxygen-carrying capacity in the blood but also increase the blood's viscosity, forcing the heart to work harder to pump this denser fluid. Capillary beds, where gas exchange actually occurs in the tissues, are more extensive in highland natives, and a greater proportion of existing capillaries are open. Increased capillary beds allow for greater diffusion of oxygen and carbon dioxide across the thin capillary membranes. All of these cardiovascular and respiratory adaptations allow for an increased flow of oxygen from the lungs to the bloodstream, an efficient transport of oxygen, and a greater degree of diffusion and delivery of oxygen to the tissues of the high-latitude native. The result is the high level of work capacity that high-altitude natives are capable of sustaining. In fact, Andean populations are capable of the same level of sustained aerobic work at high altitude as lowland South Americans are capable of at sea level, in spite of the great disparity in atmospheric pressure and available oxygen. At high altitude, natives are capable of higher work capacity than even the most highly acclimatized lowland natives.

Having established that high-altitude Andean natives show a high degree of adaptation to the stresses of hypoxia, anthropologists are intensely interested in understanding the origin of these adaptations. Are they the result of genetic adaptations acquired through natural selection over the perhaps ten thousand years that South American populations have been living at high altitude? One approach to answering this question involves the study of individuals who have migrated between the lowlands and the highlands in South America. Can lowland natives migrate to the highlands as adults and through the processes of acclimatization attain the same degree and

BOX TWO

Coca and High-Altitude Life in South America

What did Sigmund Freud, Sherlock Holmes, and Tony Montana have in common? They were all enthusiastic users of cocaine, the alkaloid that comes from the coca leaf (genus *Erythroxylum*) grown in the highlands of Peru and Bolivia. And it is true that in the late 19th century, Coca-Cola really did contain trace amounts of cocaine. Archaeological evidence suggests that the coca plant was domesticated about 3,500 years ago, and during the pre-Columbian period it was an important trade item throughout South America, moving from the Andes to the Amazon and the Pacific Coast in exchange for furs, fruits, fish, and shells. Today, of course, coca continues to play an important role in the (underground) economic systems of North and South America: cocaine is the second most important Latin American export (after petroleum), and it has been estimated that drug traffickers reap annual revenues in excess of $10 billion, while Americans spend more than $30 billion per year to obtain cocaine. The role that coca plays in traditional Andean societies provides another case study for the value of a biocultural approach in anthropology.

Among the indigenous high-altitude dwellers of the Andes Mountains in Peru, Bolivia, and Ecuador, the traditional use of coca is an important part of daily life. Coca is extracted from the leaves of the coca plant, which are either steeped in a hot, tealike drink known as *maté de coca* or chewed in a wad mixed with chalk or ash by many millions of people daily. When visitors arrive by airplane in high-altitude South American cities such as Lima, Peru; Quito, Ecuador; or La Paz, Bolivia, they are often greeted at their hotels with a (perfectly legal) hot cup of *maté de coca*, which often helps the visitor cope with some of the discomfort associated with hypoxia, including headaches, fatigue, and shortness of breath. Local farmers and mine workers claim that chewing coca leaves helps them work hard and stay warm in the very difficult conditions that they work in at high altitude. And there is good evidence that chewing coca acts as a mild stimulant and peripheral vasoconstrictor, as well as some indication that it may suppress hunger, pain, and fatigue.

The variety of ways in which highland South Americans have used coca leaves is wonderfully diverse: as an anesthetic for childbirth, broken bones, and headaches; to stop nosebleeds; to treat sicknesses including malaria, asthma, and ulcers; as a digestive aid; and even as an aphrodisiac. Coca has also played a large role in the traditional religious worldviews of the indigenous people of the highlands, perhaps for thousands of years. Today, chewing coca is a symbol of the cultural and religious identity of the Quechua speakers of Peru and the Aymara speakers of Bolivia, who make up the great majority of coca chewers in the Andes. Urban, nonnative dwellers of the Andean highlands tend to take their daily coca in the form of *maté*.

kind of adaptive response to hypoxia as highland natives? If they could, this would suggest the absence of any genetic adaptation to high altitude among natives. If, on the other hand, lowlanders were never able to achieve the level of adaptation to hypoxia attained by highlanders regardless of how long they were to live at altitude, this would support the presence of a genetic adaptation to high altitude among highland natives. Interestingly, the data support neither of these scenarios. Instead, it seems that lowland natives who migrate to the highlands at very young ages and who spend their entire childhood at high altitude tend to exhibit the same adaptations to hypoxia as high-altitude natives (larger chest and lung volumes, higher hematocrit, denser capillary beds, etc.). This situation, in which the adaptive traits are attained as a result of exposure to the stress during growth and development, has been termed *developmental acclimatization*. Although the presence of genetic adaptations to hypoxia among high-altitude natives in South America should not be completely discounted, there is little solid evidence in support of it at this time.

DIVERSE ADAPTATIONS TO LIFE AT HIGH ALTITUDE

Several decades ago, biological anthropologists thought that the pattern of high-altitude adaptation found among the Quechua- and Aymara-speaking peoples of highland South America and European "sojourners" at high altitude was the whole story. Research over the past few decades, however, has shown that human adaptations to hypoxia are actually more diverse and much more interesting than the early work on "Andean man" had indicated. We owe much of our current understanding of the diversity of responses of different human populations to the physiological stresses of life at high altitude to the work of Cynthia Beall of Case Western Reserve University and her colleagues. Beall has studied physiological responses to hypoxia among the non-Quechua-speaking high-altitude population of the Andean Altiplano, the Aymara-speaking peoples of Bolivia. Most significantly, her team has also investigated high-altitude populations in Ethiopia and in Tibet and determined that the South American pattern of physiological adaptation is not universal among modern human populations residing at high altitude. In fact, her work demonstrates the existence of different patterns of physiological adaptation to the stresses of life at high altitude in the three locations (South America, Asia, and Africa) where the majority of the world's high-altitude native populations reside. In the comparison of physiological adaptations to hypoxia among these populations, we have a natural experiment that can elucidate the workings of natural selection and perhaps tell us something about one of the mechanism through which evolution has created physiological diversity in human populations.

The first inklings of the diversity in human response to hypoxic stress came with the early studies of the cardiovascular physiology of Sherpas living at high altitude in the Tibet Autonomous Region of China in the 1970s. Four features related to oxygen transport by the cardiovascular system were considered essential components of the "Andean man" model of adaptation to life at high altitude, but in each of these traits, the Tibetans differed from the Andeans. The four features are hemoglobin concentration in the blood, oxygen saturation of arterial hemoglobin, resting ventilation, and hypoxic ventilatory response. We will examine the new light that Beall's work has thrown on each of these characteristics of high-altitude adaptation in that order, and in so doing, we will reveal the surprising diversity in human adaptation to life at high altitude.

The first two traits on our list are aspects of oxygen transport in the blood. For example, the Andean pattern included a marked increase in the number of red blood cells as measured by the concentration of hemoglobin in the blood over the levels typically found among sea level inhabitants. Increased *hemoglobin concentration* was considered an adaptive response because it also occurs among low-altitude natives who visit the highlands and because it would increase the amount of oxygen carried by the blood, since hemoglobin is the actual carrier of molecular oxygen in the bloodstream. But in Tibet, populations living at around 4,000 meters have barely higher hemoglobin concentrations than U.S. sea level populations. Even the Tibetan residents of the Phala District, at

4,850 to 5450 meters (15,912 to 17,881 feet) the highest human settlement in the world, have significantly lower hemoglobin concentrations than Aymara living at a mere 4,000 meters (13,123 feet) in Bolivia. Not only do Tibetans have lower hemoglobin levels than Aymara, but they also have lower levels of *oxygen saturation of the hemoglobin* in their arteries. As atmospheric pressure and oxygen availability decrease with higher altitude, the proportion of hemoglobin molecules that bind oxygen in the arterial blood also decreases. The resulting lowered oxygen saturation in arterial blood is known as *arterial hypoxemia*. Although hypoxemia is found in both Aymara and Tibetans, the Tibetans have significantly lower oxygen saturation levels than Aymara living at similar elevations. Both of these traits suggest that Tibetans are doing something different from what the Bolivians are doing with respect to the work of transporting oxygen that hemoglobin performs in the blood.

The second pair of features on our list pertain to differences in the ventilation of the lungs in response to hypoxic stress among Tibetans and Aymara. *Resting ventilation* is a measure of how much air is moved into and out of the lungs every minute while the subject is sitting comfortably at rest. Among Tibetans, resting ventilation is 40 to 70 percent higher than among Aymara. This results mainly from larger tidal volumes rather than higher breathing rates among Tibetans. *Hypoxic ventilatory response* (HVR) is a measure of the increase in ventilation that typically occurs with increased hypoxic stress. It is measured experimentally by having subjects rebreathe their own exhaled air. A large HVR is a typical response of low-altitude natives to exposure to high altitude, but among Andean high-altitude natives, the HVR is very slight. Among Tibetans, HVR is on average twice as large as among Aymara.

This discussion highlights the extremely different ways in which Asian and South American populations have adapted to the stress of life at high altitude. The Andean approach relies on hematological (i.e., blood-related) changes and adaptations, mainly involving increased red blood cells counts or *erythrocytosis* and associated increased levels of hemoglobin. The Tibetan approach favors pulmonary (i.e., lung-related) adaptations, which serve to increase the ventilation of the lungs. While both Andeans and Tibetans suffer from arterial hypoxemia (lower oxygen levels in the arterial blood), Andeans are able to maintain higher levels of oxygen saturation (i.e., they suffer less from arterial hypoxemia).

The third major high-altitude population and currently the least well studied lives in the Ethiopian highlands of East Africa. Since the mid-1990s, Beall's group has been studying a high-altitude Ethiopian population living at 3,530 meters on the Semien Plateau of northern Ethiopia and discovering a third pattern of adaptation to life at high altitude. Although the full details of the physiological response of Ethiopians to hypoxia are not yet available, what Beall has discovered is that they are able to maintain essentially sea level values for oxygen saturation of arterial blood with no more hemoglobin than one finds in sea level populations. Thus Ethiopians living at an elevation of 3,500 meters do not respond to hypoxia with erythrocytosis, and they do not suffer from arterial hypoxemia. Whether they manage this balancing act through adaptive responses in hematology, pulmonary ventilation, modifications in the functional characteristics of their hemoglobin, or some other method is presently unknown but under active investigation by Beall's research team. An intriguing new result from Beall's research suggests that the production of nitric oxide (NO) in the lungs may be a part of the adaptive response of both Tibetans and Aymara to regulating pulmonary circulation of blood by dilating the pulmonary vessels. NO production has not yet been investigated among Ethiopians. Even without knowing the detailed physiology of adaptation to hypoxic stress among Ethiopians, we can state with certainty that three very different solutions have independently evolved among far-flung human populations that have lived at high altitude for millennia. This variation demonstrates the opportunistic nature of evolution and highlights the polytypic variation that is such an important feature of the biology of *Homo sapiens*.

Discussion Questions

1. Describe the variety of stresses that make life difficult for humans living at high altitude (above 3,000 meters).

2. Using the anthropological studies of South American lowland and highland natives, describe what is meant by "developmental acclimatization."

3. Why do you think the U.S. Olympic training facility for track and field athletes is located in Colorado Springs, Colorado?

4. Describe the pattern of adaptation to life at high altitude that is demonstrated among natives of the Andean highlands.

5. What are the major differences between the Andean and Himalayan patterns of adaptation to hypoxic stress?

6. During their nearly fatal hydrogen balloon trip of 1862, James Glaischer and Henry Coxwell experienced (and survived!) a barometric pressure of 247 millimeters of mercury at an elevation of 8,800 meters. Can you calculate the partial pressure of oxygen at this elevation? Remember that oxygen makes up 21 percent of atmospheric air.

7. Describe the history and the reasoning behind using millimeters of mercury as the units of barometric pressure.

8. What are the various kinds of high-altitude illnesses that mountain climbers must be aware of? Describe the symptoms and treatments for each.

9. Explain the physiological role played by each of the following parts of the human cardiovascular system in life at high altitude: heart, lungs, veins, arteries and capillaries, hemoglobin, bronchioles, oxygen, and carbon dioxide.

CHAPTER 7

A Biocultural Examination of Nutrition, Health, and Growth

"Tell me what you eat, and I will tell you what you are."

ANTHELME BRILLAT-SAVARIN, *THE PHYSIOLOGY OF TASTE*, 1825

INTRODUCTION

One of the dimensions of culture that affects human biological diversity in a number of important ways is nutrition. Because we truly are what we eat, it makes sense that differences in nutrition between peoples or populations can have an important impact on biological differences between them. Another fertile field for the study of biocultural evolution is the study of human health and illness in different cultures and parts of the world. In particular, looking at the intersections between genetic and infectious diseases in certain populations will allow us to critically consider the notion of "racial illness." Finally, a consideration of growth and development will provide insight into the proximate mechanisms whereby human diversity in form or morphology is developed.

In light of the facts that food choice and food preparation are clearly within the realm of culture and that nutrition directly influences biology through its effects on human health and growth, these topics provide excellent material for the biocultural anthropologist. Topics in nutritional anthropology can have major implications for the study of human growth, development, health, and sickness and can help explain many of the biological differences between human populations. To explore the role nutrition plays in biological differences among humans today, let's begin by considering the evolution of the human diet from our earliest hunting-and gathering ancestors to the modern diet of processed fast food that has come to dominate the Western world and increasingly, for better or worse, the rest of the planet.

THE HUMAN DIET BEFORE AND AFTER THE AGRICULTURAL REVOLUTION

The starting point for any discussion of the historical and evolutionary changes to the human diet must be the realization that during the overwhelming majority of the perhaps 200 thousand years that *Homo sapiens* has existed, we have been foragers who hunted game and gathered wild plant foods. As a result of this long history, our digestive tract and physiology are the products of evolutionary adaptation to a diet with perhaps 30 to 50 percent meat, 50 to 70 percent plant foods, and no dairy products or cereal grains. In addition, the foraging or hunting-and-gathering lifestyle involves far higher daily activity levels than even the hardest-working laborer today. Both hunters (usually males) and food gatherers (typically females and children) routinely travel many miles each day in pursuit of food, often burdened by heavy loads of food and children (Eaton et al. 1988). Not only are this diet and this way of life very different from the actual diets and sedentary lifestyles of most Americans today, it is also quite different from the dietary recommendations of most government agencies and medical authorities. For example, the dietary pyramid advocated by the U.S. Department of Agriculture in 2005 includes fruits, vegetables, meat and beans, milk, and grains in varying amounts depending on one's age, sex, and activity level. When did human diets begin to change from the ancient foraging pattern that we are adapted to, and what have been some of the consequences of these changes for human morbidity (sickness) and mortality? Furthermore, what role do diet and nutrition play in the growth and development of humans, and how can the study of human nutrition contribute to our understanding of human diversity in body size and other aspects of morphological differences between human populations?

Many archaeologists consider the beginnings of agriculture and animal domestication among the most revolutionary innovations in human prehistory. One could certainly argue that in many ways, it was agriculture that fashioned the modern world. Without agriculture, we would have no cities, little or no craft specialization or division of labor, no organized religion or political hierarchies, and far fewer people alive in the world today. But like most revolutions in human history, the *Agricultural* or *Neolithic Revolution* had a series of crucial impacts and consequences that could not have been predicted. Without the Agricultural Revolution and all that has followed it, we would not die in such great numbers from cardiovascular disease or cancer, infectious disease would be a much reduced cause of human sickness and death, and childhood malnutrition would be almost nonexistent. Although many things of great value have resulted from the shift to agriculture as the primary means of human subsistence, much has also been lost (Cohen and Armelagos 1984).

BOX ONE
The Agricultural Revolution

From the beginnings of human evolution in the distant past to about 10 or 11 thousand years ago, all human subsistence was based on foraging for and collecting wild plant and animal foods. During these long ages, human populations were small and nomadic, cultural and social complexity was minimal, and people routinely carried all their possessions with them as they periodically moved their simple villages in search of sustenance. With the beginnings of plant and animal domestication, the era of food production ushered in a revolution in human biology and culture whose effects have been enormous even to this very day. Known as the Agricultural or Neolithic Revolution (or the New Stone Age), the beginnings of food production changed human life forever, and as detailed in the text, not always for the better.

The earliest evidence for the origins of agriculture and animal domestication can be found in Southwest Asia, in the area known as the Fertile Crescent, extending from the Nile River valley of Egypt northward along the Mediterranean coast (through modern Israel, Jordan, Lebanon, and Syria) to Turkey and then south through Iraq and Iran to the Persian Gulf. Wheat, chickpeas, and olives were some of the important plants first domesticated in the Fertile Crescent more than 10,500 years ago. These plant domesticates were followed shortly (around 500 years later) by the domestication of goats and sheep, and from Southwest Asia the notion of plant and animal domestication spread throughout much of Eurasia and Africa. Agriculture arose independently in at least four other places after it first appeared in

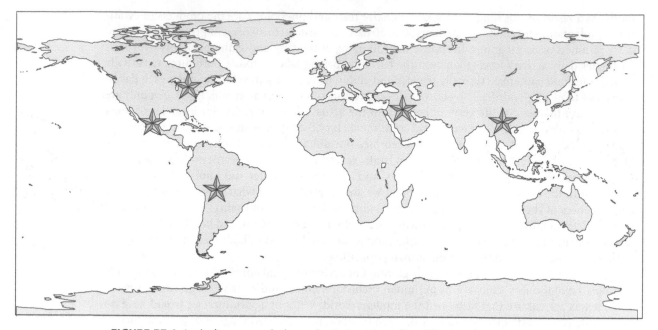

FIGURE B7.1 Agriculture arose independently in at least five different places: Mesopotamia, China, South America, Mexico, and eastern North America. From these beginnings, agriculture spread throughout the world.

Southwest Asia, including China (rice, millet, pigs, and silkworms by 7500 B.C.E.), Mexico and Central America (corn, beans, squash, and turkeys by 3500 B.C.E.), the Andes of South America and the Amazon (potatoes, manioc, llamas, and guinea pigs by 3500 B.C.E.), and eastern North America (sunflowers and goosefoot by 2500 B.C.E.). Archaeologists still debate whether agriculture also arose independently in several other places, including Ethiopia (coffee and teff), the Sahel of northern Africa (sorghum and rice), tropical West Africa (yams and oil palms), and New Guinea (sugarcane and bananas).

In addition to new subsistence techniques and kinds of foods, the Agricultural Revolution replaced nomadism with sedentism, villages with towns and cities, and patterns of social and economic equality with rampant inequality. Many of the problems discussed in this chapter concerning human health, nutrition, and patterns of morbidity and mortality in the modern developing world can trace their beginnings to the changes wrought by the Agricultural Revolution. The synergy between poverty, disease, and malnutrition is ancient, with its roots in the early agricultural towns and cities of the Fertile Crescent in the first millennia after the beginning of agriculture. These early farming populations already show distinct economic differences between the poor and poorly nourished masses and the elite members of society. Health and longevity among poor farmers was already beginning to suffer as a result of the nutritional deficiencies associated with nearly complete reliance on single crops (wheat in the Fertile Crescent), as well as the infectious diseases to which these city dwellers were now exposed. Both of these conditions are reflected in the lesions found on the skeletons and teeth of early farmers. It seems that wherever and whenever agriculture was developed or spread, the same ill health effects have been noted by skeletal biologists, making a strong case for the argument that the Agricultural Revolution was at best a mixed blessing for human populations.

Human populations first began the gradual shift from a foraging to an agricultural way of life at different times in different parts of the ancient world. Agriculture developed independently in at least five different places at five different times and spread from these areas to most of the rest of the world. The spread of agriculture eventually relegated foragers to the most marginal of habitats or to extinction. Foragers simply could not compete with agriculturalists for a number of reasons.

Agriculture allows for the creation of food surpluses, thus allowing for population increases far beyond the numbers that can be sustained in foraging groups. Settled agriculturalist villages become cities as population size and density increase. Food surpluses lead to a division of labor along narrower lines and to a far greater extent than among forager societies, where the division of labor is based almost exclusively on sex and age. The availability of food surpluses allows agricultural societies to support warriors, priests, government bureaucrats, artists, and many other kinds of specialists. Whereas foraging societies tend to be remarkably egalitarian, social and economic inequality generally appear for the first time among agricultural societies. Political power and wealth become concentrated in the hands of the elite few, while the masses exist in poverty. We can see the results of this process, and in particular the effects of the Agricultural Revolution on human health, in greater detail by examining the work of archaeologists and biological anthropologists at a series of thousand-year-old burial mounds in Illinois known as Dickson Mounds. The significance of the Dickson Mounds site is that it documents the transition from a nomadic, hunting-and-gathering way of life to a settled village life based on intensive maize agriculture that archaeologists call the *Mississippian tradition*. Since they were first excavated in the 1920s, more than one thousand skeletons have been excavated from these mounds and from neighboring pre-Mississippian sites, and their analysis has yielded some very surprising conclusions about the health effects of an intensive agricultural way of life (Harn 1980).

What do the skeletons from Dickson Mounds tell us about the health and manner of death of these early settled agriculturalists of the Mississippian tradition in central Illinois? Skeletal biologists can identify a number of health indicators from their analyses of the skeleton, including the presence and frequency of bony lesions resulting from infections or nutritional deficiencies, degenerative changes to joint surfaces, traumatic injuries to the skeleton, dental developmental defects due to nutritional or medical stresses suffered during childhood, stature, and age at death. By essentially all of these measures, the bulk of the Mississippian population seemed to suffer from poorer health than their foraging ancestors (Goodman and Armelagos 1985). The agriculturalists had more numerous and more serious bony lesions resulting from bacterial infections, most frequently occurring on the tibia (shinbone). They also had more frequent examples of skull lesions known as porotic hyperostoses due to anemia resulting from a diet deficient in iron, owing to a lack of meat in the diet. Mississippian agriculturalists lived a harder and often more violent life than their foraging predecessors, as judged from the greater incidence of arthritic degeneration of their joints and healed fractures of their bones. Finally, a higher frequency of developmental defects in the tooth enamel known as dental enamel hypoplasias, shorter stature as children and as adults, and earlier age at death and lower life expectancy round out a picture of significant decreases in health and longevity accompanying the transition from foraging to the intensive agricultural way of life of the early Mississippian people of the Illinois River valley.

What can explain the overwhelming evidence that the Agricultural Revolution was a disaster from the perspective of the health and well-being of our species? Theory suggests that although agriculture can produce the kinds of surpluses that allow for population increase, craft specialization, and the development of political and economic elites, serious nutritional problems can occur when populations subsist largely on a single crop. These problems often result from the inherent nutritional limitations of individual plants. For example, maize is deficient in lysine, one of the eight essential amino acids that are not synthesized by humans and must therefore be ingested to allow for normal protein synthesis. Similarly, a near-complete reliance on wheat, manioc, or any other domesticated plant can also lead to nutritional deficiencies, some of which will leave their mark on the skeleton in the guise of a lesion or scar (e.g., porotic hyperostosis as a mark of iron deficiency). Poor nutrition during infancy and childhood are known to lead to the formation of dental enamel hypoplasias and to shorter stature than might be attained with a better diet. All of these growth problems related to poor nutrition can be exacerbated if the individual is coping with illness, and we know that many forms of infectious disease were more prevalent in settled agricultural villages and early cities than in small nomadic villages. Many infectious agents require a large pool of available hosts, so they spread more successfully in the more densely populated settlements that agriculture made possible. City-dwelling populations also have to deal with issues of sanitation, waste disposal, and access to clean water that, if not handled properly, can lead to the spread of infectious diseases. For all these reasons, we can see that living in settled agricultural villages had substantial negative effects on human health and longevity. Early farmers and villagers in Mississippian Illinois died shorter and younger after having endured far more numerous bouts of sickness and episodes of malnutrition than their healthy and long-lived hunting-and-gathering ancestors.

NUTRITION AND MALNUTRITION AMONG MODERN POPULATIONS

The nutritional requirements of modern people are an indication of the nutritional intake necessary for maintaining basic bodily functions and providing sufficient energy for daily activities. One can distinguish between calorie or energy requirements and the need for sufficient quantities of essential nutrients such as minerals, vitamins, protein, carbohydrates, and fat. Although *malnutrition* has historically referred to insufficiencies in the intake of either energy or specific nutrients, the term today can also refer to overnutrition, the intake of calories in excess of daily nutritional requirements, resulting in the storage of excess calories as fat deposits and, in extreme cases, obesity. No single value expresses the exact nutritional requirements of all humans: individual nutritional requirements vary widely, and all general statements concerning "recommended daily allowances" of nutrients or calories are based on population *averages*. The nutritional requirements of any given individual can vary throughout the person's lifetime, being greater during periods of rapid growth (infancy and adolescence), lower in adults and seniors, and extremely high during metabolically costly activities such as pregnancy, lactation, or training to run a marathon. Malnutrition is a problem of enormous magnitude to human health and well-being, as well as an issue of increasing importance to national development and economic productivity throughout the developing world. In spite of the declaration by the World Health Organization (2000) that proper nutrition should be considered a fundamental human right, malnutrition affects 800 million people worldwide, including approximately 20 percent of the population of the developing world.

Micronutrient deficiencies are deficiencies in vitamins, minerals, and other substances that make up a tiny proportion of our total dietary intake but play critical roles in human well-being, good health, and proper development. *Iron deficiency* and the resulting clinical condition known as *anemia* is the most common nutritional disorder in the world. The number of people, most of them in the developing world, who are affected is absolutely staggering: four to five billion people suffer from iron deficiency (66 to 80 percent of the world's total population); more than two billion of them have developed full-blown anemia (30 percent of the world's population). Ninety percent of anemia sufferers live in the Third World, where, on average, half of all pregnant women and four out often preschool children suffer from anemia. The results of all this sickness include low birthweight and elevated death rates among infants and impaired physical and cognitive development among children. For adults with anemia, one of the major consequences is extreme fatigue and muscular weakness resulting in a greatly reduced capacity to perform work. The economic effects of anemia in missed days of work and lowered economic productivity may approach 20 percent on a worldwide basis, equating to many billions of dollars lost per year. And as is true for all of these forms of malnutrition, the burden of iron deficiency and anemia falls most heavily on the sickest and poorest among us, especially in the developing world (World Health Organization 2000).

Iodine deficiency disorder (IDD) is the major cause of brain damage and reduced mental functioning in the world today, and it is also the most easily preventable of the deficiency diseases. It affects nearly 750 million people, approximately 13 percent of the world's population, and like iron deficiency and anemia, it strikes mainly the poor and the young in the developing world. The effects of IDD are passed on from generation to generation as poor, pregnant women with the disorder give birth to babies with an irreversible form of serious mental retardation known as *cretinism*. Children and adults who suffer from less serious conditions of IDD have reduced IQs of 15 points on average, resulting in significant mental impairment throughout their lives. Iodine deficiencies have been greatly reduced in much of the world as a result of the production—at an incredibly inexpensive 5 cents per person per year—of iodized salt. If the current Universal Salt Iodization program that has been in effect since 1993 can completely rid the world of IDD, it will be hailed as "one of the greatest public health triumphs of the coming decades" (World Health Organization 2000:7).

The third micronutrient deficiency with major worldwide medical and economic effects is *vitamin A deficiency* (VAD). As the leading cause of preventable blindness in children, VAD affects over 100 million children, with more than half a million losing their sight every year. It also contributes to the substantial risks concerning the health of pregnant women in the developing world, for of the perhaps 600 thousand women who die of childbirth-related causes each year, the great majority are poor and poorly nourished.

Although deficiencies in any essential nutrient can cause illness, we will focus on the two most important childhood nutritional disorders worldwide and their ramifications for childhood growth and development and human differences. These two conditions, marasmus and kwashiorkor, are parts of a larger syndrome known as *protein-energy malnutrition* (PEM) that constitutes the most serious and deadly form of malnutrition, according to the World Health Organization (WHO). In its 2000 report titled *Turning the Tide of Malnutrition*, the WHO presents some sobering estimates of the challenges presented by PEM. It is estimated to affect one-fourth of all the children in the world and to play a role in more than half of the 10.4 million premature deaths of children younger than 6 years of age in the developing world each year. The WHO estimates that 150 million children

FIGURE 7.1 A child suffering from kwashiorkor in southern Ethiopia, and a malnourished child suffering from marasmus in Niger. a) © Christine Osborne Pictures / Alamy b) Courtesy of Daniel Berehulak/Getty Images

worldwide are underweight and another 182 million experience stunted growth as a result of differing degrees of PEM. *Marasmus* is a serious nutritional disorder involving insufficient intake of protein and calories. It occurs most commonly during early childhood and results in significant weight loss as subcutaneous fat and muscle are metabolized to provide enough energy to sustain life. Children who suffer from marasmus experience greatly reduced rates of growth and many never again approach age-appropriate growth standards. Lethargy and other behavioral changes are common as sufferers greatly reduce their energy expenditure in the face of insufficient nutritional energy (i.e., calories). *Kwashiorkor* refers to the malnourished condition of protein deficiency resulting from a high-carbohydrate diet with insufficient protein. Unlike in marasmus, individuals suffering from kwashiorkor have enough calories in their diet: they simply lack sufficient protein. Children are most susceptible to kwashiorkor during periods of rapid growth, and it is a common illness among recently weaned children. Affected children can be extremely emaciated yet have swollen abdomens: they experience stunted growth, edema (swelling) due to water retention, peeling and spotting of the skin, and decreased muscle mass. They also tend to be irritable, lethargic, and apathetic, with little energy for physical activities.

What causes malnutrition is a more complex question than one might think. Obviously, access to insufficient food is at the heart of it, but social and political factors are often critical. Famines frequently occur even in fertile countries with high agricultural productivity where more than enough food to feed the people is produced. They result when social unrest, civic disorder, or warfare leads to a diminished availability or distribution of food among certain segments of a society, typically its poorest members. Ultimately, poverty and inequality are the primary causes of malnutrition among the children of the world. Due to their elevated nutritional requirements during growth, their lack of autonomy, and their dependence on adults, children and adolescents are at much higher risk of malnutrition than adults under conditions of scarcity and inequality. Pregnant women also have extremely high nutritional requirements because they have to eat not only for themselves but also for the small but rapidly growing fetus. Children in agricultural societies who have been recently weaned are often the victims of malnutrition due to a lack of access to nutritious food items to replace mother's milk. Kwashiorkor is very common among these children as a result of their being fed starchy but protein-deficient weaning foods.

The effects of malnutrition on children can be greatly exacerbated by the presence of chronic diseases and gastrointestinal infections. Illness leads to poor digestion and absorption of food, reduced food intake, and diarrhea, and all these factors limit one's ability to gain nourishment. One can think of malnutrition and illness as a synergistic pair in which each magnifies the impact of the other and the effects of both are magnified by poverty. Malnourished kids are more likely to get sick, and sick kids are more likely to become malnourished—and these conditions strike overwhelmingly at the children of the poor. The combined effects of poverty, sickness, and malnourishment add up to a great burden on childhood health and growth throughout the world, especially the undeveloped world. But getting back to the issue of differences between human populations and human adaptation, how is malnutrition relevant to our biocultural critique of race and human biological difference?

MALNUTRITION AND HUMAN GROWTH AND DEVELOPMENT

As a result of the close connection between nutrition and growth and development in human populations, one of the standard benchmarks that anthropologists use to determine the overall health status of a population is the average height of its members. The idea is that individuals in poorly nourished populations or those with a large burden of infectious disease will grow at a slower rate and less than individuals in better-nourished and healthier populations. You have already seen numerous examples of the connections between nutrition, illness, and human development in this chapter. To understand more directly the role that malnutrition plays in human development and in the generation of human diversity, we will need to explore a number of important concepts and ideas from the realms of evolution and adaptation. The first of these is *phenotypic plasticity*. This notion holds that most phenotypic traits are not fixed and determined by genes alone but rather that many aspects of our adult morphology can be molded or changed to varying degrees by the kinds of environmental conditions under which we grow up. We can think of phenotypic plasticity as a reaction to the notion that our biological or genetic heritage fully determines our phenotype. This is really one aspect of the age-old *nature–nurture controversy* about which scientists have been arguing for years. Supporters of the primacy of our biological *nature* in determining who we are can be called *biological determinists*, and their position is that we are who we are because of the genes we inherited from our parents. Biological determinists minimize or ignore the importance of our *nurture* or upbringing—the environment in which we develop—in influencing the adults that we become. Most biological anthropologists today consider themselves *interactionists* with respect to these issues because they recognize that biological nature (our genetic and biological heritage) and social nurture (the social environment in which we develop) interact during the development of many or most of our morphological, behavioral, and psychological traits. In this approach, neither nature nor nurture fully determines who we are or what we become. Rather, our adult phenotypes and personalities are influenced by the interaction of our genes and our environments during the entire period of growth and development.

Some examples may help clarify these theoretical positions. Think of genes as providing a certain potential for the development of a trait such as adult stature, while the environment during growth and development influences how close to the full potential any individual will develop for that given trait. For example, the children of tall parents may have the genetic potential to be quite tall themselves, but if they are severely malnourished or sickly during childhood, their adult stature may be quite a bit shorter than one might have predicted based on their genetics alone. The combination of good genetics and good environment would certainly lead to taller adult stature in these children, allowing them to perhaps reach their full genetic potential. This interaction of genes and environment seems to be the norm for many, but perhaps not all, aspects of human development and adult phenotype. An example of a phenotypic trait with little or no apparent plasticity resulting from postnatal environment is the ABO blood group. There is no evidence that growing up rich or poor, well or poorly nourished, or healthy or sickly has any effect on one's blood type: if one inherits an A and a B allele, one will have blood type AB, regardless of the nature of the environment during growth and development. By contrast, adult stature is an extremely plastic trait that is strongly affected by a variety of pre- and postnatal environmental influences, beginning with the mother's state of nutrition and health during pregnancy and continuing throughout the entire period of growth and development of the child. Adequate nutrition, clean water, freedom from infectious disease, and generally good environmental conditions will allow the child to develop to his or her full genetic growth potential. Periods of childhood malnutrition, infectious disease, and generally poor environmental conditions will lead to stunted growth, skeletal lesions, dental developmental defects, and sometimes premature death.

So in light of the concept of phenotypic plasticity, how can we tell if a population that is relatively short has experienced nutritional stress, perhaps in combination with frequent bouts of infectious disease and other poor environmental conditions, or if it is short for purely genetic reasons? If both genes and environment influence our stature and body type, how can we tease apart these influences to determine their relative importance in any particular population? A series of studies by the biological anthropologist Barry Bogin (1999) provides an example. Bogin's studies of growth and development among children of relatively wealthy Guatemalans known as Ladinos, of mixed European and native ancestry, and among a Mayan population from the same country indicates that the Mayans are relatively stunted in growth. Adult male Ladinos are on average 176.9 centimeters tall, compared to adult male Mayans, who average 162.9 centimeters. A similar difference can be found among the adult women of these two communities: female Ladinos average 169.15 centimeters in height, while female Mayans average 151.8 centimeters. The Ladinos in this study were typically middle-class or higher in economic status, generally well nourished, and relatively free of gastrointestinal and respiratory infections. The Mayans were quite poor, were generally malnourished, and frequently suffered from infectious diseases. While it may be tempting to some to argue that the Ladinos are taller than the Mayans because of genetic differences related to their European ancestry, there is little biological evidence in support of this hypothesis. Seeing that the growth-stunting effects of poverty, disease, and malnutrition are well known, it seems likely that the differences in stature are the result of the stark differences in the environments to which Ladino and Mayan children are exposed during childhood. So although genetic differences between the two populations may play a role in the height differences, the burden of proof must be placed on those who would support the biological argument of genetic difference.

Another approach to this problem might involve the study of growth and development in the context of migrant populations. This research design involves studying a poorly nourished population in its original environment and then studying migrants from the original population who have moved to a new and improved environment. Barry Bogin has performed just this kind of study, investigating the growth and development of Mayans in their native Guatemala and after migrating to Los Angeles and to Florida (Bogin and Loucky 1997). In San Pedro, Guatemala, the local Mayans are quite poor, have little or no access to clean drinking water, suffer from serious parasitic infestations and infectious diseases, and have a diet of mostly maize tortillas with little meat or other sources of protein. They average 7.6 cm shorter than the richer, better-fed, and healthier Ladino inhabitants of San Pedro. Bogin's work showed that the first generation of Mayan migrants to the United States averaged 5.6 centimeters taller than their parents and relatives in Guatemala. This is a clear example of phenotypic plasticity in which a changed environment leads to significant change in a phenotypic trait between generations, and it lends further support to the environmental hypothesis for the difference in height between Mayan and Ladino populations in Guatemala. Furthermore, the increased height seen in Mayans living in the United States strongly suggests that the short height of Mayans living in Guatemala is, to a large extent, the result of a poor environment and not due to genetic deficiencies or differences.

A particularly informative type of plasticity involves change in some phenotypic trait in a population from one generation to the next and is known as *secular trend*. Secular trends result from changes to the environment that affect the expression of plastic developmental traits, such as the attainment of adult stature, the timing of the onset of adolescence, and the age at completion of growth in height. Most examples of secular trend are thought to be the result of improved conditions of life, including better nutrition and improved access to health care, that allow individuals and populations to more closely attain their genetic potential.

Secular trend in stature has been documented in many different countries over the past century, and in most cases, it seems to be associated with improvements in nutrition, medical care, and other aspects of a healthy environment for raising children. One of the most striking examples of secular tend in height can be found in Japan since the end of World War II. Whereas adult Japanese males averaged 150 centimeters in height in 1950, by 1995, the average height of a Japanese male was 172 centimeters! The rate of increase in height documented in Japan was 4 centimeters per decade in the 1950s but has recently slowed to about 1 centimeter per decade. A similar trend can be found in most European countries and the United States: rates of secular increase in height have recently slowed down from their faster earlier rates. This change can be explained by improvements to the environment of development for children in the industrialized world early in the 20th century and the fact that middle- and upper-class Americans and Europeans probably raise their children today in near-optimal environments, which allows these children to come close to reaching their genetic potential. The main place where secular trend in height continues today is the Third World, where much improvement remains to be made in the environments in which children are raised.

We can conclude that the differences in stature between different races or ethnicities are the result of a combination of genetic and environmental differences, with nutrition, poverty, and infectious diseases being critical environmental factors that can have a strong positive or negative effect on stature. If a significant part of the differences in stature between populations were the result of environmental influences, stature would seem to be a poor benchmark for any biological theory of race or racial classification. Furthermore, seeing that secular trend seems to be a general phenomenon found in many populations and linked to modernization and the associated changes in diet, access to clean water, and better medical care that often accompany life in much of the modern industrialized world, one can perhaps look to a future when many of the height differentials between populations will be further reduced as economic disparities and inequality diminish and more and more people enjoy the benefits that modern life can bring. The message for would-be racial classifiers is that one should never assume that morphological differences between populations are solely the result of biological or genetic differences and therefore supportive of racial classification. It is now clear that unequal environments can yield substantial differences in adult morphology regardless of the degree of biological difference between populations, and these "plastic" traits cannot form part of any racial theory of human difference.

BOX TWO

Lactose Intolerance: An Example of Biocultural Evolution

Since the time of the ancient Greeks, people have recognized that many adults experience a series of uncomfortable gastrointestinal symptoms after ingesting dairy products such as milk and, to a lesser extent, soft cheeses or yogurt. Bloating, cramping, flatulence, and diarrhea are a few of the unpleasant symptoms that some people experience shortly after drinking milk. Many readers of this book will, I am sure, know from personal experience exactly what I am writing about. What you may not know is that there is an interesting biocultural tale of evolution by natural selection hiding within this story of bodily functions and flatulence (Kretchmer 1972; McCracken 1971; Simoons et al. 1977). The story begins with the birth of an infant and the substance that makes its mother's milk taste sweet.

The sugar *lactose* is the major carbohydrate found in the milk that is synthesized in the mammary glands of female mammals. Because mother's milk is the first meal of most infant mammals, lactose is typically the first carbohydrate that infant mammals ingest. Before digestion of lactose can proceed, however, each molecule of this disaccharide must first be broken down into its two constituent monosaccharides, glucose and galactose. This process occurs in the intestines as a result of the action of the digestive enzyme *lactase*, which is produced by intestinal cells. After being weaned, most nonhuman mammals no longer have the opportunity to drink milk, and consequently their intestines stop synthesizing lactase. If an adult mammal were to drink milk, the gastrointestinal problems I've described would occur as undigested lactose in the intestines is fermented by bacteria, producing gas. But most nonhuman mammals do not have access to milk after they are weaned. This shutdown of the production of lactase in the intestines after weaning must be considered the normal mammalian condition. But in this respect, as in many others, humans are not normal mammals. In fact, *Homo sapiens* can be characterized as the only mammal that routinely drinks milk as an adult.

How do we do it? That is, how are some adult humans able to digest the lactose in milk? It turns out that the key to enjoying and digesting a tall glass of milk can be found in a genetic mutation on chromosome 2 that first occurred in some human population perhaps six thousand years ago, probably in the Middle East. This mutation would have interfered with the genetic shutoff switch for the production of lactase, and its bearers would have continued to produce lactase after weaning and throughout the rest of their lives. It is hypothesized that this mutation would have increased the fitness of its bearers and been selected for through natural selection if it occurred among pastoral peoples who would have been able to drink the highly nutritious milk and other dairy products from their goats without getting sick. The same mutation may have occurred among foraging or farming peoples, but it would not have been positively selected for among these people because they would not have had access to milk or dairy products as adults. Only among the early herders of milk-bearing mammals would this mutation have been nutritionally advantageous and hence selected for.

It would seem to make sense that the descendants of these early milk-drinking pastoralists would be found among living people who are able to consume milk and other dairy products without any intestinal distress. We call these individuals *lactose tolerant*. On the other hand, we would expect that modern *lactose-intolerant* people (those who cannot digest milk sugar) would be the descendants of foragers or agriculturalists who did not maintain herds of milk-bearing mammals in the past. This is precisely what we find when we look at the geographic distribution and historical development of lactose-tolerant and lactose-intolerant people today. The modern populations where the great majority of individuals are lactose tolerant and are able to absorb or digest lactose throughout their lifetime are clustered in regions of the world with a long history of animal husbandry and milking, typically of camels, goats, cows, and sometimes horses. This includes much of northern Europe and a few sub-Saharan pastoralist groups (e.g., the Masai of East and the Fulani of West Africa). In eastern Asia, sub-Saharan Africa, and the Mediterranean region, as well as among the aboriginal inhabitants of the Americas, malabsorption of lactose predominates among present-day lactose-intolerant people with no history or tradition of keeping and milking domestic mammals.

What is the moral of this gastrointestinal tale? One point concerns the definition of illness and suggests the question "Are lactose-tolerant or lactose-intolerant individuals the sick ones?" Seeing that lactose-intolerant individuals experience symptoms of gastrointestinal distress, and perhaps because most white Americans of European origin are lactose tolerant, the medical establishment considers lactose intolerance a disease state. But the observant reader will notice that from the perspective of the evolutionary biology of mammals, the lactose-intolerant individuals are "normal" in the sense of resembling all other adult mammals. The lactose-tolerant phenotype is the result of a mutational change that was favored by natural selection among herding and milking peoples in the past and spread throughout the world as a result of this positive selection. The story of lactose tolerance and intolerance is another story about human diversity, with a plot involving the evolution of human culture and subsistence patterns and an adaptive scenario that can help us make sense of human biological diversity without even mentioning race or racial classifications.

RACIAL DISPARITIES IN MORBIDITY AND MORTALITY

While it may be true that in the United States, at least, "all men are created equal," it is indisputably *not* true that all Americans suffer and die from the same diseases at the same rates. One of the most important public health issues today is the apparent health disparity that exists between different racial or ethnic groups. By health disparity, we mean the "differences in morbidity, mortality, and access to health care among population groups defined by factors such as socioeconomic status, gender, residence, and race or ethnicity" (Dressler et al. 2005:232). The political scientist Andrew Hacker (1992) discussed segregation in modern American life in a book he titled *Two Nations: Black and White, Separate, Hostile, Unequal*. According to Hacker, black and white Americans for the most part work, live, worship, go to school, and recreate in a segregated fashion. The medical evidence suggests that blacks and whites (and other racial or ethnic groups) in America today also suffer illnesses and die in distinctly different ways. For example, whites have higher suicide rates than blacks, and Native Americans are more commonly victims of motor vehicle accidents than members of other races. During the 1990s, blacks suffered a mortality rate two to ten times higher than that of other American populations on a long list of causes, including heart disease, lung and breast cancer, stroke, and homicide (Keppel et al. 2002). What are we to make of these enormous disparities in patterns of sickness and dying? Do these data suggest that certain diseases can themselves be characterized as "racial" in nature? Are different races genetically more or less susceptible to different forms of illness or patterns of mortality? Or can these health disparities be explained by different lived experiences or environmental exposures between racial or ethnic groups in America? The perceptive reader will notice that we are dealing once again with the nature–nurture controversy. Put differently, we seek to understand whether health disparities are the result of biological (i.e., genetic) or environmental differences between racial or ethnic groups. Let's take a closer look from the biocultural perspective at several medical conditions that have been characterized by some authors as race-related to determine if these health disparities reflect differences in biology or environment.

LOW BIRTHWEIGHT AND PREMATURE BIRTHS

As most parents would no doubt agree, giving birth to children can be a terrifying experience with only one possible happy outcome (i.e., the birth of a healthy newborn) and a multitude of distressing but thankfully rare outcomes (e.g., a wide variety of congenital birth defects, miscarriage, low birthweight, or premature birth). *Low-birthweight infants* are technically defined by a birthweight of less than 2,500 grams (roughly 5.5 pounds), and they are at significantly higher risk of dying in infancy than infants born at more than 2,500 grams. If they survive infancy, low-birthweight infants will often develop serious health problems later in life (e.g., increased risk of developing heart disease and diabetes) and may suffer from lower IQ and impaired cognitive functions as children and adults. *Preterm* or *premature infants* are those born at less than 37 weeks of postmenstrual age (i.e., weeks since the mother's last menstrual cycle), normal term being on average 40 postmenstrual weeks. Preterm infants suffer from greatly elevated risks of neonatal mortality and may be saddled with a wide variety of health problems throughout their lives, including cerebral palsy, mental retardation, and blindness.

It should be clear that from an evolutionary perspective, being born prematurely or at low birthweight has a seriously detrimental effect on a person's fitness by decreasing the likelihood that the afflicted individual will survive to reproductive age and have healthy children. As a result, natural selection would be expected to strongly select against these conditions, if there were a genetic basis underlying either. What we hope to understand are the differential rates of low-birthweight and premature infants born to white and black mothers in America today, and the differences are substantial. Low-birthweight infants are born to black women nearly twice as frequently as to white women (13.3 percent to 6.9 percent), and premature infants are born to 11.5 percent of all white mothers and 17.6 percent of all black mothers. How can we explain (and perhaps reduce) these significant racial disparities in morbidity and mortality? While the possibility certainly exists that these racial disparities are due to genetic differences between whites and blacks, there is no biological evidence in support of such a racial explanation. A far simpler and more likely hypothesis suggests that environmental differences between populations and individuals can account for these and many other racial disparities in health and wellness in America. More specifically, we might suggest that the root cause of this and perhaps of many other forms of "racial" disease is poverty, acting through its close correlations with poor nutrition and limited access to health care. Poor or absent prenatal care, often as the result of a lack of health insurance, could also play a large role in the high rates of premature and low-birthweight infants born to African American women. Most social scientists support such an environmentalist rather than a biological or genetic explanation of these "racial" differences in birth outcomes.

HYPERTENSION AND THE "SLAVERY HYPOTHESIS"

Another medical condition that is sometimes referred to as a racial disease is high blood pressure or *hypertension*. Blood pressure is measured by the familiar cuff around the upper arm which yields the amount of pressure in the blood vessels in millimeters of mercury at every heartbeat (the systolic pressure) and between heartbeats (the diastolic pressure). High blood pressure is clinically defined by a persistent systolic pressure of greater than 140 millimeters of mercury or a diastolic pressure of greater than 90 millimeters of mercury (or both). The statistics on hypertension show several major disparities between white and black Americans with very serious medical and perhaps evolutionary repercussions. More than a third of all adult black men and women but less than a quarter of all adult white men and women suffer from hypertension. By age 50, nearly half of all black men in the

United States have developed hypertension, and this leads to some very serious medical issues. In terms of mortality, blacks are ten times as likely as whites to die of hypertension-related causes—mainly heart disease, stroke, and kidney failure. In fact, because they are 18 times more likely than whites to suffer from kidney failure resulting from hypertension, blacks account for two-thirds of all kidney failure patients, though they make up only about 12 percent of the American population. On a worldwide basis, American blacks die from strokes at a higher rate than any other population except the Japanese. These morbidity and mortality statistics have led many medical anthropologists and physicians to explore the reasons behind the apparent racial health disparities. A result of this attention has been one of the most controversial hypotheses about racial patterns of disease, the *slavery hypothesis of hypertension* (Wilson 1986a, 1986b; Wilson and Grim 1991).

The slavery hypothesis suggests a historical story and a genetic explanation for high rates of hypertension among African Americans that has its roots in West African populations long before the Atlantic slave trade. It suggests that these populations lived in areas of low salt availability and as a result evolved a kind of "thrifty genotype" that allowed them to store dietary salt more readily and use it more efficiently. This "salt-sparing" physiology (Dressler et al. 2005) would have been strongly selected for when these populations suffered the hardships of the Middle Passage and subsequent life as slaves in the New World. It has been estimated that more than 50 percent of the slaves captured from West Africa died en route to their new plantation homes in America. Although the causes of their deaths would have been numerous, a contributing factor may have been extreme salt loss due to the rampant diarrhea and vomiting associated with gastrointestinal infections resulting from the crowded and unsanitary conditions to which they were subjected onboard. Survivors of the rigors of the Atlantic crossing and life as a slave may have been the individuals with the most efficient or thriftiest physiological means of regulating sodium levels. After hundreds of years of strong selection, African Americans are thought to have evolved very efficient kidneys and other physiological mechanisms for maintaining adequate sodium levels for normal physiological functions. Whereas these genotypes would have been positively selected for during the period of slavery, the modern environment has changed significantly such that the thrifty or salt-sparing genotype is no longer favored. With the high sodium levels present in most modern American diets and the low activity levels of most modern Americans, genes for retaining high levels of sodium are no longer advantageous. In fact, modern African Americans may suffer from the aforementioned epidemic of hypertension and its related health problems as a result of possessing the once-favored thrifty genotype.

The slavery hypothesis is an example of what has been called a "racial-genetic" model for explaining racial disparities, and it is clear that the story it tells contains a substantial amount of internal logic, coherence, and believability. But one thing that this hypothesis lacks is any significant biological or genetic evidence in its favor. The notion of a thrifty or salt-sparing genotype remains a completely speculative idea: no geneticist has ever located a gene that might explain such a difference in salt physiology. In spite of the popularity of the slavery hypothesis, it remains a highly controversial idea that has been seriously critiqued by historians of the African slave trade. The authors of one paper go so far as to suggest that in spite of the fact that the slavery hypothesis is "based on virtually no empirical evidence" (Dressler et al. 2005:236), it remains a popular explanation because of its simplistic genetic determinism in the context of comfortable notions of biological racial diversity. Thus it reinforces our belief that the races are deeply different in their biological makeup while at the same time providing a simple genetic-determinist model to explain the origin of these differences. One historian who critically analyzed the slavery hypothesis found it to be mistaken or unsupported by the best historical evidence on a number of critical points. For example, Curtin (1992) disputes the suggestion that salt was in short supply among the African source populations for the slave trade or that it would have been unavailable in their diet during the Atlantic crossings. During the period of the slave trade, salt was cheap and widely available as a result of trade networks that moved it throughout the West African coastlines and into the interior. Curtin also argues that African slaves did not die overwhelmingly of salt depletion and dehydration but that a variety of diseases took a substantial toll, including lung diseases such as pneumonia and tuberculosis and "eruptive fevers" such as smallpox. It seems that an explanation of the current high rates of hypertension among African Americans must be sought in some other domain than the racial-genetic model suggested by the proponents of the slavery hypothesis.

If a genetic-determinist argument like the "slavery hypothesis" fails to adequately explain the prevalence of hypertension among modern African Americans, perhaps an argument from the environmentalist perspective can be more successful. One explanation might be sought in the behavior of individuals or populations that might put them at greater or lesser risk of certain diseases. For example, since it is generally recognized that dietary salt intake is strongly positively correlated with blood pressure, one might hypothesize that the typical diet of African Americans may be higher in salt than the typical diet of European Americans, but it turns out that this is not true. Another environmentalist model might argue for the importance of poverty as a determining factor behind patterns of disease and suggest that socioeconomic status of different populations predisposes them to different diseases. Again, while plausible, this argument is not supported by the data. When one controls for socioeconomic status by comparing disease statistics between poor whites and poor blacks, we still have a major discrepancy, with much higher rates of hypertension in the black population. A far better explanation takes into account other, more subjective aspects of the environment and lived experience of African Americans to explain persistent health disparities. What Dressler et al. (2005) refer to as the "psychosocial stress model" suggests that poorer health in African Americans can best be explained as a result of the everyday stresses associated with being black in a racist society. This model suggests that the combination of structural racism in society and the individual's lived experiences of discrimination lead to conditions of psychological and social stress that affect health in a variety of adverse ways. The connection between the stresses of being a member of a discriminated-against minority group and hypertension is certainly plausible, for we have good evidence of the blood pressure–raising effects of generalized stress. It ultimately seems that a full and satisfying explanation of the racial disparities in diseases such as hypertension can best be explained by a combination of environmental causes and conditions (e.g., poverty, discrimination, access to health care) that are experienced differently by members of different races in America. While there is good evidence in support of a familial, most likely genetic component to hypertension, there is little or no biological evidence that group or population differences in rates of hypertension can be explained by genetic differences.

SICKLE-CELL ANEMIA AND MALARIA

Sickle-cell anemia has long been considered the epitome of a racial disease, found as it is in high frequency among many African populations and African Americans. As you will soon see, however, the story is a bit more complex and far more interesting than that. Sickle-cell anemia (SCA) is one of a large class of genetic diseases that affect hemoglobin (Hg), the oxygen-carrying protein molecule found in red blood cells. *Hemoglobin* is a large protein molecule known as a tetramer because it is made up of four polypeptide chains: two alpha chains with 141 amino acids each and two beta chains with 146 amino acids each. The polypeptide chains that make up hemoglobin are coded for by two different genes: the alpha gene (Hga) resides on human chromosome 16, while the beta gene (Hgb) is found on chromosome 11. Each alpha and beta chain also has at its center a *heme group*, an iron-bearing unit that is the actual site where O_2 molecules are bound to hemoglobin and which is responsible for the deep red color of well-oxygenated blood. Hemoglobin makes it possible for red blood cells to pick up oxygen in the capillaries within the alveoli of the lungs and to carry this oxygen along the arteries, arterioles, and capillaries of the circulatory system to all of the body's cells and tissues that require oxygen for metabolic and physiological functions.

Sickle-cell anemia is a genetic disease that occurs when an individual has two copies of a recessive hemoglobin beta gene that results in the production of an abnormal form of hemoglobin. The normal human beta chain has an amino acid known as glutamic acid at the sixth position of its 146 amino acids: the allele responsible can be abbreviated as Hgb_A and is the dominant form of the hemoglobin beta gene. An alternative, recessive version of this gene known as Hgb_s has only a single difference in its amino acid sequence in that valine occurs at the sixth position of the beta chain. When individuals are heterozygous for these two alleles (Hgb_As), they are perfectly healthy, and their phenotype is called "sickle-cell trait." Individuals who are homozygous for the normal hemoglobin beta gene (Hgb_AA) are also phenotypically normal with respect to hemoglobin, but clinical problems arise for the Hgb_ss homozygotes in the form of the disease known as sickle-cell anemia. The disease gets its name from the sickle shape of the affected red blood cells after they give up their oxygen in the capillaries. Sickle-cell anemia is a serious and debilitating disease that is especially common throughout much of Africa, where approximately 200 thousand infants are born with it each year. The disease has many symptoms but is at heart a form of anemia or reduced red blood cell count resulting from the body's own destruction of millions of red blood cells, which block circulation and clog the narrow capillaries due to their abnormal shape. High fevers are common, damage to the spleen often occurs, and life expectancy is seriously shortened, especially in parts of the world with little or no access to modern medical care.

Because this genetic disease is clearly deleterious and often lethal and has especially serious effects on children long before they reach reproductive age, we should expect that natural selection would tend to weed out the Hgb_s gene from the human gene pool and that its gene frequency, like that of nearly all lethal recessive genes, would be extremely low. This is exactly the situation in most human populations—for example, those of northern European descent—but it is not at all what we see in much of sub-Saharan Africa, Saudi Arabia, and many other parts of the Mediterranean region of Europe and Asia. In these latter regions, the Hgb_s gene is very common, reaching gene frequencies in some populations as high as 20 percent. This is an extraordinarily high frequency for a lethal recessive gene, and the situation begs for an evolutionary explanation. The basic paradox can be stated in the following manner: if Hgb_ss homozygotes who suffer from sickle-cell anemia tend to die in greater numbers and at younger ages than people who do not have this disease, why is the gene frequency of the Hgb_s gene so high in certain populations? Natural selection would be expected to reduce the frequency of deleterious and lethal genes to very low values, yet in some parts of the world and in some populations, the lethal Hgb_s gene is at very high frequencies. How can we explain this in the context of evolutionary theory?

It turns out that the mystery of the high frequencies of the sickle-cell gene and of sickle-cell anemia in certain parts of the world, including but not limited to sub-Saharan Africa, can be solved by examining its relationship to the geographic distribution of an infectious disease known as

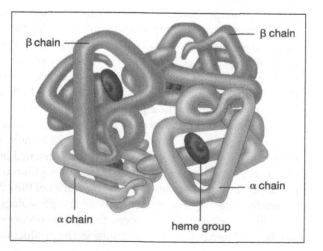

FIGURE 7.2 The hemoglobin molecule is a polypeptide comprised of two alpha and two beta chains, each carrying an iron-bearing heme group that bonds to oxygen. Hemoglobin is found in red blood cells and serves as the body's carrier of oxygen.

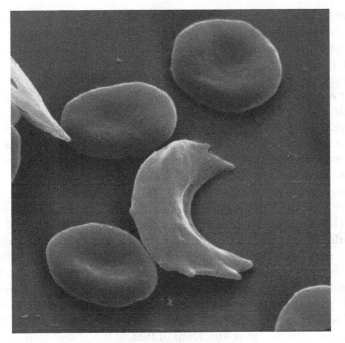

FIGURE 7.3 Normal red blood cells and sickle cells.
Courtesy of Eye of Science/Science Photo Library.

malaria (Livingstone 1958). *Malaria* is a tropical disease that occurs widely throughout the tropical zones of the Old and New Worlds and carries a heavy burden of suffering, death, and lost economic productivity in the places where it is found. Unlike sickle-cell anemia, malaria is an infectious rather than a genetic disease, but interestingly, it resembles the former in that it also affects red blood cells. Malaria is caused by infection with a protozoan parasite of the genus *Plasmodium*, which is transmitted by the bite of a female anopheles mosquito (actually, via an exchange of the mosquito's saliva with the victim's blood). Upon entering the human bloodstream, the parasite reproduces rapidly and greatly increases its numbers, eventually entering the liver and along the way destroying many infected red blood cells. Symptoms of malaria include high fevers, chills, nausea, body aches, enlarged liver and spleen, and often death. The WHO estimates that more than 500 million people become ill with malaria each year and that about one million die from it annually, mostly poor African children and women.

Let's now return to the puzzling genetic paradox and seek to explain the surprisingly high frequency of the lethal sickle-cell gene in certain parts of the world. It turns out that the places around the world where sickle-cell anemia is common are the same places where malaria is found, and this geographic overlap is the critical clue that allows us to understand why sickle-cell anemia is so common among some populations. In malarial zones of the world, individuals who are heterozygous for the hemoglobin beta gene (Hgb_As) tend to be resistant to malaria. That is, although these heterozygotes may become infected with malarial parasites as a result of being bitten by a female anopheles mosquito, they tend not to suffer greatly from malaria, and their life expectancy and fitness are not compromised by the low levels of infection they incur. Conversely, individuals who are homozygous for the dominant Hgb_A allele (Hgb_AA) have no inborn resistance to malaria and suffer greatly from this disease. The Hgb_ss homozygotes are, of course, the individuals who suffer from sickle-cell anemia: malaria is quite beside the point for these unfortunates. As a result, we can see that the best or most fit genotype in the Darwinian sense that one can have in a malarial zone of the world is to be an Hgb_As heterozygote for the hemoglobin beta gene, for these individuals neither suffer from sickle-cell anemia (because the normal A allele is dominant to the s allele) nor have much to fear from malaria (because they have a high degree of resistance to this infectious disease). In the malarial zones of the world, natural selection strikes deeply against the Hgb_AA homozygotes who succumb to malaria in high numbers and against the Hgb_ss homozygotes who fall victim to sickle-cell anemia. Because the heterozygotes are the fittest genotype in these malarial environments, the Hgb_s gene is maintained at very high frequencies in these populations because a good proportion of the healthy adults who survive to reproduce and pass their genes on to their offspring are heterozygotes, carrying one copy of both Hgb_A and Hgb_s alleles. We can consider these heterozygotes as screening the lethal sickle-cell gene from the gaze of natural selection, while a balance of selection is maintained against both homozygous genotypes. This situation has been called a *balanced polymorphism*, and in explaining how lethal recessive genes can be maintained at high frequencies in populations, it provides much insight into how evolution by natural selection can work in the world.

Evolutionary theory tells us that the effects of natural selection must be measured in particular environments and that if environments change, the relative fitness of different genes and genotypes will also change. An example might be to consider how the fitness of polar bears would decline in a world subject to significant global warming. The reduction in polar sea ice that has already occurred in the Arctic has begun to have deleterious effects on the ability of polar bears to hunt and to survive. What happens to the balanced polymorphism involving sickle-cell anemia and malaria if the environment changes and malaria is no longer a threat to human health? This experiment is actually playing out as I write this chapter. The 2000 U.S. census counted approximately 35 million self-identified black Americans, out of a total population of 280 million, most of whom can trace their ancestry back to West Africa, one of the Old World regions with high rates of malarial infection and high frequencies of the sickle-cell gene (Hgb_s). But for black Americans today, malaria is not a relevant factor because it is a tropical disease that doesn't typically occur in the New World north of Mexico. What would you predict would happen to the Hgb_s gene frequency among African Americans who live in the malaria-free temperate zones of North America over several generations? If you think that the frequency of the sickle-cell gene would drop, you are absolutely correct. Among African Americans, the balanced polymorphism is no longer in balance. Natural selection still reduces the number of Hgb_s genes in the population because people still suffer and die from sickle-cell anemia, but in the absence of malaria, there is no longer any advantage to being heterozygous. As a result, the most fit genotype in North America is Hgb_AA, and we can confidently predict that the frequency of the sickle-cell gene among African Americans will continue to decline as more and more Hgb_ss homozygotes are selected against due to the ill effects of sickle-cell anemia. In fact, the incidence of heterozygotes for sickle cell (Hgb_As) among African Americans is today around 8 percent, much lower than the 20 to 30 percent commonly found in some West and Central African populations. This is the typical situation for deleterious or lethal recessive genes, which are kept at very low levels in most populations by the "cleansing action" of natural selection. The balanced polymorphism example of sickle-cell anemia and malaria reveals the importance of the environment in determining what constitutes a "good" or a "fit" genotype. It clarifies the fact that in the Darwinian world, fitness is not an absolute characteristic associated with a particular genotype. Rather, fitness must be measured relative to the particular environment in which one lives. As the environment changes, the relative benefits or detriments of particular genes and genotypes will change, often in unpredictable ways.

Let us now return to the original question posed at the beginning of this section: Is sickle-cell anemia properly considered a "racial disease"? Several relevant facts would argue strongly against an exclusive association of sickle-cell anemia with an African race. Although sickle-cell anemia is found among many sub-Saharan African populations, it is also present in a wide variety of other tropical populations of the Old World. In Europe, sickle-cell anemia can be found in many Mediterranean populations, including Sicilians, Sardinians, Corsicans, Cypriots, Italians, Portuguese, Spanish, and Greeks. In Asia, the disease can be found in India and Sri Lanka, Turkey, and Saudi Arabia and in many other Middle Eastern countries, including Yemen, Lebanon, Israel, and Kuwait. Geneticists have suggested that the disease arose through genetic mutations at least four different times and places in Africa and once in India or Saudi Arabia. The clear association of sickle-cell anemia is with tropical environments in which malaria is an endemic disease, rather than with any particular racial group, and in this respect, it makes absolutely no sense to consider it a racial disease of Africans or African Americans. Any child could be born with this disease, and many health professionals advocate that all newborns be screened for sickle cell and other forms of abnormal hemoglobin.

We can also pose a larger question concerning the utility of the sickle-cell gene in terms of human populations and human evolution. Is sickle cell a "good" or a "bad" thing? This question may seem odd at first: after all, exactly in what sense can a disease that affects tens of millions and kill millions each year be considered a "good" thing? Certainly from the perspective of the individual afflicted with sickle-cell anemia and his or her family and loved ones, the disease is a tragic condition that leads to much pain and suffering and an early death (the life expectancy of individuals with sickle-cell anemia in America today is somewhere in the mid-forties). Yet if we ask this question from another perspective, from that of the population as a whole, we will perhaps reach a very different conclusion. The fact is that without the sickle-cell mutation, many human populations would be absolutely unable to survive and sustain themselves in the tropical regions of the world where malaria is and has been an endemic disease. While the cost to the individual can be great (much suffering and an early demise for those with two copies of the sickle-cell gene), the benefit to the population as a whole can also be great, allowing human societies to survive and prosper in the malarial zones of the world. In this sense, we can view the mutations behind abnormal forms of hemoglobin such as sickle cell as being population-level adaptations that increase the fitness of the population as a whole and make it possible for humans to survive in particularly difficult environments such as those where malaria is common. Although we must never forget or minimize the cost borne by the members of these societies who suffer from sickle-cell anemia, these individual tragedies are to some extent balanced out by the resistance to malaria that is conferred on the heterozygotes, and the population as a whole can survive and flourish.

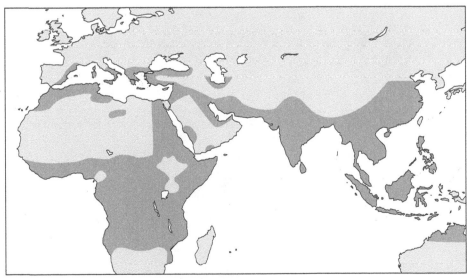

Distribution of falciparum malaria before 1930 (Boyd, *Malariology*).

FIGURE 7.4 Malaria is an endemic disease in many parts of the Old World, including much of sub-Saharan Africa, the Mediterranean region, the Arabian peninsula, much of southern Eurasia from Turkey to China, and mainland and island Southeast Asia. In most of these areas, either sickle-cell anemia or other abnormal forms of hemoglobin are present in high frequency in a balanced polymorphism.

Discussion Questions

1. What is meant by a "racial" or "ethnic disease," and is there any good evidence that this is a useful concept for the medical anthropologist?

2. Explain the evolutionary scenario known as a balanced polymorphism in the context of the connection between sickle-cell anemia and malaria.

3. List some of the major nutritional challenges facing the Third World in the 21st century.

4. What happened to human health at the Neolithic Revolution? Why?

5. Critically evaluate the slavery hypothesis to explain the high rates of hypertension among modern African Americans.

6. What are some of the causes of low birthweight, and how can the rates of low birthweight and premature infants be reduced?

7. Why do you think members of racial minorities often die younger and suffer from more illnesses than members of the majority group?

CHAPTER 8

Race, Intelligence, and Genetics

> *"I advance it therefore as a suspicion only, that the blacks,*
> *whether originally a distinct race, or made distinct by time*
> *and circumstances, are inferior to the whites in the endowments*
> *both of body and mind."*
>
> THOMAS JEFFERSON, *NOTES ON THE STATE OF VIRGINIA*, 1781

RACE AND INTELLIGENCE

For as long as societies have created racial classifications of *Homo sapiens*, the notion of innate differences in intelligence between groups has been with us. Referring to these differences by the term "innate" means that racial differences in intelligence are hard-wired, genetic, biological, and therefore deterministic of the kinds of people that we are or can hope to become. While no one would deny the fact that some individuals are smarter than others (however we might measure intelligence), is there good evidence suggesting that certain races are, on average, smarter than other races? And if such evidence does exist, what is the basis for suggesting that it is due to differences in our biological nature, rather than a result of environmental nurture or some combination of the two? And what about the very definition of intelligence? Is there only one kind of intelligence, and can it be measured by IQ tests and represented by a single score? Although *intelligence* is a word we routinely use and the meaning of which would seem to be easily understood, a closer examination will reveal that it is not a simple concept to define or measure. In this chapter, we will explore the history of the notion that human races have different genetically determined levels of intelligence and the evidence both for and against it. Is there really a biological connection among race, intelligence, and genetics? Or is the apparent inequality on IQ test scores between different social or racial groups simply a by-product of the unequal distribution of wealth, access to education, and other forms of social status and power in society? In a word, does the evidence support the existence of racial differences in intelligence, and if it does, are these differences the result of nature or of nurture? These are some of the questions and issues we will discuss in this chapter.

The worldview that suggests that people are the way they are largely as a result of their genetic heritage is known as *biological determinism* or *hereditarianism*. When Thomas Jefferson suggested that blacks "are inferior to the whites in the endowments of body and mind," he was reflecting what we would call today a hereditarian worldview. His statement concerning the "endowments of body and mind" refers to the biological heritage of physical and mental traits that we inherit from our parents. This viewpoint has always been popular among supporters of racial classification and racial stereotypes, but a moment's reflection indicates that the mere existence of some phenotypic or behavioral feature in a group says nothing about its origin (i.e., whether it is the result of genes or environment). For example, if we find a family that is full of shy individuals, can we conclude that shyness is an inherited feature and that the shyness of these individuals reflects their biological heritage? Absolutely not, for an equally likely alternative is that shy parents raise their own children to be shy and that shyness is thus passed on from parents to offspring as a form of cultural inheritance resulting from the environment in which they were raised. Further study of the differences between the rearing environments of children in shy and outgoing families, as well as a search for the presence of genes that influence shyness, must occur before we can conclude anything about the cause of shyness. The story is quite different for features with a simple and well-understood genetic background (e.g., red hair, sickle-cell anemia, hemophilia). We can easily predict the statistical likelihood of inheriting hemophilia among the offspring of two hemophiliac parents because genetic studies have revealed that the gene for hemophilia is a recessive, sex-linked gene found on the X chromosome. But intelligence is by no means a simple Mendelian trait with a known pattern of inheritance that results from a single gene on a chromosome. Evidence suggests that there are many genes that interact with each other and with the environment to influence (not determine) how intelligent we become. Furthermore, most of these genes are still waiting to be discovered (like the putative genes for shyness).

Environmental determinism refers to the worldview that suggests a dominant role of the environment (i.e., nurture) for shaping our personality and other aspects of the kinds of people we are. Environmental determinists tend to downplay the importance of genes when they explain human differences. Rather, they argue for the dominance of environmental, social, and cultural differences in making individuals and societies different from each other. Many modern anthropologists reject both biological and environmental determinism as approaches to the study of human difference, opting instead for a middle ground that takes account of both biology and environment, both nature and nurture. Often referred to as *interactionism*, this approach recognizes that most phenotypic features, whether of morphology, personality, or behavior, are the result of the interaction between genes and the environment in which the individual develops. In many respects, the interactionist approach is the most reasonable and balanced way to explore the origins and meanings of many aspects of human difference, and it will be the approach we take in this chapter toward understanding the connections between race and intelligence.

LINNAEUS AND RACIAL STEREOTYPES

As noted in chapter 4, the first scientific classification of human races was proposed by Carolus Linnaeus, in the tenth edition of *Systema Naturae*, published in 1758. In this influential volume, Linnaeus names and describes the four major geographic races of mankind that are still recognized by many people today: the Asian, European, Native American, and African races. The distinctions that Linnaeus makes between his four geographical races or subspecies are a curious collection of traits, including physical features, personality traits, and aspects of culture. More important for our purposes in this chapter, we can find one of the earliest examples of the scientific argument that the white and black races are unequal in their natural intelligence in Linnaeus's classification. Europeans, according to Linnaeus, are "very smart and inventive," while Africans are said to be "crafty" and "foolish." Remember that the sources that Linnaeus drew on for his classification of the non-European human races were essentially anecdotal accounts of travelers, traders, slave traders, and sailors during the Age of Exploration and the early days of European colonization. So although the classification into four geographic races that Linnaeus created may look similar to modern, scientific racial schemes, we should realize that it is actually closer in its details to medieval than modern worldviews. Furthermore, Linnaeus's racial classification begins the long-standing tradition in the Western world of ranking human races by presumed intelligence that continues to be a hallmark of much racial thought today. We have also seen that Samuel George Morton and the polygenists continued in this tradition, with Morton collecting much "data" on brain size in different races to confirm the widely held belief among 19th-century Europeans of their own intellectual superiority to the other races of the world.

Finally, a consideration of Linnaeus's classification suggests that one of the unspoken pedestals on which it is built is the notion of racial hierarchy and inequality. With respect to many of the personality and cultural traits that he uses, a clear Eurocentric bias is present. Who could argue that being ruled by law is not better than being ruled by caprice or that being characterized as active, very smart, and inventive does not trump being crafty, slow, and foolish? The notion of linear hierarchy in the racial classification of Linnaeus is clearly a remnant of the Judeo-Christian concept of the "great chain of being" or "ladder of creation." In this conception, all of God's creatures, from the simplest and most primitive life forms to the most complex, were thought to be arrayed in a linear fashion, like the links in a chain or rungs of a ladder. At the top of the earthly chain were humans, below them the apes and monkeys, and lower still, in a continuous and linear chain of decreasing complexity of design, all the other living things. Above humans would be found the angels and other heavenly beings, with God perched at the very top. Clearly, the notion of hierarchy was central to the visual metaphor of the great chain: being closer to God was a sign of greater worth in the universal creation. When Linnaeus created his four subspecies or races of humans and under the influence of notions like the great chain, it was only natural for him to build into his scheme a linear hierarchy, with some races closer to the angels and others closer to the apes. So it seems that the first scientific classification of race resembles modern racial classifications in several important respects, including the notion of inequality with respect to innate intelligence and a linear ranking or hierarchy of races and the broad-brush stereotyping of millions of people with supposedly Platonic essences.

THE SCIENCE OF MEASURING INTELLIGENCE

Thus race and intelligence have been linked since at least the time of Linnaeus, and he was not the only one to think such thoughts. Thomas Jefferson famously suggested ("a suspicion only") in *Notes on the State of Virginia* (1781) that blacks were "inferior to the whites in the endowments both of mind and body," and this was certainly a commonplace and unsurprising opinion at the time, even for the writer of the Declaration of Independence. Abraham Lincoln, the Great Emancipator himself, similarly felt that blacks should not be allowed the right to vote, serve on juries, or hold elective office because of the "physical difference between the white and black races which will ever forbid the two races living together on terms of social and political equality."* In this chapter, we will explore 20th-century scientific debates among anthropologists, psychologists, and geneticists concerning the purported association of race and intelligence. You will see that despite a complete lack of supporting evidence, the theory of an innate racial hierarchy of intelligence has been one of the most persistent (and pernicious) ideas in social science. Like the biological theory of race itself, which continues to thrive in the absence of supporting evidence, the purported nexus of race, IQ, and hierarchy also refuses to die. As you survey the history of scientific measurement and ranking of human intelligence, you should take note of the connections between attempts to measure human intelligence and a set of persistent racial biases and prejudices with respect to intelligence. These ideas have been at times closely associated with proposed eugenic solutions to the "problem" of

---

* From the fourth Lincoln–Douglass debate, September 18, 1858. Lincoln continued his discussion of black–white differences in the following manner: "And inasmuch as they cannot so live, while they do remain together, there must be the position of superior and inferior, and I, as much as any other man, am in favor of having the superior position assigned to the white race."

biologically inferior people, including institutionalization and even forced sterilization of people with low IQ and financial incentives for high-IQ individuals to have more children. This ugly bit of scientific history is worth revisiting from the perspective of our attempt to unravel the role of cultural conceptions of race in the ongoing debates about human biological variation with respect to intellectual endowment.

The first tests of intelligence were developed by the Frenchman Alfred Binet in the first decade of the 20th century. Binet's stated goal was to devise a practical test of intelligence that would allow him to identify youngsters whose poor performance in school might be improved by special education or other forms of educational intervention. He explicitly denied any interest in ranking or labeling children with respect to intelligence, and he proceeded without any dogmatic position concerning the causes of low or high intelligence among children. Binet's intelligence tests included a variety of tasks and activities, to each of which he assigned an age level, defined as the youngest age at which a child of normal intelligence would be expected to complete the task successfully. A child's mental age was recorded as the age of the last task the child could complete in the sequence of tasks. This figure soon came to be defined as the ratio of an individual's mental age to his or her chronological age; multiplied by 100, the result was the child's *intelligence quotient* or *IQ score*. Thus a 12-year-old child (chronological age of 12) of average intelligence (mental age of 12) would have an IQ of 100 (12 divided by 12, times 100). Conversely, a 10-year-old who was as intelligent as the average 12-year-old would have an IQ of 120 (12 divided by 10, times 100).

Although Binet regarded mental age and IQ score as a rough guide for identifying students who could benefit from help, his benign interpretation of intelligence was not destined to survive for long. After his ideas crossed the Atlantic to be further developed and greatly popularized by American psychologists, Binet's conception of intelligence was replaced by a hardened hereditarian doctrine whose main goals were to rank and label individuals, races, and even nations with respect to intelligence. IQ quickly became a single, scalable, and immutable numerical score that

FIGURE 8.1 Alfred Binet (1857–1911), the French psychologist who invented the first intelligence tests. His intention was to identify slow-learning children who might benefit from special attention in school. Courtesy of Universal History Archive/Getty Images.

represented an individual's genetic inheritance and full lifetime complement of intelligence. Ultimately from the perspective of biological determinism and hereditarianism, IQ came to represent the limits of what one might expect out of life based on one's innate amount of intelligence. Individuals, races, or nations of low intelligence could expect to be dominated by those with high intelligence, and one could not expect to rise above the level of achievement indicated by one's IQ. As the hereditarian view hardened and intelligence was increasingly seen as an innate and unchangeable quality of individuals, races, and nations, Binet's original conception of the meaning and usefulness of intelligence testing was forgotten. The results of these "academic" debates concerning the nature and quantification of intelligence would prove to have significant, and often tragic, implications for millions of people later in the 20th century.

MEASURING THE IQ OF IMMIGRANTS AND SOLDIERS

Intelligence testing came of age during the first few decades of the 20th century as a result of the determined efforts of several influential American psychologists, in particular Henry Goddard, Lewis Terman, and Robert Yerkes. Terman, a professor at Stanford University, modified Binet's original test to create the most popular and best-known IQ test of all time, the Stanford-Binet. But it is in the work of Goddard and Yerkes where we can more fully trace the development of a scholarly argument for the hereditarian approach to the study of human intelligence that has played such a large role in recent ideas and debates concerning the meanings of race. At the same time as these developments in the science of intelligence testing were occurring, another strand of scientific thought known as *eugenics* was evolving on both sides of the Atlantic. First explored in the late 19th century by Francis Galton, the first cousin of Charles Darwin, eugenics represented an attempt to develop a science of breeding for humans in order to improve the quality of the human gene pool. With their hereditarian and hierarchical leanings, the intelligence testers were very receptive to the vision of the early eugenicists. The full practical implications of the emerging scientific synthesis of intelligence testing and eugenics would not be realized until the years leading up to World War II, when the theory of eugenics was put to horrific practical use as part of Hitler's Final Solution.

FIGURE 8.2 Henry H. Goddard (1866–1957) popularized and mass-produced intelligence testing through his work with immigrants at Ellis Island.
Courtesy of Heritage Images/Getty Images.

Goddard's contributions to the development of intelligence testing were many: he was the first popularizer of Binet's test in America; he created a taxonomy of the feeble-minded in which *idiot, moron,* and *imbecile* became recognized clinical terms for different grades of mental defect; and beginning in 1913, he instituted a large-scale intelligence-testing program for newly arrived immigrants at Ellis Island in New York harbor. The goals of this program were clearly eugenic in nature, and Goddard's work contributed greatly to rising levels of fear and distrust of the perils posed by the enormous number of immigrants coming from eastern and southern Europe at the time. What exactly was it about these new immigrants that concerned Goddard? The results of the IQ tests suggested that 80 percent or more of the adult immigrants from certain populations (e.g., Hungarians, Russians, and Jews) should be classified as feeble-minded, which at the time was a technical term for individuals with a mental age of less than 12 years on the Binet scale. If this were true, and if intelligence were mostly a matter of genetics (rather than environment and schooling), these data would indeed be of real concern to both scientists and policymakers. Furthermore, since Goddard was convinced that people of low intelligence were more prone to criminal and immoral behavior, these immigrants were thought to pose a threat to both the American gene pool and American society. Goddard and many others were convinced that masses of feeble-minded immigrants flooding our shores placed the nation in real danger and suggested two courses of action: raise the standards for allowing immigrants to enter the country and limit the breeding of the feeble-minded already here. Historical evidence suggests that both courses of action were followed. Compared to the average from the preceding five-year period, deportations rose by 350 percent in 1913 and 570 percent in 1914 (Gould 1981:198), and tens of thousands of American citizens (mostly women) were forcibly sterilized as a result of their supposed low intelligence (36 thousand in 1941 alone, according to Kevles 1985:116).

World War I presented an opportunity for Yerkes to move the field of intelligence testing further along in the eugenic direction when he convinced the U.S. government to support a massive program of intelligence testing for nearly two million newly recruited soldiers. Presented as a scientific approach for determining the best military occupation and rank for these soldiers, the Army Mental Tests played a large role in the mass-marketing and mainstreaming of intelligence tests in American life and further stoked eugenic fear and resentment against the growing numbers of ethnic and racial minorities of apparently low mental quality. Gould (1981) highlights three major conclusions of the Army Mental Tests: (1) the average mental age of American adults was 13.08 years, a shockingly low number, barely above the level of the moron; (2) the intelligence level of immigrants from different European countries could be ranked, with the highest levels of intelligence being attributed to northern and western Europeans; and (3) African-Americans were at the very bottom of the racial scale of intelligence, with an average mental age of 10.41 years. Assuming a normal distribution of intelligence among African Americans, this would suggest that well more than 50 percent of adult African Americans had a mental age of 12 or lower and thus were officially feeble-minded.

In addition to providing a degree of scientific respectability to preexisting prejudices and long-lived stereotypes concerning race and intelligence, the work of Yerkes and Goddard and their colleagues had real political repercussions in the following decades. For one thing, their work was seen as a crucial support for immigration restrictions passed by the U.S. Congress and signed into law by President Calvin Coolidge in April 1924. This law greatly limited the number of immigrants allowed into the United States from countries of eastern and southern Europe, the countries with the lowest measured intelligence on the Army Mental Tests. No such restrictions were enforced against the "higher-quality" immigrants from places like England or the Scandinavian countries. With the rise of Nazi Germany only a decade after this law was passed, one possible escape route for many European Jews and other persecuted groups was effectively shut down, and they were left in Europe to play their roles in the historical tragedy that we refer to today as the Holocaust.

Could the results of these intelligence tests really be accurate? Were most American citizens really as intelligent as the average 13-year-old? Did the feeble-minded really comprise more than

FIGURE 8.3 Robert M. Yerkes (1876–1956) instituted the mass IQ testing of millions of World War I soldiers.
© Bettmann/CORBIS.

three-fourths of many immigrant groups? And was the American republic at serious risk due to the burden of the unintelligent masses? The Army Mental Tests and the IQ tests given to Ellis Island immigrants have been analyzed and critiqued in great detail by many scholars, and the consensus is that none of the conclusions drawn from these tests are true. Many of the questions used in these tests were obviously culturally biased and many measured familiarity with the English language and with mainstream American culture. The conditions under which the exams were administered left much to be desired, and illiterate people and people who spoke little or no English were often given tests that required English literacy. Gould (1981) cites several particularly egregious examples of some of these problems, ranging from vocabulary items that asked test takers to identify *Crisco* (a brand of shortening) and *regatta* (a type of boat race) to tests on which the most common score attained was zero, suggesting some major breakdown in the administration or scoring of the tests. Immigrants who had just crossed the ocean in steerage, many with little or no schooling in their own language and with rudimentary or no English, were upon arrival given tests whose content and significance they could not hope to understand. Yet in spite of the ludicrous results and the many problematic questions used, these tests were interpreted at the time as providing a good measure of innate intelligence, and the ethnic and racial differences in average IQ were considered real, substantial, and important. The hereditarian perspective was strong, and because the results were consistent with common social beliefs about the relative worth of different ethnic groups, most people found it easy to believe them. Perhaps people would have questioned the results if they suggested that whites (and particularly Nordic and Scandinavian whites) were inferior to blacks in intelligence, but few at the time had any reason to question or doubt white superiority.

ARTHUR JENSEN AND THE HEREDITARIAN VIEW RESTATED

The hereditarian and eugenic views of the early mental testers would be challenged by worldwide events that played out during the 1930s and 1940s so that by the end of World War II, this perspective was on the decline. Certainly, the realization that Hitler's program of racial cleansing and genocide used both the theory (i.e., innate differences in intelligence and morality of different ethnic or racial groups) and the practices (i.e., institutionalization and forced sterilization) of eugenics that had been advocated by America's leading academics must have played a role in the demise of this worldview. But while eugenics has gone from cutting-edge science to discredited and reviled pseudoscience in the past half century, what is the current status of the broader issues of race and intelligence raised by this brief historical sketch? Although few people today would suggest that individuals of low IQ should be sterilized to preserve the gene pool, are we as dismissive of claims of racial inequalities in the genetic allotment of intelligence? Or is there still a lingering strain of hereditarianism and perhaps eugenics lurking below the surface of our outwardly egalitarian worldview? What does modern psychological and anthropological science tell us about issues of race, ethnicity, intelligence, and equality?

In 1969, Arthur Jensen, a psychologist at the University of California at Berkeley, published an important and controversial article about race and intelligence titled "How Much Can We Boost I.Q. and Scholastic Achievement?" Jensen's argument can be broken down into several components: (1) there is a substantial difference of 15 points between the average IQ test scores of blacks and whites in America, (2) this difference is the result of genetic differences between whites and blacks, and (3) since the difference is genetic, it cannot be significantly reduced by Head Start or other social and educational programs designed to improve the environment or education of blacks. Taken as a whole, Jensen's argument was seen as a blow struck in favor of the hereditarian position for a genetic basis of intelligence, but it also elicited a storm of protest from many professors, students, people of color, and politicians. These critics questioned the scientific basis of each of the three main conclusions of Jensen's article, and some suggested that Jensen's piece was a political attack against affirmative action and other social policies designed to minimize economic and educational inequalities in our society. It may be beyond our ability to deduce Jensen's political intentions in writing this article more than four decades ago, but a sober analysis of his argument and the relevant scientific evidence suggests a very different conclusion than the one that Jensen drew concerning the effectiveness of improving the learning environment for minority children in America. Let's take a look at the science behind each of Jensen's three assertions concerning race and IQ.

The first point we want to consider concerns the evidence for and the meaning of the suggested IQ difference between blacks and whites in America. There is truth to the claim that the average IQ scores of blacks have traditionally been lower than those of whites; in fact, Asians have the highest average IQ among people of different ethnicity in America today, scoring, on average, 15 points higher than whites. The actual point difference between black and white IQ scores was 15 points at the time that Jensen was writing, although recent studies suggest that the gap may have shrunk to 7 points today (Nisbett 1995). The larger question, though, concerns our interpretation of the meaning of IQ scores and differences in these scores between different races, ethnicities, or populations. Anthropologists have long argued that IQ tests may be biased measures because by their very nature, they often seem to require knowledge common to members of the majority culture at the expense of minority knowledge. In an attempt to address this issue, Robert L. Williams (1972) developed an intelligence test that was explicitly designed to test for what he called "black intelligence," and it worked! Blacks performed at a much higher level than whites on his Black Intelligence Test of Cultural Homogeneity by correctly answering questions about the meaning of such phrases as "the eagle flies" (payday), "main squeeze" (best girlfriend), and "playing the dozens" (insulting a person's parents). If this little experiment sounds a bit absurd, think back to some of the vocabulary words that were on the early IQ tests (e.g., *Crisco* and *regatta*). Stephen Jay Gould (1981) tells the amusing story of administering one of the early multiple-choice IQ tests to his Harvard students, most of whom had no idea who Christy Mathewson was (he was a baseball pitcher famous in the early 20th century) and consequently did quite poorly. In fact, there is substantial evidence in support of the general statement that minority populations, whose social status is lower than that of the majority, score lower on IQ tests than the majority populations in many different countries (Fisher et al. 1996). This evidence strongly supports the notion that group differences in IQ scores are to a large extent the result of environmental and cultural differences.

A larger question raised by many critics of the hereditarian view of racial differences in IQ involves the actual meaning of IQ scores and in particular the often-unstated assumption that IQ scores are equivalent to intelligence. Recent work in psychology has firmly established that intelligence is a much more subtle and multifaceted entity that cannot be reduced to a single, ranked number. In his 1983 book *Frames of Mind: The Theory of Multiple Intelligences*, Harvard psychologist Howard Gardner first developed the theory that there are many different kinds of intelligence that people have in different quantities. Gardner wrote of bodily-kinesthetic, interpersonal, verbal-linguistic, musical,

FIGURE 8.4 Harvard professor Howard Gardner (b. 1943) developed the notion of "multiple intelligences" as an alternative to a single IQ score. Courtesy of Kris Connor/Getty Images.

and logical-mathematical forms of intelligence (as well as several others) and argued that each could be measured and that a much more realistic and practical picture of intelligence could be gained by exploring the various forms that intelligence takes in different people. Gardner's view of a multifaceted intelligence certainly makes intuitive sense: many of us will recognize people who have, for example, strong math and musical skills but poor interpersonal or verbal-linguistic skills. How can we capture in a single number the rich mosaic of different intelligences and skills that lead some people to become dancers (e.g., bodily-kinesthetic, spatial, and musical intelligence) while others become engineers (e.g., logical-mathematical, spatial) or philosophers (e.g., intrapersonal, verbal-linguistic, logical-mathematical)? Does knowing that someone's IQ is 120 tell you if that person is a talented musician, a quick learner of foreign languages, or skilled at investing in the stock market? In what way is a medical doctor with an IQ of 120 "more intelligent" than an athlete with an IQ of 115? In what realms might the athlete be more intelligent than the doctor? For all these reasons, it makes a lot of sense to be skeptical of claims that IQ in some sense "equals" intelligence and to conclude that intelligence is not easily reduced to or equated with one's score on a test. In this way of thinking, the black–white gap in IQ score may be essentially meaningless because reducing intelligence to a single number may conceal more than it reveals about the skills and talents of individuals or races.

The second conclusion of Jensen's work, that the black–white gap in IQ scores is mostly due to genetic differences, may also be questioned. In making this point, Jensen suggested that as much as 70 percent of the variation in IQ scores between individuals was the result of genetic variation, with the remaining 30 percent due to environmental differences. Although the 70 percent value may be a little higher than some recent estimates, most behavioral geneticists today would support a value for what they call the *heritability* of IQ scores of between 50 and 60 percent. However, there is an important problem in Jensen's logic. The heritability estimates for IQ scores are based primarily on studies of middle-class whites in America, and these estimates are therefore limited in their applicability to the populations on which they were calculated. Furthermore, Jensen uses studies of heritability of IQ *within* a population to explain differences in IQ scores *between* populations. When one says that the heritability of IQ in middle-class white Americans is high, all it means is that high-IQ white, middle-class American parents tend to have children with high IQ, and the same is true for low-IQ parents. This is not relevant at all for explaining the gap in IQ scores between different populations such as American Asians and blacks, each of whom live in different kinds of environments and have different educational and cultural experiences.

An example used by Stephen Jay Gould (1981) may help explain why this is so. Gould asks us to imagine a comparison in stature between a healthy and prosperous American population and an undernourished and poor Third World population. We would not be surprised to note a "stature gap" between the two, in which the Americans were on average quite a bit taller than the Third World population. We also know that stature has a very high heritability among middle-class Americans: estimates are much higher than for IQ, probably approaching 90 percent. Thus tall Americans tend to have tall children. But what explains the height differential between these two populations: genes or environment? In this case, it should be obvious that if we were to improve the environmental conditions of our Third World population by increasing the people's daily caloric intake, providing clean drinking water, and delivering improved health care to children and pregnant women, we would see increases in height in this population. We clearly recognize, both in this hypothetical situation and in the real world itself, that poor, malnourished, and sickly individuals do not typically realize their genetic potential for even such highly heritable features as stature. We say that their growth is stunted due to their poor environmental conditions. But isn't this exactly analogous to our consideration of an "IQ gap" between black and white Americans? How can we discount the greater levels of poverty, poor health care, malnutrition, and discrimination in discussing the lower IQ scores of African Americans? Do we really think that these factors play no role in stunting the growth of those who are subjected to them? So even though the heritability of IQ scores (and remember, these are not necessarily the same as intelligence) within a population is substantial, the differences between populations may be overwhelmingly due to environmental differences.

Finally, Jensen argues that all attempts at improving IQ scores of blacks are doomed to failure as a result of the high heritability (and consequently low environmental effects) of this trait. He thus uses his data to support a political position that suggests that Head Start programs, free breakfast programs, and all other attempts to intervene and thereby improve the environments of learning for minority children will have little effect on improving their IQ scores. The obvious conclusion that must be drawn from Jensen's argument is that we should not invest in attempts to minimize inequalities in our society for the purpose of creating healthy environments for all children to develop and learn in. Even if we do "level the playing field," we should not expect any significant improvements in IQ scores in black children, since IQ is hard-wired and genetic and thus impervious to all attempts at improvement. Thus he answers the question posed in the title of his 1969 article as to how much we can boost IQ and scholastic achievement: not much. A more chilling and pessimistic statement of the hereditarian viewpoint can hardly be imagined. But happily, Jensen is simply wrong on this score, as the previous paragraphs have documented. If growth in height is subject to stunting in a poor environment, certainly intellectual growth would also be expected to suffer in the nonoptimal environments of poverty and discrimination in which many black children live. The interactionist approach to this problem is much more successful at explaining the black–white gap in IQ scores than a strictly hereditarian approach. While there is certainly an important genetic component to intelligence, one simply cannot discount the importance of environment, both for explaining individual differences in IQ between members of a single population and especially for explaining differences between populations.

RETURN TO THE FUTURE: *THE BELL CURVE*

After a long period during which the views of hereditarians concerning race and IQ were superseded by interactionist viewpoints of scholars like Stephen Jay Gould, the hereditarian position came roaring back in 1994 with the publication of *The Bell Curve* by Richard J. Herrnstein and Charles Murray. In many ways, the arguments of *The Bell Curve* should be familiar because they are quite similar to earlier arguments by people like Jensen and because Herrnstein (1971) had already published the essence of the argument nearly 25 years earlier in a controversial article titled simply "IQ" in the *Atlantic Monthly*. The essential argument of Herrnstein and Murray is that our modern society is becoming more and more stratified into upper, middle, and lower classes based on intelligence (as measured by IQ score). They suggest that a strong relationship exists between status and success in society and intelligence and that IQ is therefore a good predictor of a whole series of measures of success or failure in society. For example, their analysis suggests that the people who are most likely to be unemployed, in jail, single and pregnant, or addicted to drugs are people of low IQ. Conversely, they suggest that the movers and shakers of society and all manner of successful people are those with high IQ. Specifically, they suggest that IQ is a better predictor of success or failure than socioeconomic status (SES), the often-stated alternative explanation of poor social outcomes that is favored by many social scientists.

At this point, their argument seems basically sociological rather than biological and not particularly controversial. Hereditarianism creeps into their argument, however, when they assert the old and discredited idea that IQ is largely determined by one's genes and little influenced by the environment in which development and learning occur. Race enters the story when they support the contention of Jensen (and others) that the black–white gap in IQ scores is determined by genetic differences between the races and thus not likely to be lessened as a result of environmental improvements among the underprivileged segments of society. Their view of the future includes the development of a "cognitive elite" in positions of power, wealth, and influence, who are not only intellectually but also physically segregated from the poor and dull drones of low IQ, who serve as laborers and janitors and in all job descriptions that pay minimal wages and require little thought to perform. By reducing this argument to its essence, we can clearly see its racial and hereditarian

FIGURE 8.5 Charles Murray (b. 1943) and Richard Herrnstein (1930–1994), the controversial authors of *The Bell Curve* (1994). a) © ZUMA Press, Inc. / Alamy b) © Ira Wyman/Sygma/Corbis

perspective: success in life is the result of high IQ, and failure is the result of low IQ; biology, through the action of genes, determines how intelligent we are, and environmental differences exert very little influence on the development of intelligence; and finally, races differ significantly in their genetic component of intelligence.

The publication of *The Bell Curve* in 1994 was greeted with an enormous amount of media attention (much of it complimentary), and it quickly became a best-seller. The scholarly attention it generated was also voluminous, but that was almost entirely critical, sometimes scathingly so (Fraser 1995; Fisher et al. 1996). The critical response to *The Bell Curve* came from all corners of academic life, including psychologists, anthropologists, sociologists, biologists, political scientists, historians, and journalists. Indeed, there is much to criticize in the book, but we will focus on only a few areas of disagreement and critique. Many readers of Herrnstein and Murray's book were impressed by its size (over 800 pages) and its aura of supporting scientific evidence, including 100 pages of appendixes, 100 pages of footnotes, and a 60-page bibliography. But the data and interpretations presented in its pages are drawn almost entirely from a single statistical analysis of data collected during a long-term study of nearly 13 thousand individuals known as the National Longitudinal Survey of Youth (NLSY). As the authors state, the NLSY data set is important because it combines "detailed information on the childhood environment and parental socioeconomic status and subsequent educational and occupational achievement and work history and family formation and—crucially for our interests—detailed psychometric measures of cognitive skills" (Herrnstein and Murray 1994:119). The data analysis technique that Herrnstein and Murray apply to this data set is known as *logistic regression analysis,* and it is designed to determine the importance of a series of predictor or independent variables for a particular dichotomous (either–or, yes–no) outcome known as the dependent variable. For example, does IQ or parental SES (the independent variables) have a stronger statistical relationship to whether or not a individual has spent some time in jail, been addicted to drugs, or been unemployed (the dependent variables)? Logistic regression analysis allows one to determine both the direction (i.e., whether high IQ is related to a higher or lower probability of being a drug addict) and the strength of the statistical relationship between independent and dependent variables.

So what does the analysis offered by the authors of *The Bell Curve* indicate about the direction and strength of the statistical relationship between IQ and SES and a long list of social and behavioral measures of success or failure in life? For the direction of the relationships, the answer is simple and unsurprising: the ranks of the socially unsuccessful and the antisocial are full of people of low IQ and poor people. High IQ and high parental socioeconomic status are both correlated with greater success in life. The answer to the question concerning the strength of the relationship actually depends on which part of the book you are referring to. In the text, the authors argue that IQ is consistently a much better predictor of social outcomes than SES: in their thinking, dumb people, not poor people, become criminals, unwed mothers, drug addicts, and welfare recipients. But one needs to carefully examine the actual tables of data presented in the appendixes to locate an important piece of evidence concerning the strength of the relationships between IQ and SES and the list of dependent variables. This evidence is a statistic that is associated with each logistic regression analysis that the authors performed known as the *coefficient of determination*, abbreviated R^2. R^2 values indicate the amount of variation in the dependent variables that is explained or predicted by variation in the independent variables. For example, appendix 4 (Herrnstein and Murray 1994:599) provides the data from the logistic regression analysis involving the likelihood of being unemployed for four weeks or more in 1989. These data are described in a chapter titled "Unemployment, Idleness, and Injury," in which the authors state that "among young white men who were in the labor market, the likelihood of unemployment for high school graduate and college graduates was equally dependent on cognitive ability. *Socioeconomic background was irrelevant once intelligence was taken into account*" (Herrnstein and Murray 1994:155, emphasis added). An examination of the R^2 value for this analysis, however, indicates that less than 2 percent of the variation in the dependent variable (i.e., whether or not an individual was unemployed for four weeks in 1989) was explained by variations in IQ and SES.

This result is not an anomaly: it is the norm for the logistic regressions performed by the authors on the NLYS data. For example, the R^2 value for the analysis of the dependent variable "first birth out of wedlock" was 8 percent, and for several independent variables involving criminal behavior, R^2 ranged from a low of 1 percent to a high of 9 percent. Clearly and unsurprisingly, both IQ and SES influence a variety of social measures of success or failure, but together they explain only a tiny part of the variation in these measures. Many other factors must predispose certain individuals to criminality or poor parenting, but these other factors are completely ignored in this analysis, and the reader is never made aware of this. A major critique of the argument of *The Bell Curve* must then involve the authors' highlighting of the direction of the statistical relationship between the variables (e.g., IQ is more important than SES in explaining unemployment), coupled with their hiding of the evidence that this relationship is quite weak (e.g., together, IQ and SES explain 2 percent of the variation in unemployment). Only a cynic would suggest that the reasons for this curious approach to presenting their data may be found in the fact that the direction of the statistical relationship supports their argument while the low R^2 values serve to weaken their case.

University of Michigan psychologist Richard Nisbett (1995) has taken a close and critical look at all of the scientific evidence concerning one of the stated assumptions of *The Bell Curve*, namely, that much of the 15-point black–white gap in IQ is due to genetic differences between the races. Examining all the published studies of race and IQ that control for differences in environment and thus allow one to determine the genetic component of IQ differences, Nisbett comes to some very different conclusions than Herrnstein and Murray did. One interesting study involved the analysis of the IQ of children fathered by U.S. soldiers but raised in Germany by their German mothers during World War II. There were no significant differences in the IQ of children born to black (average IQ: 96.5) or white (average IQ: 97) American fathers. Another study took advantage of the fact that many American blacks have some degree of European or white genes, often as much as 20 to 30 percent, as a result of a history of interracial breeding in America. If Herrnstein and Murray are right, one should find evidence of higher IQ in American blacks with a higher proportion of white genetic heritage and lower IQ among those with few Caucasian genes. Nisbett found instead a completely nonsignificant relationship between IQ and degree of European ancestry in African Americans. Interestingly, Herrnstein and Murray's 60-page bibliography omits all mention of studies like these, which serve to weaken their argument. Nisbett also summarizes the scientific literature on two other issues of great relevance to the argument of *The Bell Curve*. The first of these deals with the effects of environmental intervention in improving the IQ and school performance of poor and black children, and the second involves the evidence of a decrease in the black–white gap in IQ scores over the past few decades. On both of these accounts, Nisbett's reading of the psychological literature leads to very different conclusions from those drawn by Herrnstein and Murray. He finds good evidence that intervention in the form of enriching the environment for poor and minority children has a decidedly positive effect on their IQ and that these gains disappear only if and when the environmental enrichment program ceases. Furthermore, the bulk of the recent evidence suggests that the black–white gap in IQ scores has narrowed significantly at the rate of about 2.5 points per decade (Nisbett 1995:49). These changes are best interpreted as the result of improved socioeconomic conditions and better home and school environments for many African American children today; they certainly cannot be explained by genetic changes over this short period of time.

When one considers the bulk of the scientific evidence on genetics and the results of 100 years of IQ testing, the hereditarian position of innate racial inequality in intelligence that is presented in *The Bell Curve* and elsewhere does not fare very well. We have seen that some of the most basic assumptions of this hypothesis are problematic at best or just plain wrong: IQ may not be an unbiased measure of innate intelligence; intelligence may be too complex an entity to reduce to a single number; IQ scores and intelligence are both influenced (not determined) by the interaction of genetic and environmental effects; and racial discrimination, bad schools, and poverty may have a powerful negative influence on how well individuals or groups perform on IQ tests. Today we know that minimizing inequality among American children through improved nutrition, better schools and instruction, and enriched home environments can indeed boost IQ and scholastic achievement scores. If we truly want to eradicate the black–white gap in IQ scores, the way forward is clear. One might suggest that all we are lacking is the political will and the financial commitment as a society to create truly equal opportunities for all our children. Only when we can provide an equally rich learning environment for all children can we talk about a "level playing field" in education, and only then can we expect all our children to develop their individual intelligences to their full capabilities.

BOX ONE

Race and Sports: A Taboo Subject?

In his controversial book *Taboo*, journalist Jon Entine (2000) argues that black athletes today dominate sports that involve running, jumping, and endurance as a result of a combination of genetic advantages and environmental influences. Citing world records and Olympic medals, he claims that the best sprinters overwhelmingly share West African heritage, while elite distance runners tend to come from East Africa, mainly Kenya and Ethiopia and mainly from a single ethnic group (Kalenjin) and a single town (Eldoret) in western Kenya. He notes that the racial composition of the National Basketball Association has gone from 80 percent white in 1960 to 80 percent black in 2000. While recognizing that black athletes are as dedicated and train as hard as any other successful athletes, he suggests that black athletic superiority is at least partly the result of genetic differences between the races. Conversely, other sports that rely on different skill sets (e.g., golf, bowling, swimming, tennis, and baseball) do not show the same patterns of black dominance. Entine suggests that as a society, we treat the obvious natural superiority of black athletes as a taboo subject, one that is (or should be) off-limits to polite conversation and even to scientific investigation, for fear of being branded racist. Yet, he argues, science supports the claim that blacks are by nature better natural athletes than members of other races, and we need to be able to discuss these findings without repercussions or worries about "political correctness."

Actually, anthropologists and many other biological and social scientists are only too happy to discuss and critique these supposedly taboo data, as well as the author's interpretations. One can start by reiterating the definitional problems associated with concepts like "black athletes" and "white athletes." We know that most modern African Americans have widely varying amounts of European, American Indian, and African ancestry and that the African populations contain enormous genetic variation. If Entine's thesis were correct, we would expect greater athletic performance from African Americans with the least amount of non-African ancestry, yet no such data exist, to my knowledge. In fact, we have minimal data on the genetics of individual elite athletes, much less on groups of elite athletes of similar race. Simply noting the predominance of individuals of some ethnic or racial background at elite levels of sports does not tell us anything about why these individuals are dominant. Would anyone suggest that French Canadians are genetically superior hockey players simply as a result of their historical dominance in the National Hockey League or that Brazil's five World Cup championships in soccer can be explained by genetics? No, it seems that when white athletes dominate a sport, no one rushes to suggest that their dominance is the result of being "naturally gifted." Rather, hard work, cultural heritage, and intelligence are often cited to explain their success. We can certainly think of many historical, social, political, and economic reasons for the (temporary) dominance of certain ethnicities in certain sports. Sports that require expensive equipment (e.g., hockey) or user fees (e.g., golf) tend to be more popular with well-to-do individuals, while other sports tend to appeal disproportionately to inner-city, economically disadvantaged people (e.g., boxing). Like basketball, the ethnic makeup of professional boxing has changed dramatically from the 1950s, when Italians, Irish, and Germans dominated, to today's era of African American and Hispanic champions. So historical patterns of immigration and prosperity (or the lack of prosperity) have always influenced which sports appealed to which groups. There is very little reason to suggest that genetics plays a role in these changing trends, which take place on a time scale far too rapid to be explained by genes and are far more easily explained by social and historical factors. One should also not ignore the explicit role that racism has played in limiting or excluding the participation of African Americans from the ranks of professional athletes. This is most notable in major league baseball, which was first integrated by Jackie Robinson of the Brooklyn Dodgers in 1947, and in college basketball, when the first team to field five African Americans and win an NCAA championship was the University of Texas at El Paso in 1966.

Although we can justifiably criticize Entine's argument for the lack of explicit genetic evidence in support of a biological or racial argument, his case does actually have some strong points. What he refers to as the "Kenyan miracle," the incredible success of Kalenjin runners from western Kenya at long-distance events, is a unique phenomenon in sports. Seven of the ten fastest times in the marathon were set by Kenyans; the remaining slots belong to two Ethiopians and a Moroccan. Similarly, the world's best sprinters today overwhelmingly share West African ancestry, whether their nationality be American, Jamaican, or English. While Entine accepts that social and cultural factors play a large role in athletic success, especially among the Kalenjin, he argues that they are insufficient to explain the magnitude of the "Kenyan miracle." Perhaps the best solution lies in taking an interactionist approach, in which both genetics and environment (e.g., training, social and historical factors) play a role in explaining these patterns. What I mean by genetics is not the same as race but a more specific or fine-grained descriptor of ancestry. For example, I would be very interested in understanding if the Kalenjin people have special physiological or cardiovascular adaptations that predispose them to become great runners, given the right training and motivation, of course. Most anthropologists are perfectly comfortable talking about and researching human variation, and the study of patterns of athletic performance with respect to ancestry is certainly not a taboo subject. But our awareness of the sad history of racism in sports makes us leery of accepting facile arguments about racial difference. In light of the long-standing interest of earlier generations of scientists in pinpointing anatomical, psychological, and physiological differences between the races as a means of supporting racial inequality and a hierarchy in which Caucasians were always at the top and Africans at the bottom, this caution in accepting arguments about racial superiority makes good sense.

AN EVOLUTIONARY THEORY OF RACE?

In spite of the weaknesses of the hereditarian position concerning racial differences in IQ, there remain some scientific supporters of this position, notable among whom is J. Philippe Rushton, a psychologist at the University of Western Ontario. In a book titled *Race, Evolution, and Behavior: A Life History Perspective*, Rushton (1995) uses life history theory to explain the origins and inequalities between three races: Asians, Africans, and Europeans.

Life history theory comes from the biological sciences and seeks to understand behavioral and anatomical differences between species (or sometimes between individuals within species) in terms of a series of developmental and reproductive parameters and associated anatomical features. For example, life history theorists find significant correlations between body size, brain size, age at first reproduction, age at weaning or at puberty, lifespan, litter size, and duration of the interval between births for many different kinds of animals. Evolution by natural selection is thought to lead different species to different life history strategies. If we compare rabbits with monkeys, we can see two very different kinds of life history strategies at play. Rabbits have small bodies and small brains, reach sexual maturity at a very young age, give birth to large litters with as many as seven offspring several times a year, have a short gestation of about one month, and have a lifespan of about ten years. Monkeys are larger and have larger brains, take longer to mature and hence reproduce at older ages with much longer intervals between births, give birth to singletons or sometimes twins, and can live several decades. Rabbits can be said to live faster and die younger than monkeys: these are two different life history strategies, both of which are successful from the perspective of rabbits or monkeys. Biologists call species like rabbits that "live fast and die young", *r-selected*, where *r* refers to the rate of growth of population size, which is maximized in these kinds of animals. Species like monkeys are said to be *K-selected* because although their population growth (*r*) is slow, they live at population sizes close to the carrying capacity (*K*) of their environments. Notice that we can imagine organisms as inhabiting some position along a continuous *r-to-K* ecological spectrum, with rabbits closer to the *r* side than monkeys but salmon even more *r*-selected than rabbits and apes more *K*-selected than monkeys. One final point about life history theory is that some ecologists have suggested that *r*-selected species tend to be found in more unstable or unpredictable environments where the ability to reproduce very quickly is at a premium, since mortality tends to be high in these kinds of environments. Conversely, *K*-selected species tend to be found in more stable or predictable environments, which tend to be crowded with other competitors. These animals live longer and breed more slowly, but they are better adapted at competing for scarce resources.

FIGURE 8.6 J. Philippe Rushton (b. 1943) developed a controversial notion of the evolution of human races based on life history theory. Courtesy of David S. Holloway/ Getty Images.

The beauty of life history theory is that the relationships between these reproductive and morphological features of animals allow us to make strong inferences about an animal's life history strategy based on knowledge of a single trait or just a few. For example, if you tell me of an animal the size of an elephant (say, a wooly mammoth), I can tell you with a good deal of confidence that it lives a long life, develops slowly, produces few offspring one at a time, goes a long time between births, and provides much parental care to each offspring. Conversely, most shrew-sized mammals "live fast and die young." What exactly does this brief foray into ecological theory have to do with human races? Rushton's theory is that racial differences between the descendants of African, Asian, and European populations are the result of different placement of these racial populations on the *r–K* ecological spectrum. His argument is as follows. As a result of living in the unstable environments of the Old World tropics for so long, Africans are the most *r*-selected of the human races. Rushton suggests that high levels of "tropical diseases" would have killed many Africans and that the best strategy in this kind of environment would be the *r*-selected one in which rapid reproduction is emphasized, with lots of babies, but little parental care available for each. By contrast, Europeans and especially Asians are more *K*-selected because they moved out of the tropics to the temperate zones, where different strategies for survival had to be used. In this new environment, a new set of problems (food storage, shelter from the elements, etc.) had to be solved that required more brain power, smaller families, and more parental care of fewer offspring. Rushton suggests that the three continental races have each evolved different characteristics that are adaptive for the environments in which they evolved and that these can be understood in terms of life history theory and *r*- and *K*-selection. What are the characteristic profiles of each race? Essentially, Rushton asserts that Africans (and African Americans), as the most *r*-selected of the human races, have smaller brains and are less intelligent, are more aggressive and violent, mature faster, and reproduce earlier and more frequently than the other races. Asians are the most *K*-selected race, and hence they possess the largest brains and most intelligence, are the least aggressive, slowest to mature, and have smaller families in which they lavish lots of parental care on each offspring. Europeans are intermediate on Rushton's spectrum of life history variation.

Whereas many critics have accused Rushton of scientific racism, one can also criticize his work for its shoddy methods, poor documentation, dogmatic support of hereditarianism, and misapplication of recognized scientific principles and practices. Under the category of shoddy scientific methods, I would highlight his approach to collecting data from the published scientific literature in support of racial differences. For example, his data on brain size simply aggregate all the published studies and provide an average value for black, white, and Asian brain size. But the problem with this approach is that it lumps together and treats as equally valid noncomparable data sets of varying quality and sample size, collected by a variety of methods by many different investigators. His evidence of low IQ among Africans is based in part on IQ scores of black children from apartheid-era South Africa: Does he really doubt that these low numbers reflect more on the social policies and legalized discrimination of his native country than they do on the genetic endowment of all Africans? The notion that human populations have been shaped differently by evolution with respect to *r*- and *K*-selection is simplistic. How exactly can we categorize the enormous range of environmental and habitat variation found in a continent the size of Africa (or Asia or Europe, for that matter) as "unpredictable" and conclude that modern humans whose ancestors spent more time in Africa are, as a result, more *r*-selected? What exactly about life in the temperate zones of Asia and Europe requires more intelligence than life in Africa? How can the incarceration rates of blacks, white, and Asians in America today tell us anything at all about the evolutionary history of our ancestors? Are the fertility rates of all Asian populations (and associated libido, according to Rushton) lower than those of African populations, and are there not better explanations from the social, cultural, and economic realms for human variation in family size? In my opinion, Rushton's work is political advocacy and racial stereotyping masquerading as science. The science is poor, and the politics is harmful: in either case, his life history perspective on the origins and adaptive significance of racial differences contributes nothing to an understanding of the biological or social meanings of race.

Discussion Questions

1. What is the nature–nurture controversy with respect to features of human nature?

2. What is biological determinism, and how does it explain differences in human populations' IQ scores?

3. Why are many anthropologists skeptical of the proposition that IQ scores provide a reasonable measure of innate intelligence of individuals and populations?

4. What were the initial goals of the eugenics developed by Francis Galton? Were these goals ever realized?

5. Who was Arthur Jensen, and what was his position with respect to race and intelligence?

6. Critically analyze the argument developed by Herrnstein and Murray in *The Bell Curve*.

7. What were some of the results of the mass IQ tests given to Ellis Island immigrants and World War I soldiers in the early 20th century?

8. What modern racial stereotypes can you see in Linnaeus's 1758 classification of human races?

CHAPTER 9

Race as a Cultural Construction

"There is no biological basis for separation of human beings into races and . . . the idea of race is a relatively recent social and political construction."

GRAVES 2001:1

THE CENTRAL PARADOX OF RACE

How can race both exist and not exist? A clear explanation must be made here in order to clarify the basic paradox that runs throughout the modern anthropological critique of race. Let's start with the negative proposition. When anthropologists say that race does not exist, what exactly do they mean? Is this a call for a "color-blind" society in which race recedes into the political and social background because it is no longer relevant to the global human or local American experience? Does this position perhaps argue for the repeal of all affirmative action laws (as my own state of Michigan and some other states have done in recent years) because race is simply not relevant to American life anymore? Are we entering a postracial stage of American democracy in which, in the immortal words of Martin Luther King Jr. (1963), people "will not be judged by the color of their skin but by the content of their character"? In a word, has race become obsolete?

When anthropologists state that race does not exist, they are *not* claiming that human biological variation does not exist: that would be a ridiculous position for anyone to hold, considering that both polymorphic and polytypic variation are so central to evolutionary analysis and to the anthropological experience. People whose ancestors come from different parts of the globe really do vary in many different biological parameters, including skin, hair, and eye color; blood group genetics; and disease susceptibility. Nor do we mean that race has no significance for the lived experiences of modern people. What we mean to say is that biological theories of race and all resultant classifications of race within *Homo sapiens* have no significant scientific support. The problems with biological theories of race have been discussed earlier in this book and can be quickly recapped here. Race as biology involves the arbitrary selection of certain biological features (e.g., skin color or ABO blood group frequencies), followed by the arbitrary separation of these continuously variable traits into discrete groups. Since these traits tend to be discordant (i.e., all people with dark skin do not share similar ABO gene frequencies), the resulting classifications tend to be as disparate and as numerous as the individual classifiers. This is the problem discussed in chapter 1 concerning different definitions of the concepts of "tall" and "short" among humans. While we would all agree that tall and short people can be found in human populations and that much of the difference in stature is due to genetics, who among us would be so bold (or so foolish) as to suggest a universal and biologically justified classification of the world into tall and short "races"? Scandinavians are indeed taller on average than African pygmies, but does this mean that we could successfully classify all the world's populations into races based on their stature? And if we substituted the words *dark* and *light* for *tall* and *short* and *skin color* for *stature*, would we then reach a different conclusion, namely, that we could scientifically and objectively classify humans into races? I think not, and in this limited, biological sense only, I would argue that race doesn't exist.

As a result of these considerations, the notion of human race fails as a biological theory, and hence race does not exist. But what is the standing of race in other aspects of human experience, for example, in the social, cultural, political, economic, and artistic realms? If race does not stand up to scrutiny as biology, does it have any relevance or significance in any other realms of human experience? In what sense does race still have relevance and meaning for real people living today or, for that matter, in the past or future? The argument is easy to make that for much of American history, race has been a vital aspect of everyone's social, economic, and political experience. At the most basic level of political participation and of personal freedom, race was until the late 19th century the crucial dividing line between free citizens and disenfranchised slaves. Throughout much of the 20th century in America, free descendants of these slaves were discriminated against in a variety of ways: they were lynched, publicly humiliated, segregated, made to sit in the back of the bus, and forced to submit to many more indignities—all on account of their perceived inferiority as a race.

Clearly, race is real in America, but this kind of race is not biological. This version of race is what anthropologists refer to as a *social* or *cultural construction*, and here is where the real strength of race resides. Social constructions of race are the cultural beliefs and meanings associated with people of differing phenotypes such as skin color. Different societies have different ideas about the meaning of being black, for example. Even the same society attributes different meanings to races at different times and in different places. It is obvious that being black in Mississippi meant very different things in 1850 and 2010, with the result that the lived experiences of black people in Mississippi would have been very different then and now. Similarly, race can have different cultural meanings in different geographic zones of a single society or country even at the same point in time. When I lived in New Orleans during the early 1990s, I was surprised to note the existence of a range of racial categories with which I had no prior familiarity. Such categories as creole (a mixed race involving some combination of French, Spanish, African American, and Native American ancestry), quadroon (one African American grandparent), and octoroon (one African American great-grandparent) were still in everyday use there, suggesting that race was constructed very differently in southern Louisiana than it was in my native New York. So in this cultural sense, it is clear that race does indeed exist, as all anthropologists would agree. Here is the resolution of the paradox: race as biology fails completely, but race as a social construction has a continuing and significant relevance in America.

While accepting the historical importance of these cultural and social aspects of race in America, some critics have suggested a "declining significance of race" today and advocate for a "color-blind" society. In this chapter, we will consider how, in spite of its nonexistent biological status, race continues to play a vital and significant role in the cultural, social, and political life of Americans.

RACE IN AMERICAN HISTORY

"We hold these truths to be self-evident, that all men are created equal, that they are endowed by their Creator with certain unalienable rights, that among these are Life, Liberty and the pursuit of Happiness." With these stirring words from the preamble to the Declaration of Independence, Thomas Jefferson and the other Founders created a new political entity dedicated to the principles of equality, freedom, and democracy. But left unspoken in the Declaration was the reality that many of these same Founders were wealthy slaveholders who had no intention of ending the profitable institution of slavery. Some of the Founders may have wanted to abolish slavery, but the need to ensure the support of

FIGURE 9.1 Thomas Jefferson (1743–1826), third president of the United States, principal author of the Declaration of Independence, and lifelong slave owner.
© GL Archive / Alamy

the southern states required the compromise of maintaining the "peculiar institution." For example, John Jay well understood the gap between the ideals that founded our country and the contemporary practice of slavery when he wrote in 1786, "It is much to be wished that slavery may be abolished. The honour of the States, as well as justice and humanity, in my opinion, loudly call upon them to emancipate these unhappy people. To contend for our own liberty, and to deny that blessing to others, involves an inconsistency not to be excused." So at the very beginning of the American experiment, we are confronted with another paradox that continues to influence lives today: in a country founded on explicitly stated principles of equality for all, political inequality based on race has always been a part of the fabric of American society.

Thomas Jefferson himself has been strongly criticized by historians for his ownership of hundreds of slaves at Monticello, his Virginia estate. Another serious inconsistency between Jefferson's writings and the way he led his life can be found in his position on interbreeding between blacks and whites. In spite of the fact that he wrote in 1814 that "the amalgamation of whites with blacks produces a degradation to which no lover of excellence in the human character can innocently consent," recent DNA tests have proved that Jefferson had several children with one of his Monticello slaves, Sally Hemings. Ironically, Sally Hemings was probably the half-sister of Jefferson's own wife: evidence suggests that Jefferson's father-in-law, John Wayles, may have been Sally's father! Another of the Founders and icons of early American democracy, Benjamin Franklin, was also a slaveholder who was ambivalent about both the continuation and the end of the institution. He wrote in 1789 that "slavery is such an atrocious debasement of human nature, that it's very extirpation, if not performed with solicitous care, may sometimes open a source of serious evils." Better the evil that we know than the evil that we don't know.

The U.S. Constitution explicitly mentions slavery in several places, including the so-called enumeration clause in article 1, section 2, where it states that slaves should be counted as three-fifths of a person for the purpose of determining the population of states with respect to political representation in the federal government. This compromise was obviously in the political interest of the southern states, where a large proportion of the inhabitants were, in fact, slaves. Some 18 percent (700 thousand) of the 3.8 million people counted in the national census of 1790 were slaves, and the proportions were much higher in certain southern states, including North Carolina (26 percent), Maryland (32 percent), Virginia (39 percent), and South Carolina (43 percent). In section 9 of this article of the Constitution, Congress was prohibited from banning the importation of slaves until 1808, and the fugitive slave clause in article 4, section 2, ensured that slaves who escaped to another state had to be extradited back to their slave state of origin and to servitude.

It has been clear to American historians for a very long time that the conflict between supporters of slavery and those who wanted slavery ended (known as abolitionists) was one of the major causes of the American Civil War (1861–1865). In 1857, a Supreme Court decision (*Dred Scott* v. *Sanford*) concerning the rights of a slave to sue for his freedom, was one of many precipitating sparks that contributed to the conflagration that was the Civil War. Dred Scott was a slave born in Virginia but sold as an adult to a U.S. Army doctor by the name of John Emerson in the slave state of Missouri. Emerson and Scott traveled extensively together throughout the Illinois and Wisconsin territories, where slavery was forbidden. In 1846, Scott sued for his freedom in a Saint Louis courtroom on the grounds that the time that he had spent in free states made him eligible to claim his freedom from servitude. The case eventually went all the way to the U.S. Supreme Court, where in 1857 Chief Justice Roger Taney delivered the majority opinion, stating that the issue at hand was the following:

> Can a negro, whose ancestors were imported into this country and sold as slaves, become a member of the political community formed and brought into existence by the Constitution of the United States, and as such become entitled to all the rights, privileges, and immunities guaranteed by that instrument to the citizen? One of which rights is the privilege of suing in a court of the United States.

The *Dred Scott* decision struck a serious blow against the abolitionists' struggle to end slavery by denying that any blacks, free or slave, could claim citizenship in the United States. Because blacks were not citizens, they had no standing in the U.S. legal system and could not sue in court. Furthermore, the Court held that slaves, as chattel or property, could not be taken from their rightful

FIGURE 9.2 Dred Scott (1799–1858) was a slave who sued for his freedom but was denied by the U.S. Supreme Court in 1857 on the basis that blacks, both slave and free, could not be citizens of the United States.
© The Art Archive / Alamy.

owner without due process of the law, according to the rights guaranteed by the Fifth Amendment to the Constitution. Finally, the Court ruled that the federal government had no right to prohibit slavery in any federal territory. The *Dred Scott* decision was a sweeping victory for slaveholders and their supporters and a crushing defeat for black people and abolitionists and for the ideals on which this country was founded. Within two short years of the *Dred Scott* decision, the abolitionist John Brown would be hanged for his attempt to start a slave rebellion and his unsuccessful raid against a federal armory in Harpers Ferry, Virginia (1859). Two years later, on April 12, 1861, Confederate batteries in Charleston, South Carolina, began the bombardment of Fort Sumter in the Charleston harbor that signaled the beginning of the American Civil War. By the time the Treaty of Appomattox was signed on April 9, 1865, nearly 200 thousand Union and Confederate soldiers would be counted among the dead in a war fought over the contested meanings of race in America.

On January 1, 1863, President Abraham Lincoln issued an executive order that has come to be known as the Emancipation Proclamation, in which he declared the freedom of all slaves in the rebellious states of the Confederacy. The Civil War was now explicitly about freeing the slaves, and as the word spread to the slave population, more and more slaves escaped to the northern lines and to freedom, with many promptly enlisting in the Union armed forces. By the end of the war, almost 200 thousand blacks had actively fought for their own freedom in the Union Army and Navy. Because the Emancipation Proclamation was a wartime measure that explicitly freed slaves only in the rebellious states of the Confederacy and not in some of the loyal border states, the formal abolishment of slavery in the entire United States was not legislated until the Thirteenth Amendment to the U.S. Constitution was ratified on December 6, 1865, just eight months after the cessation of hostilities.

With the end of the Civil War, the country embarked on a period of reconciliation and reunification known as the Reconstruction era (1865–1877). Two additional amendments to the Constitution that had important implications for race relations in America were passed during Reconstruction. The Fourteenth Amendment (ratified on July 9, 1868) provided a new definition of citizenship that overturned the *Dred Scott* decision and for the first time guaranteed full citizenship to blacks. The citizenship clause (section 1, clause 1) of this amendment states, "All persons born or naturalized in the United States, and subject to the jurisdiction thereof, are citizens of the United States and of the State wherein they reside." The amendment's due process clause states that "no State shall deprive any person of life, liberty, or property, without due process of law," thereby extending this important restraint on government power over individuals to the states (the Fifth Amendment had already established the principle of due process with respect to the federal government). Finally, the Fifteenth Amendment (ratified on February 3, 1870) stated that the right of all citizens to vote "shall not be denied or abridged by the United States or by any State on account of race, color, or previous condition of servitude" (although only males had the right to vote at that time). In spite of these attempts by the newly united federal government to ensure the full participation in American democracy of freed black slaves and their descendants, shortly after the end of Reconstruction in 1877, many southern state governments passed laws that effectively disenfranchised freed blacks and maintained their inferior social and political status. These so-called Jim Crow laws legislated the mandatory segregation of blacks and whites in all public spaces in most southern states. This meant that separate or segregated facilities were to be provided in all aspects of public life for blacks and for whites, including but not limited to schools, transportation, hotels, and restaurants. In 1896, the Supreme Court sided with the Jim Crow segregationists in the *Plessy* v. *Ferguson* decision. In a 7-to-1 majority decision, the Court stated that forced racial segregation was constitutional, based on the principle that segregated facilities could be "separate but equal." While these laws would continue to be in effect in some places in the South until 1965, the fight to repeal the Jim Crow laws was at the heart of the civil rights movement of the 1950s and 1960s. The struggles of the civil rights era to end the post–Civil War legacy of racism and segregation and to finally live up to the high ideals and promise of American democracy for all citizens would prove to be one of the most significant social and political movements of the 20th century.

FIGURE 9.3 For most of the 20th century, Jim Crow laws ensured the segregation of whites and blacks in the southern United States. Here a barrier separates a drinking fountain "For Colored Only" from one reserved for whites.
© Bettmann/Corbis.

THE CIVIL RIGHTS ERA

Although most accounts of the civil rights era focus on the work of a few high-profile leaders of the movement (e.g., Martin Luther King) or on the major politicians of the time (e.g., Presidents Kennedy and Johnson), the former NAACP chairman and civil rights activist Julian Bond has rightly suggested that "the civil rights drama involved thousands of acts of individual courage undertaken in the name of freedom" (1987:xi). In this necessarily brief summary of some of the high points of the civil rights era, we will follow Bond's advice and look at some of the lesser-known players in this drama among the millions of ordinary Americans who participated in the struggle for equal rights and for a new meaning of race in America.

The first major blow struck against the evils of racial segregation and Jim Crow was the Supreme Court's landmark decision in *Brown* v. *Board of Education of Topeka*. The case revolved around 7-year-old Linda Brown, the daughter of Reverend Oliver Brown of Topeka, Kansas, who was required to travel across town to attend a black school in spite of the presence of a good whites-only school nearer her home. The case was argued by a brilliant young NAACP lawyer named Thurgood Marshall, aided by lawyers (notably Charles Houston, Marshall's own professor when Marshall was a law student) and law students from Howard University in Washington, D.C. Marshall's argument against "separate but equal" schools relied heavily on the results of social science research by sociologists and psychologists that indicated that segregation naturally led to feelings of inferiority on the part of black children. In addition, Marshall presented clear evidence of the poor funding and inferior facilities found at most schools reserved for blacks, both in the Topeka school district and in many other places throughout the country. On May 17, 1954, the Supreme Court returned a unanimous decision for the plaintiff. The *Brown* decision ended legal racial segregation in public schools by overturning the precedent set in 1896 by *Plessy* v. *Ferguson*. The Court determined that "separate but equal" was not only a myth in the Jim Crow South, since separate facilities for blacks were always

FIGURE 9.4 Thurgood Marshall (1908–1993), the lawyer who in 1954 successfully argued the *Brown v. Board of Education* case before the U.S. Supreme Court. He later became the first African American to serve on the Court (1967–1991).
© Bettmann/Corbis.

inferior to those reserved for whites, but also unconstitutional. Chief Justice Earl Warren's decision read in part:

> Does segregation of children in public schools solely on the basis of race, even though the physical facilities and other tangible factors may be equal, deprive children of the minority group of equal educational opportunities? We believe it does. . . . To separate them from others of similar age and qualifications solely because of their race generates a feeling of inferiority as to their status in the community that may affect their hearts and minds in a way very unlikely ever to be undone. We conclude, unanimously, that in the field of public education the doctrine of "separate but equal" has no place. Separate educational facilities are inherently unequal.

The reaction to the *Brown* decision was mixed. While it was welcomed by civil rights advocates and many ordinary Americans, both black and white, segregationists and many whites in the South violently resisted its call for full-fledged integration of their social and political lives. The Supreme Court decision had actually called for an end to segregation of all public schools in the nation "with all deliberate speed," and this curious and somewhat contradictory phrase was used by politicians to argue for a slow and gradual end to segregation. Even political leaders such as Arkansas Governor Orval Faubus and Alabama Governor George Wallace fought against the forced integration of their state's schools, in open defiance of the Supreme Court's decision and the wishes of the federal government. Although the federal government forcibly integrated many school districts in the South, most famously in Little Rock, Arkansas, in 1957 with the help of the U.S. Army, many school districts continue to be segregated throughout the nation today, more than half a century after the *Brown* decision. Segregated schools today are more a result of economically stratified and segregated neighborhoods than of a legal system of "separate but equal" schools for the different races, but perhaps the end result is not all that different. If one were to compare, for example, today's inner-city Detroit schools with those of some of the wealthy outlying suburbs, one might have to conclude that in spite of the *Brown* decision, things have not changed very much.

Another reaction to the social changes of the 1950s was the resurgence of the white supremacist organization known as the Ku Klux Klan (KKK), which led to increased violence against blacks throughout the South (Thernstrom and Thernstrom 1999). One of the most shocking and perhaps the most significant of the numerous lynchings and other acts of violence perpetrated against blacks was the murder of a 14-year-old black youth from the South Side of Chicago named Emmett Till. Emmett and his cousin Curtis Jones were spending the summer of 1955 with relatives in a small town in the Mississippi delta. One day at a grocery store in town, Emmett apparently spoke a bit too freely (for 1955 Mississippi) with the white woman proprietor. Three days later, the woman's husband and another man dragged Emmett out of bed after midnight, kidnapped him, tortured him, shot him in the skull, and dumped his body in the Tallahatchie River. Another three days would pass before his body would be recovered. After his body was returned to Chicago for burial, his mother insisted on an open-casket funeral, and when *Jet* magazine published a graphic picture of the murdered boy, the case gained national prominence, and two white men were charged with kidnapping and murder. In spite of death threats to any blacks who testified against the two men who had dragged Emmett out of bed that night, his cousin's grandfather, a 64-year-old uneducated sharecropper named Mose Wright, courageously took the stand and pointed out the men who had taken Emmett. Nevertheless, after an hour's deliberations, the all-white jury acquitted both men on all counts. The two acquitted killers probably had no idea that the revulsion felt by millions of Americans in response to their murderous act would play a major role in ending white supremacy and routine violence against blacks in the South. No one was ever convicted of the torture and murder of Emmett Till, but the brutality of the Jim Crow system was now out in the open for all Americans to see.

Another aspect of daily life that was highly segregated in the Jim Crow South of the 1950s was public transportation. Blacks had to sit in the back of the bus, and in many cities, blacks had to give up their seats to whites if there was a shortage of seats. On December 1, 1955, a 43-year-old seamstress in Montgomery, Alabama, named Rosa Parks decided that she would rather go to jail than give up her

FIGURE 9.5 Fourteen-year-old Emmett Till, from Chicago, was one of the first martyrs of the civil rights movement. He was kidnapped, tortured, and murdered by white supremacists for speaking to a white woman in Money, Mississippi, in 1955.
© Bettmann/Corbis.

FIGURE 9.6 Rosa Parks (1913–2005) climbing the stairs to the Montgomery, Alabama, courthouse in 1956 to be arraigned for her act of civil disobedience: refusing to move to the back of a segregated city bus—a violation of city statutes at the time.
Courtesy of AP Photo.

seat on the bus to a white passenger. Within a few days, the entire black community of Montgomery organized a powerful and peaceful response to these injustices: the Montgomery Bus Boycott. For the next 13 months, tens of thousands of Montgomery blacks chose to walk to work and to school rather than patronize the city buses, and a new civil rights leader was born. At the time, Martin Luther King Jr. was the 26-year-old pastor of the Dexter Avenue Baptist Church in Montgomery, but his leadership of this pivotal nonviolent protest thrust him into the leading ranks of civil rights leaders, a position he would relinquish only as a result of an assassin's bullet in Memphis, Tennessee, on April 4, 1968. The Montgomery Bus Boycott ultimately succeeded when the Supreme Court affirmed a lower court's ban on racial segregation on public transportation. On December 20, 1956, just over a year since Rosa Parks decided to make a stand by remaining seated, Montgomery's blacks once again rode their newly integrated city buses.

The civil rights era can be arbitrarily said to have ended in 1965, a year in which much of the focus of the movement was on the right of all citizens to vote, regardless of color, that had been granted by the Fifteenth Amendment nearly 100 years earlier. The flashpoint of efforts to register southern blacks to vote was to occur in Selma, Alabama, a place where in 1963, "just 156 of Selma's 15,000 blacks of voting age were on the voting rolls" (Williams 1987:252). In the face of increasing violence and harassment aimed at organizers and would-be black voters, Martin Luther King Jr. came to Selma in January 1965 and began to plan for a mass march from Selma to the state capital of Montgomery in support of voting rights for blacks. On Sunday, March 7, 1965, some 600 civil rights activists began the march to Montgomery, but as they approached the Edmund Pettus Bridge across the Alabama River, they were met by a large contingent of Alabama state troopers and Selma police. When they refused to disperse, the unarmed marchers were violently attacked with clubs and tear gas by police and state troopers on foot and on horseback. As the nation watched this brutal attack on what would become known as "Bloody Sunday," a sense of outrage at the lengths to which southern segregationists and racists would go in order to maintain the racial status quo was rising in the

FIGURE 9.7 Police officers watching as civil rights protesters cross the Edmund Pettus Bridge during their march from Selma to Montgomery, Alabama, in 1965. © Bettmann/Corbis.

FIGURE 9.8 Malcolm X (1925–1965), civil rights leader and supporter of black nationalism, at a rally in 1963. He was assassinated two years later while giving a speech in New York City. © Bettmann/Corbis.

federal government and among much of white and black America. When President Johnson spoke to a joint session of Congress on March 15, 70 million Americans watched on television as he called the recent events in Selma "an American tragedy" and promised to "strike down all restrictions used to deny people the right to vote." One week later, on Sunday, March 21, the march from Selma to Montgomery finally went off with four thousand people undertaking the 54-mile journey on foot to protest for their right to vote. Six months later, the president signed the Voting Rights Act. One week later, the first of the urban race riots of the 1960s occurred in the Watts neighborhood of Los Angeles, California, to be followed by similar violent riots in 1967 in Newark, New Jersey, and Detroit, Michigan. The era of the nonviolent protest, guided by the principles of civil disobedience of Martin Luther King Jr., was now over. In its place was the more assertive and often openly violent approach advocated by Malcolm X, Stokely Carmichael, and the Black Panthers.

RACE, ETHNICITY, AND AMERICAN CITIZENSHIP

What makes an American citizen? This seemingly simple question has been a highly contested issue throughout our more than 225 years as a nation, and race has always played a major role in answering this question. If we look at the racial or ethnic composition of the United States as revealed by the American Community Survey of 2006, we will find a very diverse nation of nearly 300 million inhabitants, 74 percent of whom are white, 12 percent black, 1 percent Native American, and 4 percent Asian. In addition, the 2000 census estimated 12.5 percent of the U.S. population was of Hispanic origin (this question was separated from questions referring to race). This particular snapshot of the racial and ethnic makeup of the American people can be seen to result from at least three different factors: (1) historical patterns of transnational migration, (2) demographic patterns such as birthrates and family size, and (3) the conscious design of U.S. immigration and naturalization laws (Haney López 1996).

Historically, waves of immigrants have come to America from all over the world, including the author's own ancestral Irish during the 19th century and Italians during the early 20th century. Between 1892 and 1954, more than 12 million immigrants came to the United States through Ellis Island in New York harbor. As the earlier waves of English, Dutch, and Scandinavian immigrants gave way to new immigrants from Ireland, Italy, Russia, and China, the biological and cultural diversity of the country was forever changed, constantly renewed, and ultimately enriched. The importance of demographic trends is made very clear by recent estimates suggesting a tripling of the Hispanic population in the United States by 2050 as a result of extremely high birthrates among Americans of Hispanic descent. But perhaps the most interesting and important way in which race has played a role in the making of the American citizenry can be found by an examination of how the U.S. government has designed its immigration and naturalization policies over the span of our history as a nation.

The important point is this: the racial and ethnic diversity of the American people is today, and has always been, to a large extent the result of deliberate government policies aimed at defining who is or is not eligible to become an American. Our government has accomplished this goal through two major activities: by controlling the requirements for citizenship and by controlling immigration. Obviously,

FIGURE 9.9 Ellis Island, at the mouth of the Hudson River in New York harbor, was the first stop for most European immigrants entering the United States between 1892 and 1954.
Courtesy of MPI/Getty Images.

determining citizenship requirements and immigration policies are perfectly reasonable things for a national government to do, and all functioning governments perform these tasks. But what may be unique to the United States is the degree to which racial thinking has influenced government policy in both these areas. As you will see, federal law restricted immigration to the United States on the explicit basis of race for nearly a century (from 1882 to 1965). With respect to citizenship, our record is even worse: race was an explicit barrier to becoming a naturalized citizen of the United States from 1790 until 1952! Let's take a closer look at the historical record of the immigration policies and citizenship requirements of the United States to gain a better understanding of how the racial and ethnic composition of our country has been steered in particular directions over the past several hundred years.

BECOMING AMERICAN

The historian Eric Foner has drawn attention to an interesting contradiction relating to American and Western debates on race and citizenship. Foner writes, "If the West . . . created the idea of liberty as a universal human right, it also invented the concept of 'race' and ascribed to it predictive powers about human behavior" (1998:38). We have already seen a version of this contradiction regarding liberty and race slavery starkly represented in the persons of Thomas Jefferson and Benjamin Franklin, but Foner suggests that it may also be seen in the historical and continuing struggle over determining "who is an American." One can become a citizen of the United States in one of two ways: by being born on American soil (this is known as *birthright citizenship*) or, for those born in other lands, through the process of *naturalization*. Although the U.S. Constitution does not explicitly define the citizenry, the notion of citizenship by birthright, that all who are born in a country are automatically granted citizenship, is a principle of English common law that was well known and accepted by the Founders. Yet in direct opposition to the standard of common law, the *Dred Scott* decision of 1857 explicitly denied citizenship to blacks born in the United States. Native Americans were also placed outside of the boundaries of the citizenry, but they were considered members of independent political entities ("tribes") and were exempted from taxation. With respect to blacks, however, there is no doubt that Chief Justice Taney's decision was based on his belief in the inferiority of blacks as a race. The framers of the Constitution left the question of naturalization to Congress, which obliged by passing the Naturalization Act in 1790, just a few months after the Constitution was ratified. This law restricted naturalization to "any alien, *being a free white person* who shall have resided within the limits and under the jurisdiction of the United States for a term of two years" (emphasis mine).

The situation with respect to race and birthright citizenship would seem to have been resolved during Reconstruction with the passage of the Civil Rights Act of 1866, which stated that "all persons born . . . in the United States and not subject to any foreign power, excluding Indians not taxed, are declared to be citizens of the United States." The intent of this law was to overturn the *Dred Scott* decision and thereby guarantee citizenship to all people born in the United States, regardless of race. Two years later, the principle of birthright citizenship was again institutionalized in our legal system in the form of the Fourteenth Amendment, which stated that "all persons born or naturalized in the United States, and subject to the jurisdiction thereof, are citizens of the United States and of the state wherein they reside." Yet in spite of these two seemingly crystal-clear legal precedents, there has been and continues to be a struggle over the application of the principle of citizenship by birthright to members of many minority groups, especially Native Americans, children born in America to noncitizen parents, and Asians. All Native Americans were finally granted U.S. citizenship in 1924, but the struggle over the citizenship status of U.S.-born children of undocumented aliens continues to be a potent political issue today, especially in the southern and western border states. In many ways, we are still debating the *Dred Scott* decision, in spite of the fact that these issues were ostensibly settled by law in the 1860s.

With respect to naturalization, the story is no less complicated or less interesting. As noted earlier, Congress in 1790 limited naturalization to "free white persons," and this "whites only" provision was maintained until 1870, when Congress opened up naturalization to "persons of African nativity or African descent." Chinese, Japanese, and many other groups considered to be "nonwhite" were restricted from becoming naturalized American citizens until the 1940s, when these groups were, in piecemeal fashion, eventually added to the list of suitable applicants for naturalized U.S. citizenship. The end to legal racial restrictions on naturalization came in 1952 when Congress ended all restrictions based on "race or sex or because such person is married." As this quotation implies, there was also a time when the requirements for citizenship included sex (i.e., males only) and marital status (i.e., women who married aliens could lose their U.S. citizenship). Finally, it is sobering to learn that in 1935, when the Nazi government formally limited German citizenship to members of the "Aryan race," the only other country in the world that racially restricted naturalized citizenship was the United States of America, where only blacks or whites could become citizens.

A NATION OF IMMIGRANTS

The United States is a country whose inhabitants are overwhelmingly either recent immigrants or the descendants of immigrants. In one of the stories that we tell about ourselves, we are a nation that has always welcomed immigrants from distant shores, and these immigrants come to America because of the freedoms that we offer and the opportunities that are available here to all. These sentiments are famously engraved on the pedestal of the Statue of Liberty in a poem by Emma Lazarus titled "The New Colossus":

> *Give me your tired, your poor,*
> *Your huddled masses yearning to breathe free,*
> *The wretched refuse of your teeming shore.*
> *Send these, the homeless, tempest-tost to me,*
> *I lift my lamp beside the golden door!*

Another aspect of this story is that all immigrants eventually become fully American by blending into the "melting pot" of American society by willingly giving up their old ways and adapting to the new, American way of life and culture. A homogenous American culture is thereby created out of the various immigrant nationalities and races through assimilation and enculturation. Although this story is certainly true and accurate for many immigrant populations, a consideration of the

FIGURE 9.10 Newly arrived European immigrants leaving the Great Hall at Ellis Island in the early 20th century. Courtesy of the Library of Congress Prints and Photographs Division.

history of government restrictions on immigration leads to the inescapable conclusion that race has always played a powerful role in determining who would be welcomed to these shores and into the melting pot and for whom access would be blocked or limited.

How, then, have government immigration policies shaped the racial and ethnic makeup of modern America? Simply put, federal law restricted immigration to the United States on the explicit basis of race or ethnicity for nearly a century, from 1882 until 1965. The first group that was excluded from immigration was the Chinese, when the U.S. government passed the Chinese Exclusion Act of 1882. Chinese immigration to the United States had been mostly to the West Coast, beginning with the California Gold Rush in 1849 and continuing with the building of the transcontinental railroad in the 1860s. With declining economic prospects after the end of the Civil War and the completion of the railroad, anti-Chinese sentiment grew, at times exploding into urban riots of violence against Chinese workers and their families (e.g., in Los Angeles in 1871 and Rock Springs, Wyoming, in 1885). The Chinese Exclusion Act prohibited Chinese laborers or miners from entering the country for a period of ten years, but it was amended in 1884 to exclude all Chinese indefinitely. In 1917, Congress passed a new immigration restriction act prohibiting entry into the United States of all Asians in what was dubbed the "Asiatic Barred Zone." The animosity toward Asians, an outgrowth of fears of the "Yellow Peril" of Asian immigration, was based to some extent on racism but also on *nativism* (a tendency to favor native inhabitants of the country over immigrants) and on *xenophobia* (a fear of strangers or of "the other"). Even today, we can see these familiar strains of racism, nativism, and xenophobia in many calls by politicians for immigration restrictions to be placed on Mexicans or Arabs. Interestingly, shortly after the passage of the legislation creating the Asiatic Barred Zone, the U.S. Senate passed a bill restricting all immigration from Africa. The bill was narrowly defeated in the House after intense lobbying by the NAACP.

In 1924, a landmark immigration restriction act was passed by Congress and signed into law by President Calvin Coolidge. A consideration of the details of this bill will allow us to revisit themes touched on in earlier sections of this book, notably, the social and political impact of mass intelligence testing of immigrants and soldiers and the biological determinist ideology of eugenics during the first two decades of the 20th century. Recall that the overwhelming message of the intelligence testing done by American psychologists such as Goddard, Terman, and Yerkes was that different races and ethnicities had different levels of innate intelligence and that the American gene pool was in danger of being swamped by the increasing numbers of feeble-minded immigrants who were flocking to our shores. In particular, the newer immigrants from southern and eastern Europe were thought to pose the greatest peril to American intelligence as a result of the enormous proportion of feeble-minded individuals supposedly found among these ethnicities. Both Terman and Yerkes had presented data that suggested that the average Italian, Pole, Russian, and African American was technically a moron (someone with the intelligence of the average 8- to 12-year-old). Under the sway of the hereditarian theory of innate intelligence, these new immigrants were said to pose a serious threat to American democracy. Morons in particular were seen as a threat because, unlike the even more mentally debilitated idiots (technically defined as have the average intelligence of a 3-year-old) and imbeciles (those having a mental age of between 3 and 7 years), morons were close enough to normal intelligence to blend into society and escape detection. Something had to be done to preserve the American way of life and gene pool from these "high-grade defectives."

The proposed solution was to restrict immigration from countries with the highest proportion of mentally deficient individuals, and the result was the Johnson-Reed Immigration Act of 1924. This law created a permanent quota system for different countries of origin that was based on the number of immigrants from these various countries who were already in the United States. Specifically, the number of new immigrants allowed into the United States each year from a particular country was set at 2 percent of the number of Americans who could trace their ancestry to that country as determined by the 1890 census. Why was the 1890 census used for the purpose of setting the immigration quotas, rather than the most recent census at the time, that of 1920? The answer is blatantly obvious: in 1890, the United States had not yet seen much immigration from eastern and southern Europe, so the

2 percent quotas based on the 1890 numbers ensured very low quotas for those "undesirables." The 1890 census was actually known at the time as the "Anglo-Saxon census." For example, according to Nelli (1993:41), at the height of Italian immigration to the United States in the first decade of the 20th century, an average of 200 thousand immigrants came through Ellis Island each year (including both of my father's parents, from small towns in southern Italy near Naples); after the new quotas were set, only 4,000 Italians were allowed in each year (i.e., 2 percent of the 200 thousand Italian Americans in the 1890 census). At the same time, the new quotas allowed for annual entry of 57 thousand of the more desirable German immigrants; other nationalities that benefited from the new quotas were the British and the Irish. The losers in this new system included immigrants from Hungary, Russia, Italy, Poland, and other nations in eastern and southern Europe. These were, of course, the countries whose inhabitants were tarred by the accusation of feeble-mindedness through the work of some of the leading psychologists of the day. In a statement that reflects a total lack of understanding of the true nature and meaning of America, President Coolidge said upon signing the 1924 immigration act into law, "America must be kept American."

Racial restrictions placed on legal immigration to the United States in 1924 were to remain on the books until 1952, and the quota system based on ethnicity or national origin would remain in force until 1965. Although the 1952 Immigration and Nationality Act, also known as the McCarran-Walter Act, repealed all racial restrictions on immigration, it continued the earlier policy of restricting immigration based on national origin with annual quotas. In addition, it added an ideological clause that restricted immigration of (and allowed deportation of) people thought to be engaged in "subversive activities." This clause was used repeatedly to keep out of the United States prominent individuals with dissenting political views and communist sympathizers, including writers Doris Lessing and Gabriel Garcia Marquez and the poet Pablo Neruda, among a great many others. The 1952 McCarran-Walter Act set the limit of "ordinary immigrants" (i.e., those without special skills, excluding political refugees and wives and children of men already in the United States) at 270 thousand a year. Although President Harry Truman vetoed the bill, decrying the "absurdity, the cruelty of carrying over into this year of 1952 the isolationist limitations of our 1924 law," his veto was overridden by the House and Senate, and the McCarran-Walter Act became law. In 1965, President Lyndon B. Johnson signed into law two of the legislative cornerstones of the civil rights era and of his Great Society program: the Voting Rights Act and the Immigration and Nationality Act. This latter law was the final nail in the coffin of the national origins quotas put into place in 1924, and although legal immigration to the United States retained a ceiling level, these limits were now based on geographic rather than racial or ethnic considerations.

What is the status of U.S. immigration policy in our current post-9/11 world, in which an estimated 11 million immigrants are living in America illegally? In some respects, American immigration policy is still heavily influenced by the Cold War, and in no place is that better seen than Cuba. Although the U.S. government considers Cuba one of four official state sponsors of terrorism (along with Sudan, Syria, and Iran) and a travel ban by American citizens has been in place for more than 40 years, Cuba is also perhaps the only place in the world from which illegal immigrants are welcomed to our shores. The reasons for this policy are obviously political and relate to the Cold War ideological struggle between American democracy and free enterprise and Cuban socialism: each Cuban immigrant is seen as another victory in the ideological struggle against communism and the Castros. America is, of course, a terribly attractive place for the many impoverished people of the Caribbean, including not just Cubans but also Jamaicans, Haitians, and Dominicans. Each year, many poor people from such places as Haiti and Cuba risk their lives by trying to cross the Florida Strait to enter America illegally, but only Cubans are welcomed with open arms upon arrival. Traditionally, illegal immigrants from Haiti have been rounded up and returned as soon as possible. Does race have anything to do with these decisions? Because many Cubans are just as dark-skinned as many Haitians, it would seem that Cold War politics rather than racism can best explain these different outcomes. But if one compares U.S. immigration policy toward African countries with those of European countries, perhaps race has not yet been completely eliminated from U.S. policy. U.S. government figures show that 94,711 individuals from Africa (out of a total population of 922 million in 2005) and 120,821 from Europe (with a total population of 728 million in 2005) obtained permanent legal status in the United States in 2007. Perhaps with so much attention being focused on the "war on terror" and the threat of Islamic fundamentalism, the next group to be denied entry into the United States will be individuals of Arab descent. A poll taken shortly after September 11, 2001, suggested that more than 75 percent of Americans favored restrictions on Arab or Muslim immigration.

AFFIRMATIVE ACTION AND THE DREAM OF A COLOR-BLIND SOCIETY

On August 28, 1963, Martin Luther King Jr. gave a speech to a quarter of a million civil rights supporters at the Lincoln Memorial in Washington, D.C., in which he articulated the desire for what has become known as a "color-blind society." In the beautiful prose and lilting cadences of the "I Have a Dream" speech, King shared his dream of a just, equal, and color-blind society in which "my four little children will one day live in a nation where they will not be judged by the color of their skin but by the content of their character." Less than five years later, in Memphis, King would lose his life to an assassin's bullet, with his dream deferred. But what about today? How close are we in America to finally creating a truly color-blind society, one in which we are all judged by the "content of our character" and not by the "color of our skin"? Can we hope to realize King's dream any day soon?

Two years before the "I Have a Dream" speech, President John F. Kennedy signed Executive Order 10925, which created the Committee on Equal Employment Opportunity and directed all government contractors to "take affirmative action to ensure that applicants are employed, and that employees are treated during employment, without regard to their race, creed, color, or national origin." With the stroke of his pen, President Kennedy had affirmed the federal government's support for civil rights and its stand against racial discrimination and inequality, creating the concept of "affirmative action" to ensure equity in hiring and education. In the early 1970s, affirmative action began to generate intense opposition from a segment of society that argued that racial quotas, two-track hiring schemes (one for blacks and one for whites), and other attempts to restrict discrimination against certain groups had become "reverse discrimination" against whites. This issue reached the Supreme Court in 1977 in the case of *Regents of the University of California* v. *Bakke*.

Allan Bakke, a white applicant to the medical school at the University of California at Davis, had been denied admission in both 1973 and 1974, in spite of the fact that his grades and test scores

FIGURE 9.11 Several hundred protesters rallied against the Supreme Court's decision in the *Bakke* case at the Federal Courthouse in Foley Square, in New York City.
Courtesy of AP Images

were better than many minority candidates who had been admitted under a two-track admissions policy that used lower standards for minority applicants in the interest of affirmative action. Bakke argued, and five Supreme Court justices ultimately agreed with him, that the medical school admissions policy had practiced "reverse discrimination" by holding him to a higher standard than other applicants on the basis of race. Four justices presented the dissenting argument that the Constitution should be interpreted to distinguish between "benign" and "malign" uses of race and that affirmative action, as a benign use of race intended to right social wrongs and to level the playing field between the races, should be allowed. The Court's decision held that although race could be used as one among many relevant factors on which to base college admissions decisions, UC Davis's medical school admissions policy involved the use of a strict racial quota, and this was deemed unconstitutional because it discriminated against nonminority candidates.

This issue of racial quotas and of the use of race as a "plus factor" was revisited by the Supreme Court in two higher-education admissions cases from the University of Michigan in 2003. In *Grutter* v. *Bollinger*, the Court upheld an admissions policy at the University of Michigan Law School that involved a "narrowly tailored" use of race for the pedagogically sound reason of creating a superior learning environment by ensuring a diverse student body. Significantly, the majority opinion (written by Justice Sandra Day O'Connor) suggested that affirmative action's days were numbered and that the days of race-based admissions policies at prestigious universities would soon be over:

> Race-conscious admissions policies must be limited in time. The Court takes the Law School at its word that it would like nothing better than to find a race-neutral admissions formula and will terminate its use of racial preferences as soon as practicable. The Court expects that 25 years from now, the use of racial preferences will no longer be necessary to further the interest approved today.

Gratz v. *Bollinger* concerned the undergraduate admissions policy at the University of Michigan. In this case, the Supreme Court ruled that the admissions policy, in which a 150-point scale was used to rank all applicants and minority candidates were automatically given 20 points, was unconstitutional. In the Court's interpretation, this point-based system was not "narrowly tailored" and thus violated the equal protection clause of the Fourteenth Amendment. Taken together, the two University of Michigan cases upheld the *Bakke* decision by arguing that race could be used as a plus factor in university admissions decisions but that racial quotas and other blunt applications of affirmative action amounted to reverse discrimination and violated the right to equal protection of the law guaranteed by the Constitution.

The proper role that affirmative action should play in American life continues to be a highly contested social and legal issue, with the locus of these arguments shifting from the Supreme Court to the voting booth. At present, voters in three states have passed propositions restricting the use of affirmative action. California started this trend in 1996 when the passage of Proposition 209 prohibited all public institutions in the state from taking race, ethnicity, or sex into account in employment, education, or contracting decisions. The state of Washington passed a similar law known as Initiative 200 in 1998 that banned both discrimination against and preferential treatment of "any individual or group on the basis of race, sex, color, ethnicity, or national origin in the operation of public employment, public education, or public contracting." In 2006, voters in Michigan banned affirmative action when they passed a ballot initiative known as Proposal 2.

What does this apparent backlash against affirmative action tell us about ourselves? For one thing, it tells that many Americans support the idea of a color-blind society in which both racial discrimination and racial preferences have become things of the past. Might Supreme Court Justice O'Connor have overestimated how many years it would take for American society to move beyond the need for racial preferences? Are we then on the verge of attaining Martin Luther King's dream of a color-blind society, or are equality and equal opportunity still determined by skin color or some other ascribed or inborn trait? And what about the hidden benefits that automatically accrue to whites simply by virtue of their membership in the majority group and the fact that they are *not* black? There is no denying the reality of what social scientists call "white privilege" as a result of the lingering effects of structural racism in our society. Would an end to affirmative action and the resulting color-blind society completely rid ourselves of race-based favoritism, or would it just end favoritism toward minorities while maintaining the traditional "white privilege" enjoyed by generations of white Americans?

One way in which we might attempt to answer some of the questions about the status and importance of race in American society would be to look at a variety of social, economic, and medical measures of the "quality of life" among blacks and whites today. The sobering results of such a look might give us pause from proclaiming an end to race and to racism. For in nearly every sphere of life that we might explore, we would find blacks still lagging far behind whites, in spite of the many advances and improvements that have occurred in recent years. For example, U.S. Census Bureau data clearly indicate the continuing significance of race with respect to income in America. While median family income for both whites and blacks increased between 1980 ($21,904 for whites, $12,674 for blacks) and 2005 ($59,317 for whites, $35,464 for blacks), the gap between black and white income has barely changed over this 25-year period: black income was 58 percent of white income in 1980 and 60 percent of white income in 2005. It is possible that factors other than race may be responsible for this ongoing economic inequality, but the census data suggest otherwise. For example, even controlling for attained educational level, blacks earn significantly less than whites, with the sole exception of black women with four years of college.

Education and Earnings of Blacks per $1,000 Earned by Whites

Education Level	Men	Women
High School Not Finished	$797	$974
4 Years of High School	$764	$942
1 to 3 Years of College	$825	$925
4 Years of College	$798	$1002
5+ Years of College	$771	$973

Source: Hacker 1992:95.

Another important aspect of wealth in America can be gauged by home ownership. While recent census data indicate that home ownership is currently at an all-time high, they also show large racial inequalities. Whereas three-fourths of white households owned a home in 2005, only 46 percent of black and 48 percent of Hispanic households owned their homes. Home ownership is a critical aspect of family wealth in America for a variety of reasons, including associated tax benefits and the ability to pass on wealth as home equity to one's children, and whites have clearly benefited to a much greater extent than blacks or Hispanics in this respect.

Criminal justice is another area of American life where race continues to play a large and contested role. The crime statistics indicate that with respect to crime in America, blacks are overrepresented "in virtually all spheres—offenders, victims, prisoners, and arrests by the police" (Hacker 1992:181). Recent U.S. Bureau of Justice statistics on homicide show that proportional to their population sizes, victimization rates for blacks are six times higher than among whites and offending rates are seven times higher. It is also interesting to note that the great majority of homicides in America are intraracial: between 1976 and 2005, 86 percent of white victims were killed by whites, and 94 percent of black victims were killed by blacks. More than the numbers might suggest, many white Americans seem to have an inordinate fear of being victimized by violent crimes committed by young black males, in spite of the overwhelming evidence that blacks, and especially poor blacks, are much more likely to be the victims of violent crime than whites. In fact, one could easily argue that being black in many white neighborhoods in America is much more dangerous than the reverse and that so-called hate crimes are much more commonly committed by whites against blacks. For example, on June 7, 1998, in Jasper, Texas, white men seized an African American named James Byrd, chained him to the bumper of a truck, and dragged him to his death (Temple-Raston 2002). Another example is the 1986 case of Michael Griffith, a 23-year-old black man of Trinidadian ancestry who lived in Brooklyn, New York. Michael and three black friends apparently committed the offense of being black in a white neighborhood of the New York City borough of Queens known as Howard Beach. They were beaten and chased by a group of about ten white men, and Michael was killed by a car as he tried to escape his attackers. Finally, the case of Yusuf Hawkins further demonstrates the life and death significance of race in America today. Yusuf was a 16-year-old African American who, with three other black youths, was attacked by a gang of whites on a summer evening in 1989 in Bensonhurst, a working-class neighborhood in Brooklyn. Yusuf had come to Bensonhurst that night to look at and possibly purchase a used automobile. The white mob had been alerted to the presence in the neighborhood of a black male who had been dating a local white girl, and their attack on the four young black men can thus be traced back to the long-standing and irrational fear among many whites of interracial mating. Some of the white attackers wielded baseball bats, and one had a handgun; Hawkins was shot twice in the chest and died later that night.

Finally, the areas of health, wellness, and health disparities can provide further insights into the persistence of racial inequality and the continuing significance of race in modern America. In short, a wide variety of illnesses have a far more negative effect on the health of African Americans than they do on whites. According to the Centers for Disease Control and Prevention, African Americans in 1999 could expect to live nearly five years less (73.1 years) than the average American (77.8 years), while infant mortality among African Americans (14.1 deaths per 1,000 live births) was more than twice the national average (6.9) in 2000. Though representing less than 13 percent of the U.S. population, African Americans accounted for more than 50 percent of all new HIV infections reported in 2001. Finally, with respect to a number of diseases that can lead to premature death, African Americans have much higher age-adjusted death rates than whites, including cancer (25 percent higher), diabetes (113 percent higher), heart disease (30 percent higher), and stroke (41 percent higher). Rather than reflecting any important health-related genetic differences, it is clear to most medical practitioners and anthropologists that the reasons for these race-based health disparities can be found in environmental conditions that differ between the races, including poverty, limited access to health care, diet and lifestyle, and discrimination. In a word, the legacy of slavery, segregation, and discrimination continues to make people ill and causes them to die prematurely in a way that reflects the importance of race as a cultural construct in American society today. Perhaps we should not be so quick to dismantle the governmental mechanisms of affirmative action in favor of a "color-blind society" until the conditions of life for all Americans are truly equal.

RACE AS A CULTURAL CONSTRUCTION

How can we sum up our brief consideration of the historical, political, and cultural dimensions of race in America? As demonstrated repeatedly in this book, the notion of human race fails as a biological concept. Human biological diversity is real, but it is of a nature that doesn't lend itself to an objective, scientific, nonarbitrary classification into races. Yet race continues to exist and to thrive as a social or cultural construct, something that can be found in our heads rather than in the world. Race is not so much about skin color as it is about the meanings that we assign to skin color. And we have seen that these attributed meanings have a history and can and do change over time and space. As we have also seen, the cultural or social meanings we attribute to skin color and racial differences have real, life-and-death significance for individuals.

To the anthropologist, culture is a complex and interrelated matrix of ideas and beliefs about the world and about how to behave in the world that is shared by some group of people. Different cultures pose different answers to questions such as what foods should one eat, what kinds of clothes should one wear, and the ways in which men and women are the same or different. Different cultures also pose a variety of solutions to larger, existential questions about the meaning of life (e.g., which God or gods one should worship, what happens after we die) and the value of individuals, of groups, and of life itself. The concept of race developed in the West over the past 500 years as a partial and imperfect solution to questions about the meanings of human biological and cultural differences. It incorporated earlier ideas about hierarchy, religion, inequality, and biology into a new theory of human diversity that posited the existence of several intrinsically different racial groups. And it suggested that these were real or natural groups, supported by the prestige and authority of both biological science and Christian religion.

It has taken a long time for scientists and anthropologists to unmask the racial worldview and to strip it of its spurious biological justification. In the first two decades of the 20th century, Franz Boas's study of European immigrants in New York argued for plasticity via environmental influence in the development of human skull shape and called into question all previous (and subsequent) classifications of human race based on the cephalic index. Boas also was the first anthropologist to clearly distinguish between the biological and cultural realms of the human experience and to insist on the independence of cultural achievement from biological endowment. Near the midpoint of the last century, Ashley Montagu famously criticized much of the anthropological world for its unyielding focus on human races in spite of the obvious weakness of the theory of biological race. Montagu (1942) was the first anthropologist to clearly see the connections between a racial worldview and a racist agenda when he declared race "man's most dangerous myth." In the 1960s, Frank Livingstone and C. Loring Brace further clarified the biological nature of human diversity with their support of the notion of clinal or gradual morphological variation over geographic space. They argued that because the human species varied gradually and continuously across and between the continents and the different racial traits (e.g., skin color and blood groups) varied in a discordant fashion, all racial schemes were arbitrary exercises in futile classification.

Montagu, Livingstone, and Brace all suggested that rather than engage in racial classification, anthropologists ought to study the dynamic processes that lead to human biological variation from an evolutionary perspective. In the last quarter of the 20th century, a number of anthropologists made major contributions to the debunking of scientific theories of race and the recognition that race is a cultural construct. Leonard Lieberman surveyed the changes in anthropological research and teaching about race to demonstrate a changing paradigm within the discipline with respect to the declining status of the concept of biological race. Alan Goodman has thoughtfully critiqued the continuing use of the race concept within skeletal biology and forensic anthropology, perhaps the last remaining bastions of support for biological race in the field of anthropology. Goodman has also been an eloquent supporter of the importance of different cultural constructions of race and has noted that the true significance of race occurs at the level of the lived experiences of individuals. Finally, Audrey Smedley has written the definitive anthropological treatment of the roots and historical development of the concept of race in the Western world. It should be clear from the foregoing that anthropologists have come full circle from being the main scientific supporters of the notion of race as biology to being the main critics of this notion and supporters of the idea that race is a product of culture and society rather than biology.

In an essay titled "Black, White, Other," the anthropologist Jonathan Marks (1994) tells the story of the attorney Lani Guinier, who was described at two different places in a single *New York Times* article of 1993 as being "black" and "half black." This curious inconsistency leads Marks to question the biological (and algebraic) nature of the race concept. He describes racial categories as "cultural constructs masquerading as biology." In the movie *Race: The Power of an Illusion*, a historian describes the differing legal definitions of a "Negro" in several southern states in the early 20th century. One-eighth black ancestry (i.e., one of a person's eight great-grandparents) made one legally black in Florida, one-sixteenth black ancestry (i.e., one of a person's 16 great-great-grandparents) was the threshold in Virginia, and in Alabama, a single drop of "black blood" marked someone as a member of the black race. If one's racial identity and legal status can change by crossing state lines, it is very clear that we are in the realm of cultural construction and social meanings and very far indeed from the world of biology.

The notion that race fails as a biological theory but can be of life-or-death significance as the lived experiences of individuals and of groups is the new standard anthropological interpretation of race. In 1903, the great American civil rights activist and scholar W. E. B. Du Bois presciently wrote that "the problem of the twentieth century is the color line." In the 21st century, anthropology provides us with a new and improved understanding of the biological and cultural meanings of race and human diversity. Let us hope that we can construct an American society that truly lives up to the glorious ideals of freedom, democracy, and equality for all that were laid out by the Founders and finally cross to the other side of Du Bois's "color line."

POSTSCRIPT

On the evening of April 3, 1968, the Martin Luther King Jr. delivered his last public speech at the Mason Temple in Memphis, Tennessee. King was in Memphis to support the city's sanitation workers who were on strike and protesting their poor working conditions and low pay. In his famous "Mountaintop" speech that evening, King touched on age-old themes of struggle and God's will, of death and of his own mortality.

Less than 24 hours later, King was shot and killed while he and several civil rights coworkers (including Jesse Jackson and Ralph Abernathy) were standing on the balcony of room 306 of Memphis's Lorraine Motel. He was right: he would not get to the Promised Land with us. Forty years after King's assassination, the American people elected the first African American to the presidency of our country. We still may not have arrived at the Promised Land, but perhaps we too can begin to see it.

Discussion Questions

1. In what sense do anthropologists argue that race exists *and* does not exist? How can you make sense of this seeming paradox?

2. What is meant by "white privilege," and of what relevance is it to the arguments for or against affirmative action and a color-blind society? Can you give some examples of white privilege?

3. Describe some of the major Supreme Court decisions bearing on race, segregation, and affirmative action in the past 200 years.

4. How were the intelligence tests of the early 20th century used in the debates over immigration and naturalization policies?

5. How did the Johnson-Reed Immigration Act of 1924 limit the number of legal immigrants from southern and eastern Europe compared to those from western Europe?

6. What was wrong with President Calvin Coolidge's statement upon signing the 1924 Johnson-Reed Immigration Act that "America must be kept American"?

7. Who was Sally Hemings, and what does her story tell us about the place of race in the founding of the modern American political system?

8. Why are many American cities and school still segregated more than 50 years after the Supreme Court's *Brown* v. *Board of Education* decision?

BIBLIOGRAPHY

American Association of Physical Anthropologists
1996 AAPA Statement on Biological Aspects of Race. American Journal of Physical Anthropology 101(4):569–570.

Barlow, Nora, ed.
1958 The Autobiography of Charles Darwin, 1809–1882. New York: Norton.

Behe, Michael
1996 Darwin's Black Box: The Biochemical Challenge to Evolution. New York: Free Press.

Bennett, Lerone, Jr.
1964 Before the Mayflower: A History of the Negro in America, 1619–1964. Chicago: Johnson.

Blumenbach, Johann F.
1950[1776] On the Natural Variety of Mankind. Section IV: Five Principal Varieties of Mankind, One Species. In This Is Race: An Anthology Selected from the International Literature on the Races of Man. Earl W. Count, ed. Pp. 34–39. New York: Schuman.

Bogin, Barry
1999 Patterns of Human Growth. 2nd edition. Cambridge, UK: Cambridge University Press.

Bogin, Barry, and James Loucky
1997 Plasticity, Political Economy, and Physical Growth Status of Guatemala Maya Children Living in the United States. American Journal of Physical Anthropology 102:17–31.

Bond, Julian
1987 Introduction. In Eyes on the Prize: America's Civil Rights Years, 1954–1965. By Juan Williams. Pp. xi–xv. New York: Viking Penguin.

Boyd, William C.
1950 Genetics and the Races of Man. Boston: Little, Brown.

Brace, C. Loring
1964 On the Race Concept. Current Anthropology 5:313–320.
2000 Evolution in an Anthropological View. Walnut Creek, CA: AltaMira Press.

Brody, Howard, and Linda M. Hunt
2006 BiDil: Assessing a Race-Based Pharmaceutical. Annals of Family Medicine 4:556–560.

Carter, Mary
2006 Heart Disease Still the Most Likely Reason You'll Die. CNN.com, November 1. http://www.cnn.com/2006/HEALTH/10/30/heart.overview/index.html, accessed January 6, 2010.

Cavalli-Sforza, Luigi Luca, and Walter F. Bodmer
1971 The Genetics of Human Populations. San Francisco: Freeman.

Cohen, Mark N., and George A. Armelagos, eds.
1984 Paleopathology at the Origins of Agriculture. Orlando, FL: Academic Press.

Cold Spring Harbor Laboratory
N.d. James Watson's Personal Genome Sequence. http://jimwatsonsequence.cshl.edu, accessed January 3, 2010.

Collins, Francis S.
2004 What We Do and Don't Know about "Race," "Ethnicity," Genetics, and Health at the Dawn of the Genome Age. Nature Genetics 36(suppl. 11):S13–S15.

Coon, Carlton S.
1962 The Origin of Races. New York: Knopf.

Coon, Carleton S., Stanley M. Garn, and Joseph B. Birdsell
1950 Races: A Study of the Problem of Race Formation in Man. Springfield, IL: Thomas.

Count, Earl W.
1950 Introduction. In This Is Race: An Anthology Selected from the International Literature on the Races of Man. Earl W. Count, ed. Pp. xiii–xxviii. New York: Schuman.

Curtin, Philip D.
1992 The Slavery Hypothesis for Hypertension among African Americans: The Historical Evidence. American Journal of Public Health 82(12):1681–1686.

Darwin, Charles
1962[1839] The Voyage of the Beagle. Leonard Engel, ed. New York: Doubleday.

Dobzhansky, Theodosius
1968 Introduction to Part 2: Biological Aspects of Race in Man. In Science and the Concept of Race. Margaret Mead, Theodosius Dobzhansky, Ethel Tobach, and Robert E. Light, eds. Pp. 77–79. New York: Columbia University Press.
1973 Nothing in Biology Makes Sense Except in the Light of Evolution. American Biology Teacher 35:125–129.

Dressler, William W., Kathryn S. Oths, and Clarence C. Gravlee
2005 Race and Ethnicity in Public Health Research: Models to Explain Health Disparities. Annual Review of Anthropology 34:231–252.

Du Bois, W. E. B.
1903 The Souls of Black Folk. Chicago: McClurg.

Eaton, S. Boyd, Marjorie Shostak, and Melvin Konner
1988 The Paleolithic Prescription: A Program of Diet and Exercise and a Design for Living. New York: HarperCollins.

Entine, John
2000 Taboo: Why Black Athletes Dominate Sports and Why We're Afraid to Talk about It. New York: Public Affairs Books.

Fisher, Claude S., Michael Hout, Martín Sanchéz Jankowski, Samuel R. Lucas, Ann Swidler, and Kim Voss
1996 Inequality by Design: Cracking the Bell Curve Myth. Princeton, NJ: Princeton University Press.

Foner, Eric
1998 The Story of American Freedom. New York: Norton.

Fraser, Steven, ed.
1995 The Bell Curve Wars: Race, Intelligence, and the Future of America. New York: Basic Books.

Gardner, Howard
1983 Frames of Mind: The Theory of Multiple Intelligences. New York: Basic Books.

Goodman, Alan H.
1997a Bred in the Bone? Sciences, March April: 20–25.
1997b The Problematic of "Race" in Contemporary Biological Anthropology. In Biological Anthropology. The State of the Science. Noel T. Boaz and Linda D. Wolfe, eds. Pp. 221–243. Bend, OR: IIHER.

Goodman, Alan H., and George J. Armelagos
1985 Disease and Death at Dr. Dickson's Mounds. Natural History 94(9):12–18.

Gould, Stephen Jay
1978 Morton's Ranking of Races by Cranial Capacity. Science 200(4341):503–509.
1996 The Mismeasure of Man. New York: Norton.

Graves, Joseph L.
2001 The Emperor's New Clothes: Biological Theories of Race at the Millennium. New Brunswick, NJ: Rutgers University Press.

Gravlee, Clarence C., H. Russell Bernard, and William R. Leonard
2003 Heredity, Environment, and Cranial Form: A Reanalysis of Boas's Immigrant Data. American Anthropologist 105(1):125–138.

Hacker, Andrew
1992 Two Nations: Black and White, Separate, Hostile, Unequal. New York: Ballantine Books.

Hahn, Robert A., Joseph Mulinare, and Steven M. Teutsch
1992 Inconsistencies in Coding Race and Ethnicity between Birth and Death in U.S. Infants. Journal of the American Medical Association 267(2):259–263.

Haney López, Ian
1996 White by Law: The Legal Construction of Race. New York: NYU Press.

Harn, Alan D.
1980 The Prehistory of Dickson Mounds: The Dickson Excavation. Springfield: Illinois State Museum.

Harris, Marvin
1964 Patterns of Race in the Americas. New York: Norton.

Herrnstein, Richard J.
1971 IQ. Atlantic, September: 43–63.

Herrnstein, Richard J., and Charles Murray
1994 The Bell Curve: Intelligence and Class Structure in American Life. New York: Free Press.

Hooton, Ernest Albert
1937 Apes, Men, and Morons. New York: Putnam.

Human Genome Project
2008 About the Human Genome Project. http://www.ornl.gov/sci/techresources/Human_Genome/project/about.shtml, accessed January 3, 2010.

Hume, David
1742 Of National Characters. In Essays, Moral, Political and Literary. 2nd edition. Essay LXXI. London and Edinburgh.

Hunt-Grubbe, Charlotte
2007 The Elementary DNA of Dr. Watson. Sunday Times, October 14. http://entertainment.timesonline.co.uk/tol/arts_and_entertainment/books/article2630748.ece, accessed January 3, 2010.

Jablonski, Nina G.
2006 Skin: A Natural History. Berkeley: University of California Press.

Jensen, Arthur R.
1969 How Much Can We Boost I.Q. and Scholastic Achievement? Harvard Educational Review 33(1): 1–123.

Jorde, Lynn B., and Stephen P. Wooding
2004 Genetic Variation, Classification, and "Race." Nature Genetics 36(suppl. 1):S28–S33.

Kahn, Jonathan D.
2007 Race in a Bottle. Scientific American, August: 40–45.

Keppel, Kenneth G., Jeffrey N. Pearcy, and Diane K. Wagener
2002 Trends in Racial and Ethnic-Specific Rates for the Health Status Indicators: United States, 1990–1998. DHHS Publication (PHS) 2002-1237. Hyattsville, MD: National Center for Health Statistics.

Kevles, Daniel J.
1985 In the Name of Eugenics: Genetics and the Uses of Human Heredity. New York: Knopf.

King, Martin Luther, Jr.
1963 "I Have a Dream," speech delivered from the steps of the Lincoln Memorial, Washington, DC, August 28.

Kretchmer, Norman
1972 Lactose and Lactase. Scientific American, October: 71–78.

Lewontin, Richard C.
1974 The Genetic Basis of Evolutionary Change. New York: Columbia University Press.

Lieberman, Leonard, Raymond E. Hampton, Alice Littlefield, and Glen Hallead
1992 Race in Biology and Anthropology: A Study of College Texts and Professors. Journal of Research in Science Teaching 29(3):301–321.

Lieberman, Leonard, and Fatimah Linda C. Jackson
1995 Race and Three Models of Human Origin. American Anthropologist 97(2):231–242.

Lieberman, Leonard, and Larry T. Reynolds
1978 The Debate over Race Revisited: An Empirical Investigation. Phylon 39:333–343.

Littlefield, Alice, Leonard Lieberman, and Larry T. Reynolds
1982 Redefining Race: The Potential Demise of a Concept in Physical Anthropology. Current Anthropology 23(6):641–655.

Livingstone, Frank B.
1958 Anthropological Implications of Sickle Cell Gene Distribution in West Africa. American Anthropologist 60:533–562.
1962 On the Non-Existence of Human Races. Current Anthropology 3(3):279–281.

Maddox, Brenda
2002 Rosalind Franklin: The Dark Lady of DNA. New York: HarperCollins.

Marks, Jonathan
1994 Black, White, Other. Natural History 103(12):32–35.
1995 Human Biodiversity: Genes, Race, and History. New York: Aldine de Gruyter.

Mayr, Ernest
1963 Animal Species and Evolution. Cambridge, MA: Harvard University Press.

McCracken, Robert D.
1971 Lactase Deficiency: An Example of Dietary Evolution. Current Anthropology 12(4):479–517.

McNeil, Donald G.
2009 Bid to Stop the Killing of Albinos. New York Times, February 16. http://www.nytimes.com/2009/02/17/health/17albi.html, accessed January 13, 2010.

Messner, Reinhold
1999[1979] Everest: Expedition to the Ultimate. Seattle, WA: Mountaineers Books.

Miller, Kenneth R.
2008 Only a Theory: Evolution and the Battle for America's Soul. New York: Penguin.

Montagu, Ashley
1942 Man's Most Dangerous Myth: The Fallacy of Race. New York: Columbia University Press.
1953 The Natural Superiority of Women. New York: Macmillan.
1955 The Direction of Human Development. New York: Harper.
1963 What Is Remarkable about Varieties of Man Is Likenesses, Not Differences. Current Anthropology 4(4):361–367.
1972 Statement on Race: An Annotated Elaboration and Exposition of the Four Statements on Race Issued by the United Nations Educational, Scientific and Cultural Organization. London: Oxford University Press.
1975 Race and IQ. New York: Oxford University Press.

Myrdal, Gunnar
1944 An American Dilemma: The Negro Problem and Modern Democracy. New York: Harper.

Nelli, Humbert S.
1993 From Immigrants to Ethnics: The Italian Americans. New York: Oxford University Press.

Nisbett, Richard E.
1995 Race, IQ, and Scientism. In The Bell Curve Wars: Race, Intelligence, and the Future of America. Steven Fraser, ed. Pp. 36–57. New York: Basic Books.

Robbins, Ashley H.
1991 Biological Perspectives on Human Pigmentation. Cambridge, UK: Cambridge University Press.

Rushton, J. Philippe
1995 Race, Evolution, and Behavior: A Life History Perspective. New Brunswick, NJ: Transaction.

Sankar, Pamela, and Jonathan D. Kahn
2005 BiDil: Race Medicine or Race Marketing? Health Affairs 24(W5):455–463.

Sayre, Anne
1975 Rosalind Franklin and DNA. New York: Norton.

Simoons, Frederick J., John D. Johnson, and Norman Kretchmer
1977 Perspective on Milk-Drinking and Malabsorption of Lactose. Pediatrics 59:98–108.

Smedley, Audrey
2007 Race in North America: Origin and Evolution of a Worldview. 3rd edition. Boulder, CO: Westview Press.

Sparks, Corey S., and Richard L. Jantz
2002 A Reassessment of Human Cranial Plasticity: Boas Revisited. Proceedings of the National Academy of Sciences 99(23):14636–14639.

Sperling, Susan
  2000 Ashley Montagu (1905–1999). American Anthropologist 102(3):583–588.

Szent-Györgyi, Albert
  1957 Bioenergetics. New York: Academic Press.

Temple-Raston, Dina
  2002 A Death in Texas: A Story of Race, Murder, and a Small Town's Struggle for Redemption. New York: Holt.

Thernstrom, Stephan, and Abigail Thernstrom
  1999 America in Black and White: One Nation, Indivisible. New York: Touchstone.

U.S. Department of Agriculture
  2005 MyPyramid.gov. http://www.mypyramid.gov/index.html, accessed January 23, 2010.

Watson, James D.
  1968 The Double Helix: A Personal Account of the Discovery of the Structure of DNA. New York: Atheneum.

Watson, James D., and Francis H. C. Crick
  1953 A Structure for Deoxyribose Nucleic Acid. Nature 171(4356):737–738.

Weiner, Jonathan
  1994 The Beak of the Finch: A Story of Evolution in Our Time. New York: Knopf.

Wetzler, Brad
  2002 Reinhold Don't Care What You Think. Outside Online, October. http://outside.away.com/outside/features/200210/200210_messner_1.adp, accessed January 15, 2010.

Wheeler, David A., Maithreyan Srinivasan, Michael Egholm, Yufeng Shen, Lei Chen, Amy McGuire, Wen He, Yi-Ju Chen, Vinod Makhijani, G. Thomas Roth, Xavier Gomes, Karrie Tartaro, Faheem Niazi, Cynthia L. Turcotte, Gerard P. Irzyk, James R. Lupski, Craig Chinault, Xing-zhi Song, Yue Liu, Ye Yuan, Lynne Nazareth, Xiang Qin, Donna M. Muzny, Marcel Margulies, George M. Weinstock, Richard A. Gibbs, and Jonathan M. Rothberg
  2008 The Complete Genome of an Individual by Massively Parallel DNA Sequencing. Nature 452:872–876.

Williams, Juan
  1987 Eyes on the Prize: America's Civil Rights Years, 1954–1965. New York: Viking Penguin.

Williams, Robert L.
  1972 Racial Differences on a Black Intelligence Test. Journal of Negro Education 43(4):429–436.

Wilson, Thomas W.
  1986a Africa, Afro-Americans, and Hypertension: A Hypothesis. Social Science History 10(4):489–500.
  1986b History of Salt Supplies in West Africa and Blood Pressures Today. Lancet 327(1):784–786.

Wilson, Thomas W., and Clarence E. Grim
  1991 Biohistory of Slavery and Blood Pressure Differences in Blacks Today: A Hypothesis. Hypertension 17(suppl. 1). 122–128.

World Health Organization
  2000 Turning the Tide of Malnutrition. Responding to the Challenge of the 21st Century. http://www.who.int/mip2001/files/2232/NHDbrochure.pdf, accessed January 21, 2010.

INDEX

Sex-linked genes, 38–39
Sexual reproduction, 28, 32–35, 37, 41
Shivering, 90–93
Sickle cell anemia, 7, 139–144, 146
Skin color
    as an adaptation, 99–110
    as a racial trait, 2, 4–9, 58, 62, 68, 72–74, 81,
        83, 86
Skin reflectometer, 7
Skull lesions, 129
Skull, size and shape of, 59–60, 70–71, 97, 182
Slavery hypothesis of hypertension, 137–139, 144
Slavery and slaves, 13–14, 55, 64–68, 80
Smedley, Audrey, 55, 63–64, 182
Socioeconomic status, 9, 56, 78, 136, 139, 155–158
Solar radiation, 93–94, 99–110
South America, Darwin, 12–15, 18
South America, high altitude adaptation, 112, 117,
        121–123, 128
Special creation, 14, 18, 20, 59
Stature, 6–8, 49, 121, 129, 133–135, 154, 164
Strain
    at high altitude, 121
    in human adaptation, 83–84, 110
    and thermoregulation, 83–84, 96
Stratum corneum, 102
Stratum germinatavum, 102
Stress
    at high altitude, 111–125
    in human adaptation, 78, 82–85, 110
    thermoregulation, 86–98
Struggle for existence, 23–26, 33, 49, 83
Sunburn, 105, 108–109
Supreme Court, 17, 166–171, 178–179, 183
Sweat
    glands, 102, 105, 109
    and sweating, 84–89, 94, 96
Systemic circulation, 115–117, 121

T

Taney, Chief Justice Roger, 166
Tanning response, 85, 103–104
Temperate zones, 8, 90, 93, 96, 101, 109, 142, 161
Terman, Lewis, 149, 176
Thermal equilibrium, 86, 89
Thermoregulation, 81, 85–86, 91, 96, 109
Tibetans, 123–124
Till, Emmett, 170
transfer RNA, 46–48
tRNA. *See* transfer RNA
Tropics, 8, 81, 89, 93–98, 106, 108–109, 161

U

Ultraviolet radiation, 73, 101, 103–106, 108–109
UNESCO, 75–76
Uniformitarianism, 22, 24
Urban race riots of 1960s, 173
US Constitution, 17, 165–167, 174, 179

V

VAD. *See* Vitamin A deficiency
Vasoconstriction, 90–93
Vasodilation, 184
Vestigial organs, 16
Vitamin A deficiency, 131
Vitamin D, 104, 108–110
Volume
    blood, 117
    body, 90, 91, 97–98, 110
    brain case, 66
    lungs, 120–121
Voting Rights Act, 172, 177

W

Wallace, Alfred Russell, 25–26
Wallace, George, 169
Watson-Crick Model, 41–48
Watson, James D., 29, 41, 43–44, 49–53
Wedgewood, Emma, 20
Wedgewood, Josiah, 12, 20
Weismann, August, 21
Warm-blooded. *See* Homeothermic
Watson and Crick, 43–44, 49, 52–53
Watts. *See* Urban race riots of 1960s
White privilege, 180, 183
Wilkins, Maurice, 43, 52–53
WHO. *See* World Health Organization
Woods, Tiger, 77
World Health Organization, 130–131

X

X chromosome, 39–40, 42, 146
Xenophobia, 176
X-linked, 39

Y

Y chromosome, 39
Yerkes, Robert, 298, 300, 301, 352

Z

Zygote, 35, 37, 39, 43, 53